Nothing
Matters

Nothing
Matters

Ronald Green

BOOKS

Winchester, UK
Washington, USA

First published by iff Books, 2011
iff Books is an imprint of John Hunt Publishing Ltd., Laurel House, Station Approach,
Alresford, Hants, SO24 9JH, UK
office1@o-books.net
www.o-books.com

For distributor details and how to order please visit the 'Ordering' section on our website.

Text copyright: Ronald Green 2010

ISBN: 978 1 84694 707 0

A CIP catalogue record for this book is available from the British Library.

Design: Stuart Davies

Printed in the UK by CPI Antony Rowe
Printed in the USA by Offset Paperback Mfrs, Inc

We operate a distinctive and ethical publishing philosophy in all
areas of our business, from our global network of authors to
production and worldwide distribution.

CONTENTS

This is dedicated to my family - to those who were, who are, and who will be.

Acknowledgments

How can I even begin to thank the many people who read, discussed with me, and read again the parts that came together to form this book? Each one, whether we agreed or disagreed, was instrumental in making this book what it is. Rather than list them all and risk even one omission, I prefer to thank each one personally. All of them know how much I appreciate and value their input.

Special thanks go to those, without whom this book would never have appeared:

- to Debbie Knoller, whose advice, understanding and patience with the philosophical threads that make up so much of the book helped me through the intricacies that involved *nothing*. It is due to her that I put down in readable form the ideas and thoughts that have exercised me for years. Often we disagreed more than we agreed, and I am grateful for her structured views that helped me on many occasions. The fact that at the end we still disagreed on some points, is, in my opinion, as it should be. I did not expect this book to be non-controversial.

- to Frank Shapiro, my friend and History guru, whose wide and profound knowledge of history and religion were invaluable in giving me perspective to a subject that sometimes threatened to engulf me within the mass of detail that I faced. Above all, it was his constant encouragement that pushed me on to see the book through to fruition.

- to my wife, Lily, for whom everything I do is dedicated. Again and again she read, commented and corrected progressive drafts of the book. She heard more about *nothing* in the past four years than is humanly, and humanely, possible. That she is still smiling after all this says a lot about her. At last we will be able to talk about something, rather than nothing, together.

It goes without saying that any mistakes are mine and that nobody, apart from me, is responsible for the conclusions and views expressed in this book.

Preface

Why should *nothing* be important? If anything is important, why should *nothing* be important? And yet, mysteriously, it is, for there isn't anything, it seems, that *nothing* does not touch, or anything that does not touch *nothing*. History, philosophy, religion, science, art, literature, music – all have *nothing* as a path that winds its way through, influencing everything it touches and, in turn, stimulating questions that would otherwise not be asked.

If everything started from nothing, so we are told, then *nothing* must contain the seeds of everything. Surely, then, *nothing* is as important as everything. More so, in fact.

Nothing may be nothing, but it is pivotal in many areas and has been examined with various degrees of respect and wonder through the ages. Theologians had been disturbed by it and worried about the concept of creating something out of nothing. It was a difficult topic for Greek philosophers, Medieval and Late Ancient thinkers and for mathematicians. Definitely not nothing to worry about, *nothing* was a concept that threatened the foundation of what people held dear. The Greeks were scared of it and Aristotle wouldn't accept it, so that due to the Catholic Church's embrace of Aristotelianism, Western science and mathematics were held back for centuries.

What is this *nothing* that we can't actually see, touch or feel? Is it absolute? Is it relative to everything else? If we are able to think about it, write and read about it, is it something, and if so wouldn't it *not* be nothing?

This is precisely the mystery of *nothing* – that the more we think about it, the more there is to it.

Disarmingly invisible, the point of *nothing* – to paraphrase Bertrand Russell on philosophy – is to start with something so simple as to seem not worth examining, and to end with something so paradoxical that no one will believe it.

Far from being an esoteric subject discussed by professional thinkers or students within a late-night haze of insight, the idea that *nothing* could be something is an idea that reaches into almost all disciplines and into the arts, some of which deal with it almost obsessively.

Looking at the world through the prism of *nothing*, often seeing what there is by examining what there isn't, this book is a look at where we can go when we think; it is a meander through subjects that have worried humankind for thousands of years and is a foray into what we can discover when they are cast in a new light. In that way, it is less about what *nothing* is than about how we might attempt thinking about it.

Nothing is unique and endlessly fascinating, for the more we delve into it, the more we discover. It is, somehow, always ahead of us, leading us on while eluding our grasp of what it might be. We could say – and we do say, as we progress – that in some way, *nothing* holds the key to understanding everything.

It is not surprising then, to discover that it was because of *nothing* that European progress was held back by some six hundred years. And it is *nothing* that leads us to asking the perennial question "What is art?" and to actually provide an answer! *Nothing*, so we discover, provides the common denominator for all religions, faiths and cults, while the puzzle of *nothing* is still the subject of philosophers' head-scratching after some two thousand years.

Strangely, we know less about *nothing* than we know about anything. If we ever find out what *nothing* is, would we be further along the road to knowing everything? Possibly. After all, striving for the impossible is an important part of what makes us human.

The existence of nothing – on the surface, an oxymoron – is what we are going to explore. In other words, is there such a thing as nothing? Not for the sake of it, but to illuminate what there still is to be discovered; and by examining what we think isn't, to find what there is.

Obviously, this is not an exhaustive study of *nothing*. It can't be. Even if it were a scientific look into all aspects that I touch, there would be more, since *nothing* is what everything isn't.

One

Nothing as Zero

I get a bemused, nonplussed stare from most people when I ask what *nothing* is. It's a question, their expressions tell me, that is so frivolous as to border on lunacy. When I persist, since I rarely get an answer the first time, the reaction turns from indulgence to something akin to annoyance. Nothing is nothing, is the most common answer. Nothing, zero, zilch – what's the big deal?

As impossible as it sounds today, there was a time when merely mentioning *nothing* would have been a very big deal. So big in fact that zero – then, as now (but with decidedly less dangerous consequences), associated with *nothing* – was absolutely banned on pain of death. Dying for zero would have been dying for *nothing*.

Linking zero and *nothing* is, of course, natural. Most people, when asked, will liberally interchange them, and in the general course of events we think of zero and *nothing* as being the same. '0' is what we write, and there it is on our keyboards, alongside the other numerals. In mathematics, though, zero is not really nothing; it represents something and is, in fact, a legitimate number – a character that designates an arithmetic value and has a function, no different in this respect from the numbers 1 to 9.

Clear as all that is today, it is almost impossible to imagine that anyone could ever have questioned its legitimacy, its very right to exist. The sad fact, though, is that zero had a difficult birth and an early life that was hell, the reason it survived at all being due to its link with other numbers. It was a link akin to an umbilical cord, the other numbers having no life without it. And neither would we – not in the way we know it.

The concept that all numbers can be represented by just ten

symbols 1, 2, 3, 4, 5, 6, 7, 8, 9, 0 is something that we take for granted. Obviously we do, because they are part of our lives. Electricity, printing, computers, telephones, cars, planes... they make us what we are in the world. Yet none of it would exist if it weren't for those ten symbols, of which zero is arguably the most significant. It's unlikely that we would have those symbols at all if it weren't for the zero. Imagine our keyboards and calculators showing Roman numerals (I, II, III, IV, V, VI, VII...) and no zero, not to mention the gigantic keyboards needed just to accommodate them. But, of course, there would have been no such scenario, since without zero there would never have been computers or electronic calculating machines or electronic anything.

It's not just that they make counting and arithmetical manipulations, such as addition and subtraction, easier than the systems that had come before. After all, systems of various kinds were used for these functions from way back, possibly by the first people who walked the earth, brought on by the necessity of keeping track of food that was stored and tools that were made and collected.[1]

Every system was adequate for its time. Until, in fact, it wasn't adequate any more: when further advances required a better system. So it was that the Western world was using the Roman numeral system when the Arabs, who had picked up the new system with its zero during their seventh-century conquests of India, introduced it. And it changed the world, because without an efficient system for calculating and computing numbers, there would be no science. What we call science is, after all, the mathematical study of nature that was given a huge push by Galileo in the 16th century, using that system of numbers. If "science begins when you can measure what you are talking about and express it in numbers," as stated so succinctly by Scottish mathematician and physicist W.T. Kelvin,[2] then science really takes off and flies when it can be expressed efficiently. Earth-shattering the new system was, revolutionizing the world as much as had the invention of the wheel.

But if the system was so good, why wasn't it accepted in Europe immediately it was introduced? Why did it take till the 16th century to be used? And we're not referring to a small gap: we're talking about a delay of 700 years from when it was first introduced into Europe! Now admittedly changing the numbering system is not something you'd expect to happen overnight – but seven hundred years?

And not for the lack of trying, and certainly not because nobody knew about it. It is, in fact, astounding how many mathematicians not only understood the significance of what the Arabs had, but also tried to spread the good news. They failed miserably. Introduced into Spain, which the Muslims had conquered, and into Italy that tried to import it through travelers from North Africa, the new counting system with its zero wasn't a hit. Its reception was, to put it mildly, not encouraging. On a good day the reaction was the equivalent of 'Don't call us, we'll call you', which in those times might have meant excommunication, incarceration or even death.

It was not the numbers 1 to 9 that caused the problem in Christian Europe. The sticking point was the zero, which, like an unwanted, illegitimate child, was hated immediately and then hidden away.

Through no fault of its own, zero was associated with *nothing*, a concept that was too mind-blowingly mysterious and threatening – devilish, even – to be accepted and acceptable. And because of its linkage with *nothing*, zero as a legitimate number – something that can be used and manipulated within a counting system – took an inordinately long, tortuous path to recognition. From when the Arabs introduced it into Europe until it was finally diffused into the university system and became widely used, zero's existence was fraught with fear and intrigue bound up with religion, belief and politics. Now, of course, it is nigh impossible to envisage an efficient number system that does not have the zero. Far from zero being nothing, it is an important something: an essential element in the counting system, without which the system could not really be used.

Location, location, location

It's not size, but positioning that matters. That's what makes the Hindu-Arabic notation so much simpler to use than the others that came before: not only does the system depend on ten characters only (1, 2, 3, 4, 5, 6, 7, 8, 9, 0) but the value of a character depends on where it is placed. Taking the number 205 as an example: the 2 denotes two hundreds, the zero denotes no tens and the 5 denotes five units. Now if we change their positions, the characters have different values: in 520, 5 denotes five hundreds, 2 denotes two tens and zero denotes no units. So obviously – to put it another way – 23 is not the same as 32. We can see clearly, then, that the character has a 'meaning' only according to its position. Look how different that is to Roman numerals, in use beforehand, where each character denotes a fixed number: V is five, X is ten, and always remain so; it is the addition of the symbols that gives the ultimate value.[3]

So where does our zero come in? Obviously it doesn't – not in an 'additional' system as the Romans had, where the characters themselves, rather than their position, matter: one hundred is C, one thousand is M, two thousand is MM, and where two thousand and six would be MMVI. (However number-challenged some of us are, we can consider ourselves lucky; just reading the numbers would have been a pain in those days, never mind actually manipulating them. The number 1944, for example, would be MCMXLIV.) Zero does matter, though, in a system where position is important. And in the flexible, efficient system where only ten characters are used, the zero is essential not only as a place holder to show that there is no entry in a particular position (like 205, where there are no tens), but as a genuine number equal to the others. So the fact that zero represents *nothing* (a blank) **in a certain position** tells us what that *nothing* replaces; zero has the function of showing that there is no number in that position. Zero, in other words, has the strange function of being a different *nothing* depending on its position. That was the breakthrough – the concept of zero as a number, i.e. as something, not just a place holder ('nothing').

And that was what the Arabs saw at the time of their conquests. There it was, the blank space as something that can be counted, as part of the abacus, which, with its movable beads on wires or rods, had been used around the world since antiquity to provide a simple means of calculation. Ingenious, in fact. When it showed sums in even tens (such as number 30 or 40) the abacus kept the first right-hand column empty (void). When expert abacus users had no abacus available to them, they could remember and visualize the operation of the abacus so clearly that all they needed to know was the content of each column in order to develop any multiplication or division. They then invented symbols for the content of each column to replace drawing a picture of the number of beads, as well as a symbol for the numberless content of the empty column – that symbol came to be known to the Hindus as *shunya*, 'empty space, void'.

It was this system of ten numbers that the Arabs adopted from the Indians and brought with them to Europe (Muslim Spain), calling the empty spot *sifr*, 'void' from which the meaning of the word 'zero' originates. More than anything else the Arabs introduced, the new system gave the Arabs a huge advantage over those who insisted on using the old cumbersome Roman system of numbers and allowed the Arabs to advance in mathematics and technology. No wonder, then, that they made a qualitative leap forward, having a system of only 10 symbols that combined flexibility with the potential of infinite computations.

Holding nothing back

But if all that explains how good the positional system is, it is even more of a mystery as to why it took so long for it to be accepted elsewhere. After all, the Arabic language and culture was spread over those areas of southern Europe conquered by the Arabs, showing up a glaring difference to other parts of Europe. While Arab-Islamic civilization had been achieving great scientific and cultural advances from the 8th till the 11th centuries, comparable only with Athens and Alexandria in their eras, western Christendom was just beginning to awaken from a long dark period where it had languished in social disorder, economic depression, and intellectual torpidness.

It's not that nobody knew about the new mathematical system. To say – as it often is – that nothing happened in mathematics in Europe from the 9th to the 15th century is nonsense, as it always is when supposedly 'nothing happens'. The mathematicians of the time were not blind to the system in use by the Arabs, and, in fact, there were genuine attempts to spread the word by European mathematicians, as we shall see. But while the Muslim world in those days was open to new ideas and therefore prospered, Christian Europe turned its back on the innovation of the positional counting system.

But why? What could have been the reason for not taking up a counting system that was obviously better than the Roman one then in use? Could the sticking point have been the zero and the concept of *nothing*? And let's face it, it really is a strange animal, the zero. We take zero for granted, accepting its schizophrenic character of nothingness and numberness; so while we now accept its idiosyncrasies, its strange nature and foibles, it was looked at in a far different way when was first introduced.

Just to remind ourselves how crazy the concept must have seemed at the time, here is an explanation from the Indian mathematician Brahmagupta, who lived from about 598 to 660 AD. A genius, far ahead of his time and still writing on mathematics and astronomy till the end, Brahmagupta was the first recorded person we know of who pondered zero as a concept, at a time before mathematicians used symbols so that everything was written out in words.

A debt minus zero is a debt.
A fortune minus zero is a fortune.
Zero minus zero is a zero.
The product of zero multiplied by a debt or fortune is zero.
The product or quotient of a fortune and a debt is a debt.

Here, 'debt' is a debit, meaning a negative number, although it could apply just as nicely to 'debt' in today's world, in a somewhat similar vein to Dickens' David Copperfield:

Annual income twenty pounds, annual expenditure nineteen and six, result happiness. Annual income twenty pounds, annual expenditure twenty pounds ought and six, result misery.

So what was that strange concept, the zero, that the Arabs picked up, saw its potential, and brought with them to Europe? It has no value of its own, and when put in front of a number, the number doesn't change: 5 and 05 mean the same. When added or subtracted from a number, the number doesn't change; but when put after a number, it does (and multiplies the number by 10): 5 becomes 50. Even more bizarre: if other numbers precede the zero, the rules change – a zero in front of a number now means something: 105 is not the same as 15. And to really complicate matters, if the number includes a decimal, a final zero no longer multiplies by 10: 1.05 and 1.050 are the same. More: there is that strange phenomenon of any number to the power of zero resulting in 1. Not to mention division by zero, which has confused even great minds. How many times does zero go into ten? Or, how many non-existent apples go into two apples?

Division by zero is, of course, meaningless, as much so as attempting to answer the question "Do green ideas sleep furiously?"[4] It wasn't till the 1600s (a thousand years after Brahmagupta drove himself crazy trying to define division by zero)[5] that Isaac Newton and Gottfried Leibniz solved this problem independently and opened the world to untold possibilities. By working with numbers as they approach zero, calculus was born without which we wouldn't have physics, engineering, and many aspects of economics and finance.[6]

We should not be surprised, then, that zero was confusing to people who had never seen it before. It was nothing some of the time, but at other times it acted as if it were something. Was zero a number or not? It was supposed to be like the numerals 1 through 9, but it had no value as such, even though it had the power to hold a place and to multiply or negate the value of other numerals.

Strange it may have seemed, but that, surely, could not be the reason for the non-acceptance of the zero in Europe. After all, the Arabs were using it in North Africa and in Muslim Europe. Besides, there was no dearth of mathematicians who did understand the importance of the new system that included zero.

What happened quite simply was that the zero was killed at birth by the powers-that-be: the Church. The new numerical system had, as far as they were concerned, an element in it that was a definite no-no. To say that the introduction of zero was discouraged is an understatement; the Church did everything in its power to stop it, and this included ridicule, bribery, anti-zero laws and strong-arm tactics, in line with the general policy against anything modern, which meant anything that could be construed as heresy.

It was the conception of zero being *nothing* that had the Church up in arms, and no explanation as to zero being like the numbers 1 through 9 would have helped. The Church had no problem with 'real' numbers; in fact, numbers had long been used as mystical symbols of events and as aids within the canon of the Church. One, three, seven, twelve, forty... you name it, there was a connection to something significant. Take the numbers 1 and 3: One God and the Trinity (Three in One), a central tenet of the Church, where the basic number would have to be one – one God, the basis, the source of everything. But not zero, not *nothing*.

As far as the Church was concerned, there could not be *nothing* and there could never have been *nothing*, because God was eternal. There never was a time before God, according to Church dogma. For the Church, then, *nothing* was an impossibility, a heresy, and they came down like a ton of bricks on anyone who mentioned it.

The Greeks, of course, had said it all before: Aristotle (384-322 BC), in his theory to justify the existence of God, reasoned that there was no such thing as *nothing*, because something had to have created the heavens and the Earth. Something must be moving the sun, the stars and the moon, and that something was God. His theory was based on a logical argument, and although his concept of God was very different, some 400 years before the birth of Christ, to that of the Christian God, Christianity adapted Aristotle's theory to much of its theology.

It was not till the thirteenth century that there was a break with Aristotle's ideas, particularly with the notion of infinity, which was seen by Aristotle as a necessary characteristic of *nothing*. Infinity and eternity, though, were basic to the nature of God, and in 1277 Étienne Tempier issued a formal condemnation of thirteen doctrines held by "radical Aristotelians" that contradicted God's omnipotence. Eternity was in, but *nothing* still remained a problem with the Church even when it was later accepted, as we will see.

Looking back from where we are in the 21st century, our first reaction is to wonder what all the fuss was about, or why theology was so important. But really we don't have to go far to understand a little what it was like a thousand years ago. We only need to look at the world around us, at the host of countries today that are theocracies, such as Iran and Saudi Arabia, where theology governs all aspects of legislation. But even in the USA, a strong democracy which has official separation of church and state, there is a strong, and growing, movement to reintroduce aspects of theology into the school system, witnessed by the hard-fought battle to push creationist theory into schools. Then, as now, knowledge of 'the Truth' was important as a way to influence hearts and minds. Essential, even, in those bygone days, as **the** source of power.

Knowledge is power, and never more so than in the Middle Ages, when the Church was the keeper of the truth – the truth about God and what He wants. It went without saying that the Church, and only the Church, knew what God wanted, and it was going to do everything to make sure that the people were aware of that. If knowledge was power, power as wielded by the Roman Catholic Church had to be absolute.

Which brings us back to the new numerical system that was all the rage among the Arabs but did not exactly impress the Church. The strange thing is that it needn't have been a problem. Good market research would have identified what the trouble was with zero, and decent advertising would have separated it from *nothing*, getting it past the Church. Instead, everything went wrong, from faulty translation from Arabic to a lack of explanation of what zero actually meant in a system of mathematics.

If today's modes of communication allow us instant contact with all and sundry, in the Middle Ages the Church was hardly any less efficient at getting its own views known. With everything in the Christian world touching religion in some way, with all disciplines, including philosophy, science, mathematics, being adjuncts of God's will as prescribed by the Church, it is not surprising that the mathematicians who first translated the Arabic texts on mathematics into Latin recognized immediately the potential problem of *nothing* and tried to downplay zero.

Take Fibonacci of Pisa (Leonardo Pisano [Leonardo of Pisa], also known as Leonardo Bigollo; 1175-1250), a well-traveled and renowned mathematician, who had picked up the number system in North Africa and was one of the high-profile people bringing the new ideas to Europe. Although born in Pisa, Fibonacci was educated in North Africa and saw at first hand the advantages of the new number system. Yet when it came down to it, he held back, not daring to treat 0 in the same way as the other numbers 1, 2, 3, 4, 5, 6, 7, 8, 9; in his landmark book *Liber Abaci*, in Pisa, 1202, he referred to the 'sign' zero while referring to the other symbols as 'numbers'. For somebody who has been called, albeit with some hyperbole, "the greatest European mathematician of the middle ages," he understood enough of the political climate to downplay the significance of zero. As far as he was concerned – and there was ample justification to his thoughts – it would have been foolhardy, if not downright dangerous, to come out strongly for zero at that time.

But let's be fair to Fibonacci. We can't really blame him for being cautious at first. By the time he wrote *Liber Abaci*, the zero was already in the dog house, so that it was most probably too late to save it. The point is that he wasn't the first to publicize the Indo-Arabic numeral system, even though he liked to make out that he was. He was certainly a colorful character, having the advantage of good looks, brains and connections with the right people. These, added to the debonair charisma of one who had lived in North Africa and had traveled extensively, held him in good stead when he returned to Pisa in 1200. The son of the representative in Bugia, a town in eastern Algeria, of the merchants of the Republic of Pisa, Fibonacci had studied mathematics there, influenced by the wonders of the system used by the locals. The fact that he was a great mathematician was not in doubt, for besides translating Arabic mathematical works, he did important work of his own that spread his fame beyond Pisa, the

'Fibonacci code sequence' even achieving a 21st century cameo appearance in Dan Brown's *Da Vinci Code*. (And it is in Pisa where he can be seen today, his statue standing in Piazza dei Miracoli, not far from the Leaning Tower.) He did, though, know where his bread was buttered and where it would be hard and dry if he crossed the Church.

Lost in translation

So why did the Church see zero as *nothing*? And what did the Church find so threatening about *nothing*? To really understand these two linked problems, we need to get inside the heads of the people and to try and imagine the atmosphere of the time.

We have already touched on the theological problem – that the very concept of *nothing* was heresy. But how would marketing and advertising have helped? The remarkable fact is that there was no need for the situation to have reached the state it did; after all, zero within the new number system was not considered as *nothing* by the Arabs, who in any case didn't see any theological problem with the idea of *nothing*: the Qur'an states, "But does not man call to mind that We created him before out of nothing?"[7]

The Muslims, then, didn't see zero as a threat or as any sort of mystery, but as an essential part of an efficient numbering system. And – this is a crucial point – neither did the mathematicians who translated from Arabic and who introduced it in Europe.

Like with so many things, it started badly. As far as the Church was concerned, zero was born in sin. It was the origin of the word, the Arabic 'sifr', that set off the alarms, because it meant 'a void'. But really, all it described was the space on the abacus that represented the numberless content of the empty column when showing even tens. An empty space, that's all. Not sinister and certainly not 'nothing'. *In mathematical terms zero had a function and was not meant to be 'nothing'.*

The nature of zero should have been clear. It certainly was

clear in Latin, to which the Arabic text was translated, which did make the distinction between 'zero' used as a numeral, and 'nothing'. It did so by having a different word for each. So Latin had two words that corresponded to Arabic 'sifr': they were *sifra* and *sefirum*, which had distinctly different meanings. *Sifra* meant 'a number', 'a digit', whereas *sefirum* meant 'nothing', and these meanings were brought out in the later development of both words: **sifra** took on an extended, more general meaning to denote any of the ten numerals and became the French *chiffre* and Italian *cifra* around the 14th century, the German *Ziffer* in the 15th century, and the English *cipher*, meaning 'digit' and later, a hidden number, i.e. a secret code; **sefirum**, the word that meant 'nothing' in Latin, on the other hand, developed into Italian to *zero*, which was adopted by French and also by English.

When Fibonacci (and others), translated the Arabic texts, they did so correctly, using the Latin *sifra* ('a number', 'a digit'), so making it plain that Arabic 'sifr' in that context meant 'zero-as-something' (digit), rather than 'zero-as-nothing' (nothing). It is more than of passing interest to note that the equivalent term in Hebrew, a close relative of Arabic, is *sifra*, which means 'a numeral' and has no connotation with 'zero'.

It so happens that Latin was not lacking in words that meant 'nothing'; here is another word that existed in Latin: *nulla*, which was around because no Roman numeral for zero existed. And, believe it or not, Latin also had *nihil*, still another word for 'nothing'. Yet the translation from Arabic of the new zero was neither *nulla* nor *nihil*, proving that zero had a different connotation from *nothing*.

So what happened? If the translation into Latin was so clear, why did the Church perceive zero as *nothing*? It seems that what was clear for the mathematicians was not so for the Church, who were jealously guarding themselves from so-called heretics on all fronts. Besides, the Church did not want to take any chances, preferring to be safe rather than sorry. It did not help either, that the Latin *sifra* looked so similar to the Arabic *sifr* and that the explanations were too esoteric to be understood by non-mathematicians. This was where some real and simple clarifications would have come in handy – in other words, a good advertising campaign to calm down the potential consumers.

And a decent graphic artist would have helped too. It was an unfortunate decision – actually, more by default than an actual decision – to continue using a sphere as the symbol for zero. Whereas the Indian numerals 1 through 9 were modified by the Arabs and then by the Europeans, only zero stayed more or less in its original form as a closed sphere. It was used by the Indians (where, as we saw, *shunya* meant 'a void'), then by the Arabs (whose *sifr* was a translation), but who later represented zero as a dot, and still do nowadays.

To make matters worse, there was an additional problem, a huge stumbling block when it came to the Church and *nothing*: 'shunya' had religious significance in India – it signified the uniquely Buddhist 'no-thing-ness' paradigm of enlightenment, already appearing as a spiritual ideal in the Hinayana canon of early Buddhism which rose to prominence in India in the first century AD.

It is doubtful as to whether Fibonacci knew about spirituality in India (for if he did, he would surely not have used the round symbol for zero), but it is not unlikely that word from the East had reached the ears of Pope Innocent III from his emissaries. Did they know that in Sanskrit, the word for 'enlightenment as no-thing-ness' happened to also be the word for 'zero as a number'? This was a serious point, as far as the Church was concerned, for it backed up their theological arguments that *nothing* was a heretical notion and it reinforced what the Church had said about the ungodliness of the concept; here, after all, was proof of its use by idol-worshiping cults, as seen from the viewpoint of the Church. For the Church, then, taking a stand against zero had nothing to do with holding back progress, but of stopping the work of the devil himself.

Nothing and the devil

And they said it. They actually invoked the devil when referring to zero. Take William of Malmesbury (born circa 1090), a foremost thinker, widely regarded as the best and most conscientious English historian of his time, a man who had the breadth of vision and the stamina to set out the history of England ("Thence it came that not being satisfied with the writing of old I began to write myself," he stated, expressing his frustration), who, nevertheless, made the point that the introduction of the zero was "dangerous Arab magic."

Now although William was a Benedictine monk in Malmesbury Abbey, in Wiltshire, England, and spent his best working years there, he was not living in isolation. The fact that he had heard about the new numeral system, its source and enough details to be aware of the zero, shows that he had contact with the outside world. In fact, he traveled extensively throughout England in order to research facts for the books he was writing. By 1125, when he had completed the first edition of the *Gesta Regum Anglorum* (*Deeds of the English Kings*), his first and most ambitious work of history, he had traveled the length and breadth of England, visiting most of its cathedrals and abbeys, going to wherever there was a library, his tall, slightly stooped figure in the black robe of the Benedictine order a familiar sight among the other scholars.

Although many of those he met were monks, not all were. Some had come in from Italy or Spain, from a far different world to what they found in England, unlike William, who did not yet know anything different to the conditions that he endured. Later he would travel extensively in Europe, but now, walking or traveling by ox-pulled carts that lurched along at a top speed of two miles per hour on mud that had been churned up by others on the 'roads' between towns, it must have been hard for him to believe the descriptions of the very different conditions that prevailed in lands that lived under the Arabs. Not just the physical conditions of the towns – in England most people lived in the country, while the towns consisted of unsanitary dens in which men, women and children shared space with their animals – but of the learning, science, mathematics and almost universal literacy in those countries.

Of all the people William met on his travels, one of the most interesting would have been a fellow Englishman, Adelard of Bath, recently returned from Europe after two long sojourns abroad. Roughly twenty years older than William, Adelard was a sophisticated, if scatter-brained individual, whose harassed appearance of one constantly in a hurry seemed to be in conflict with a body that would have been overweight were it not for incessant travel.

Adelard was, as we can now say from hindsight, arguably the first English scientist and one of the most influential men of the time. Having traveled in France and in Italy, where he had spent some time in Salerno, famous for its school of medicine that was the oldest university in Europe, founded in the 8th century, some 300 years previously, he moved on to Sicily, at the time a Norman kingdom, then to Greece and probably Toledo, Spain. He traveled as well in Asia Minor and North Africa, picking up languages effortlessly; he could speak Latin, English (a Saxon, Germanic version, spoken by the masses), Norman French, as well as Arabic and Hebrew, likely picked up in Sicily, a thriving and cosmopolitan country still heavily influenced by Arabic culture. Adelard's influence on culture was enormous; his translations from Arabic into Latin of the Greek philosophers helped to reintroduce them into the West, while his translations (with commentaries) of works on mathematics and astronomy from Arabic helped introduce Hindi-Arabic numerals and the use of zero to the West.

When William met Adelard in 1130 or thereabouts, Adelard

had recently translated from Arabic into Latin the classic work on arithmetic of Al-Khwarizmi (from whom, by the way, the word *algorithm* is formed), and although others translated it as well (as we noted about Fibonacci of Pisa), it does seem as though Adelard was, if not the first, then pretty close to it.

So there they were, the two of them in a tavern, drinking their ale, the cheapest drink at the time and certainly healthier than water whose source was often suspect. Adelard might have been playing his cithar (a stringed instrument, precursor of the guitar) before William joined him. Although not a monk, Adelard as a child had attended the school of the Benedictine monastery in Bath, which became the cathedral priory, and so would have felt comfortable with the Benedictine black-robed William.

It was a riveting conversation, with both doing their best to cut out the noise around them: the hubbub and clamor of the people, plus the dogs and cats waiting for scraps from the tables, not to mention the occasional fowl that alighted on their bench and the enveloping stench of animal and human waste, none of which was conducive to quiet talk. But talk they did, the historian and the scientist, each interested in what the other had to say, what the other added from his world of acquired knowledge. It was Adelard who talked more, relating the wonders of the world he had recently left to his companion, who found it hard to imagine a life so different to what he was used to.

Adelard needed to talk; he had settled back in England, possibly unwillingly, and since then showed all the characteristics of a workaholic, churning out translations from Arabic to Latin of scientific and mathematical treatises as well as his own philosophical works and even a book on falcons. Actually, "churning out" may not quite reflect the mechanics of writing so much in such a short time: this was before the invention of printing, so that each book had to be laboriously written by hand and that any copies were exactly that — whole books copied by hand.

And now he was telling William of Malmesbury about what was happening outside England. How much was spent on discussing *nothing* we don't know but there can be no doubt that it was part of their conversation, since Adelard would have told William about the Arabic numerals with their zero. They, of course, were speaking in Latin, the lingua franca of scholars discussing professional subjects, and it would be interesting to know whether Adelard used the word *cifra* or *sefirum* to explain that strange new concept. And what was William's reaction? We don't know whether he repeated his comment about the "dangerous Arab magic" and even whether it really reflected his views, that is, whether it was merely a politically correct statement for the times. We do know, though, that William had learned to tiptoe between the puddles and that he was careful with what he wrote so as not to offend his superiors. His first love was history and it was important for him to be allowed to travel and gather the information he needed. Keeping to history and not getting involved too much in the business of the abbey – the religious matters – was what he did, and he was well aware of what to keep away from.

There was no doubt that the new numerical system with its zero that he had been hearing about was something the Church would frown upon. What he was hearing now in the tavern from Adelard about the Church's strong stand against zero in the rest of the Christian world fortified him in his opinion. Whatever the truth of his views, it does show how strongly people felt about zero in what was – or, rather, should have been – merely a method of calculation.

For Adelard of Bath, coming back to England must have been quite a shock after what he had seen on his travels. In fact, he didn't mince any words in his first book *Quaestiones Naturales*, written after returning for the second time in 1116, where he expressed his desire to discover the manners and customs of his own country. He stated that he "has learned that its chief men are violent, its magistrates wine-lovers, its judges mercenary, its patrons fickle, private men sycophants, those who make promises deceitful, and that friends are full of jealousy, and almost all men are self-seekers." Perhaps he thought he could make a difference by reintroducing the Greek philosophers that, strangely enough, were known in the Arab world but had been lost in the West after the fall of the Roman Empire. Yet with all that he reintroduced and introduced to the West from the Arabs, the one thing that completely failed to impress was the new Indo-Arabic numeral system with its weird zero.

With no one putting up a strong fight in its defense, zero didn't have much of a chance. Prejudice was widespread. A similar anti-zero reaction could be found among the sophisticated merchants of Pisa as among the monks of rural England. Everywhere in Europe, in fact, apart from the lands that were under Arab rule – southern Spain, as well as Sicily, still under the influence of Arab culture even after the Arabs had left.

The French pope, the skull and nothing
We know that Fibonacci (Leonardo of Pisa) wasn't the first to translate the 'Treatise of the Cipher' from Arabic to Latin, and that Adelard of Bath had done so a few years earlier. But even before that, the work had been translated by someone else: a Frenchman by the name of Gerbert of Aurillac (945-1003), one of the strangest characters in a field that certainly had its share of them. Perhaps it was genius that made him into an eccentric (to put it kindly) in his later years, but it also contributed to his meteoric rise to power for someone of lowly birth, from Benedictine monk to pope, with some pretty wild political machinations on the way.

It is generally not enough to be bright or even a genius if there is no input, be it formal education or at least some level of stimulation. And never was it more important than in the period that we are talking about, around the year 1000 AD. In Europe, if you didn't live in lands occupied by the Muslims, where the source of knowledge and learning was concentrated, you would be severely handicapped as far as intellectual stimulation was concerned. It's not that nothing was happening in France, where Gerbert was born and received his early education, but that so much more was happening in Al-Andalus, across the border from where he was studying in the cathedral school in Vic, Catalunya.

Just to get an idea of the difference between Christian Catalunya and Al-Andalus under the Muslims, the largest library in Christian Europe contained less than a thousand volumes, while the library in the Muslim capital of Cordoba held over four hundred thousand! It was Gerbert's luck to be living in Vic, whose proximity to the Muslims benefited him so much and gave him the backdrop for his later work.

Gerbert was a precocious boy, thirsty for knowledge and lapping it all up with ease. It didn't take long for him to be noticed by higher-ups in the church, and in 969, the bishop of Vic took young Gerbert with him to Rome, where he met and impressed Pope John XIII. And not just the pope. Gerbert's obviously-outstanding mind soon came to the attention of Otto II (973-983), emperor of the Holy Roman Empire, who persuaded him to be his adviser and tutor.

Being clever is an advantage, and it definitely was for Gerbert, who rose in influence through the patronage of Otto II. Even more important, then, as now, was not so much *what* you knew, but *who* you knew, and in those days it was definitely also the luck of knowing the right people at the right time. The fact that Gerbert hitched his star to the Emperor in his struggles against the Church served him well, at least in the short run.

Gerbert's rise in power, though, did not translate into universal popularity, which was certainly not helped by the general feeling that he was more than a little strange. To the superstitious people of that time, Gerbert's material knowledge of the world outside of the Church, not to mention the ability to make complex calculations in his head, were a clear sign of his being in league with the devil. This label stuck to him even when he was made pope in 999 by Otto III.

Gerbert, now Pope Sylvester II, the first French pontiff, was, to put it mildly, not popular, as much for the sin of being foreign as for the ever-growing rumors of his magical and mystical powers, one of the rumors being that he had built a mechanical skull that would answer any of his questions with either 'yes' or 'no'.

None of this could have come at a more inauspicious time. It was the beginning of the millennium, when the end of the world was widely and wildly expected; a crazy, French pope with magical powers just seemed to auger the expected calamities.

He was deposed after only two years due to more earthly reasons: his political interference in secular matters. Forced to flee Rome, he nevertheless came back for another two years, though certainly not to increased popularity. Earlier rumors of his dealings with the occult and his links with the devil were now firmly established as fact by the populace. That he was one of the most important mathematicians of his time had not impressed the ordinary people, but, on the contrary, had had the opposite effect. And making him even more suspect in their eyes was not only that he was conversant with, and had used, Arab science and mathematics, but that he had tried to spread the Arab system of numbers that contained the zero. If he had any thoughts that as pope he would be able to utilize his scientific knowledge to further man's spiritual salvation, he was very wrong and singularly unsuccessful.

Zero certainly had the wrong champion in Gerbert, with circumstances no better after his death. In fact, for zero it got worse: whatever Gerbert as pope had touched in his lifetime was discounted as suspect by his successors, so that zero was doomed before later mathematicians got hold of it. The fact that a pope had endorsed it did not help at all; because the pope in question was Sylvester II, the pope in league with the devil, this could – and was – used against zero whenever necessary.

Jews, Muslims and nothing

If it is ever intimated that the Middle Ages were boring and that nothing interesting was happening, this is patently untrue. It was a period of vast change, of a bubbling up of new ideas that were thrusting themselves to the fore against forces that were intent on suppressing them. Just look at what was happening with and around *nothing*, not to mention the odd bods and geniuses who were wandering across countries and continents, pushing it. So much passion there was over that circle, the zero, so much suppressed excitement by the few mathematicians who saw its potential but couldn't get it accepted.

It could be said, of course, that zero had come to the West before its time. That, though, is not entirely true, since it was thriving in large parts of Europe and North Africa, namely where the Muslims were in charge. But it definitely was introduced to Christian Europe at the wrong time, in a critical period for the Church fighting to keep its authority in a world that was going through huge changes. Zero was a hostage in all of that – a metaphor for what was, in fact, a clash of civilizations, one religion against another, entrenchment against openness, north against south, pope against emperor.

So while zero was running for cover in large parts of Europe, it was safe in others. The difference with what was happening to it in societies where learning was advanced, and what was happening in stifled closed societies, whose aim was to keep out anything that was seen as a threat to the powers-that be, was colossal. The divide between the relatively more tolerant Muslim Europe and suspicious Christian Europe was nowhere better exemplified than in Spain, where the south and north might as well have been on different planets.

Scholars and thinkers living in Spain under the rule of the

Arabs had the advantage of libraries that contained not only current works on Muslim and Jewish science, mathematics and philosophy, but also, in Arabic, tomes of the ancient Greek civilization. It was no wonder that the country (and the other counties under Arab rule) attracted people from elsewhere – people such as Adelard of Bath, William of Malmesbury and Gerbert of Aurillac – who took in what they could and went out to spread the word.

Whether being eccentric was a coincidence or whether being a little crazy came with the territory, there is no doubt that being 'different' at that time helped when dealing with zero.

But 'different' did not even begin to cover another character that wandered through the turbulent world of zero and *nothing*. A loner, not a monk, not even a Christian, another genius to add to the roster of those who couldn't get zero much further than their own writings. Meet Abraham ben Meir ibn Ezra, Jewish itinerant poet, bible scholar, philosopher, astrologer, grammarian, mathematician. (An aside on his name: 'ben' and 'ibn' are simply 'son of' in Hebrew and Arabic respectively, so that his name is actually Abraham son of Meir son of Ezra. He is referred to in the literature as Ibn Ezra, which has the effect of perpetuating his grandfather's name rather than that of Abraham himself.)

Ibn Ezra (1089-1164) was born in a part of Spain (either Tudela or Toledo) that had recently been reconquered by the Christians after more than 350 years of Arab rule. He was a restless soul, a wandering hobo, traveling south to the Muslim regions and back and forth to the Jewish communities in North Africa, returning each time to Spain, never settling down anywhere long enough to accumulate more than he could carry. He did, though, find enough time to marry and father a son, Izhak, although this did not seem to cramp his lifestyle or make him a model husband and father. On one of his trips, he took Izhak along to Baghdad and left him there, finding out later that he had converted to

Islam and had died of an illness a few years after. Devastated as he was, this did not make him rethink his lifestyle, except to care even less for his worldly appearance. He continued his wanderings, wrote poetry and delved more deeply into astrology and magic, in addition to his other intellectual activities.

In 1160 Ibn Ezra left Spain for the last time and wandered around Italy, visiting the Jewish communities of the Christian world and being well received for his knowledge and teachings. Unlike the Jews in Arab lands who spoke Arabic, those in the Christian world knew Hebrew in addition to the local languages, and it was Ibn Ezra who brought to them science and mathematics from the Muslim world that he translated into Hebrew. All of this in addition to his own works on a wide spectrum of subjects, including a codified Hebrew grammar. In exchange, he was fed and housed during his brief sojourns in every place. Chronically poor, he must have had the appearance of a wandering prophet not caring about himself in order to dispense wisdom – not only on religious, but also on secular matters – to people who were thirsty for knowledge.

Ever more unkempt and dirty, Ibn Ezra wandered from Rome to Lucca in Tuscany, where he wrote some of his most famous works, then to France and to England, where he might have crossed paths with Adelard of Bath, perhaps not literally but it is interesting that they were there during the same period. And not only in England, for they had been traveling through the same areas in Europe, visiting the same centers of learning. It's nice to speculate that they did meet, even though there is no way of knowing whether they, in fact, did. If it happened, they would have had something in common, the Benedictine monk and the wandering rabbi, for they had each translated Al-Khwarizmi's work on the new numeral system – to Latin and to Hebrew respectively – and understood its importance.

There is an element of mystery about all this. Even if Adelard and Ibn Ezra never met, they would, surely, have been aware of the other's work on the numeral system. Yet neither quoted the work of the other, neither mentioning that they had even read what the other had written. We are, after all, speaking of exactly the same period and their respective translations would have been done within the space of twenty years. And Ibn Ezra did much more than translate from Arabic; he wrote three treatises on numbers which would have brought the Indian symbols and ideas of decimal fractions to the attention of some of the learned people in Europe, and there are indications that he wrote in Latin as well as in Hebrew.[8]

Ibn Ezra's *Book of the Unit* is a work on the Indian symbols 1, 2, 3, 4, 5, 6, 7, 8, 9 that he represented through the first nine letters of the Hebrew alphabet. Zero was not dealt with, for the same reason that Fibonacci ignored it a few years later: fear. The chances are that if Ibn Ezra had written the book when he was still living in Muslim Spain, he would have included the zero, which was, after all, an integral part of the numerical system. As unearthly as he looked and as involved with Jews as he was, he was very far from unaware of the world in which he wandered. If Christian mathematicians were afraid to deal with zero, a Jewish rabbi would have been out of his mind to challenge the Church. In the second work, though, *Book of the Number*, which describes the decimal system for integers with place values from left to right, Ibn Ezra does use zero; he could not have written the book without it. Whether this was an act of courage or just a submission to fate, he must have figuratively shrugged his shoulders and wrote what he did. The information that he was hearing about the wholesale slaughter of Jews who happened to be in the path of the Crusades in the Rhine valley on the way to the Holy Land made his zero seem very insignificant.

There is, though, a clue as to why Ibn Ezra thought he could get away with writing about the zero so openly and in such detail. It was the way he referred to the symbol, the character zero, itself. Brilliantly different, he named the zero character according to its **description**; he called it 'galgal' (meaning wheel or circle in Hebrew), rather than naming it according to what it represented, as others, before and after, had done.

So Ibn Ezra did not refer to it as 'zero', with its loaded connotation of 'void' and 'nothing', but instead simply gave it a physical description. Was this a sop to the Christian authorities? Did he mean to show that the zero represented *something* rather than *nothing*? If so, he killed two birds with one stone, for in describing zero as a circle he also gave his interpretation of how the Jewish religion saw it – not as *nothing*, but as the turning wheel of life on this earth.

Ibn Ezra made an important point through naming the character according to its shape, the circle, and thus allowing it to be seen not as *nothing*. For Christianity as well, the circle of life was an important symbolism. Unfortunately Ibn Ezra was alone in the way he referred to the symbol, and other mathematicians, even his contemporaries, such as Adelard of Bath, ignored Ibn Ezra completely.

It is riveting speculation that, had other mathematicians called the character something that was not associated with *nothing*, the new numerical system might not have been censored out by the Church and that it would have been adopted a few hundred years earlier than it eventually was!

Shapes and sizes

And the shape was wrong. The circle, with its mystical Eastern origin, merely reinforced the Church's aversion to the whole idea of zero. A bad mistake it was. A mistake not due to conscious thought, but rather by default: it was the character that the Arabs took over from the Indians and was simply continued in Europe.

It so happens that the shape was not the original one for zero, which was originally denoted by a dot, used as a place-marker, as early as 200 BC by the Hindu mathematician Pingal and that only later was replaced by a circle before spreading east to China. But even as a dot, it had a symbolic connection to zero, as in this sixth-century poem, in which Vasavadatta states: "The stars shone forth... like shunya-bindu (zero-dots)." [9]

Nobody, though, thought to change it, not even Ibn Ezra, who had distanced his 'galgal' from a *void* connotation. The fact that Ibn Ezra found it necessary to use the circle to represent zero is fascinating. He could have used another symbol. After all, there is nothing inherently significant in the shapes of our numbers; the numbers in a positional system are purely conventional and are not a graphic representation of the number itself (as, for example, three slashes – III – for 'three'), and while the Western world uses the numbers 1, 2, 3, 4, 5, 6, 7, 8, 9, 0 no matter what language is used to read them, there are many languages that use different signs. So for the number 3, for example, Arabic uses ٣, Hebrew ג, Bengali ৩, Devanagari ३, Lao ໓. It doesn't matter what shape the numbers have, the principle of mathematics is the same when there are ten numbers. (As a curious aside, the numbers used in the West are called 'Arabic numerals', to indicate their source, even though they aren't used in Arabic.)

Yet when it comes to zero, we find a surprising similarity among many disparate languages, as we can see on the chart overleaf.

As different as the other numerals are in various languages, zero is more often than not represented by some sort of closed sphere. (Although strangely enough, Arabic, the language that took the system with its zero symbol from the Indians and introduced it to the West, actually uses a dot, not a circle!)

Perhaps, then, there is something special in that particular symbol, not shared by the others. Is there a perceived mysticism about the character itself, the round symbol that represents *nothing*? Or to put it another way, does the concept of *nothing* extend also to the symbol that represents it? This is a question, one of a series of interesting questions thrown out by looking at *nothing*, that we will address later, in the chapter "Believing in Nothing".

	0	1	2	3	4	5	6	7	8	9
Arabic	٠	١	٢	٣	٤	٥	٦	٧	٨	٩
Bengali	০	১	২	৩	৪	৫	৬	৭	৮	৯
Chinese (simple)	〇	一	二	三	四	五	六	七	八	九
Chinese (complex)	零	壹	貳	叄	肆	伍	陸	柒	捌	玖
Chinese 花碼 (huā mǎ)	〇	〡	〢	〣	〤	〥	〦	〧	〨	〩
Devanagari	०	१	२	३	४	५	६	७	८	९
Ge'ez (Ethiopic)		፩	፪	፫	፬	፭	፮	፯	፰	፱
Gujarati	૦	૧	૨	૩	૪	૫	૬	૭	૮	૯
Gurmukhi	੦	੧	੨	੩	੪	੫	੬	੭	੮	੯
Kannada	೦	೧	೨	೩	೪	೫	೬	೭	೮	೯
Khmer	០	១	២	៣	៤	៥	៦	៧	៨	៩
Lao	໐	໑	໒	໓	໔	໕	໖	໗	໘	໙
Limbu	᥆	᥇	᥈	᥉	᥊	᥋	᥌	᥍	᥎	᥏
Malayalam	൦	൧	൨	൩	൪	൫	൬	൭	൮	൯
Mongolian	᠐	᠑	᠒	᠓	᠔	᠕	᠖	᠗	᠘	᠙
Myanmar	၀	၁	၂	၃	၄	၅	၆	၇	၈	၉
Oriya	୦	୧	୨	୩	୪	୫	୬	୭	୮	୯
Roman		I	II	III	IV	V	VI	VII	VIII	XI
Tamil	௦	௧	௨	௩	௪	௫	௬	௭	௮	௯
Telugu	౦	౧	౨	౩	౪	౫	౬	౭	౮	౯
Thai	๐	๑	๒	๓	๔	๕	๖	๗	๘	๙
Tibetan	༠	༡	༢	༣	༤	༥	༦	༧	༨	༩
Urdu	٠	١	٢	٣	۴	۵	۶	٧	٨	٩

Ager, Simon. "Omniglot - writing systems and languages of the world."

30.2 2009. www.omniglot.com

Nothing in the world

There are things that we take for granted, so much so that without them the world would be a very different place. Some of these, such as computers, the Internet and cell phones, while now indispensable, are innovations recent enough for many of us to remember a world without them. And it is not beyond our imagination, or our collective historical memory, to envisage a world without electricity, the telephone, refrigerators and running water. Stretching our 'memories' even further, we can imagine even what it was like before the invention of printing.

Can we envisage a world without the zero, though? In many ways, the very question seems ridiculous, since zero is as much part of us as, say, our arms or the language we speak. But having asked, we can but wonder, because zero is so 'natural', whether it was a discovery, rather than an invention.

It has been claimed that mathematics developed through real needs rather than as a result of abstract problems.[10] After all, if ancient peoples needed to solve a problem about how many goats someone needed, then the answer would be real and actual; it was not going to be 0 or -6 goats. No one can argue with that; concrete problems require concrete answers; the person wouldn't **need** *no goats*, and neither would less than one goat make any sense.

But if the farmer knew what he needed, he also knew what he did **not** need. He may have needed goats and not needed, say, foxes, or rats, or fleas. And naturally he was aware of what was left when all his goats escaped, so that he would have been very capable of telling his neighbor that he had no goats left. It is clear, then, that the concept of zero meaning *nothing* – an absence of something – was not something that had to be learned, but was inherent.

That does not mean, of course, that our ancient predecessors would have been able to manipulate zero within a mathematical system, which is not intuitive and would have had to be learned.

In fact, we know that it took thousands of years for that to happen. Unlike the zero meaning *nothing* (an absence), the zero that has the characteristics of a mathematical numeral is obviously not an inborn, inherent feature.

As we know, people had been able to survive without zero as part of their numerical system; in fact, there were even place-value number systems that did not contain the zero. The Babylonians seemed to manage very nicely for over 1000 years using such a system, from around 2000 BC. They succumbed, though, around 300 BC, when they started using an empty place holder, and six hundred years later the Mayans began using zero as a place holder. It took another 150 years for the Indians to use the zero not only as a place holder but also as a number.

So was zero invented or discovered? We are, of course, not talking about the symbol, the character, itself; obviously the representation, shape of zero, was invented, as were the shapes of the other numerals. Our concern is with zero as used in the counting system.

Let's take the wheel as an analogy. When we say that the wheel was invented, we are not, of course, referring to the shape itself. It was not roundness that was invented: that existed in nature, and we can safely assume that roundness as a concept was part of the human psyche. What was invented was the physical expression of roundness – its adaptation to something practical that could be used. And so it was with zero: absence, *nothing*, like roundness, is part of the natural world and therefore a concept inherent in the human mind. It was the adaptation of *nothing* (to zero), similar to the practical use put to roundness (the wheel), that was invented.

But if we have made that case for zero – that it is based on an inherent understanding – would it not apply to all numbers? Why would zero be different from the other numbers in that sense? The question, in other words, is whether humans have an inherent sense of numbers.

Now here we have to be careful to differentiate between the ability to count (which is taught) and an inherent (untaught) numerical perception, a number sense.[11] The difference is between a sense of **numbers** and a sense of **number**. We can get some idea by looking at children of around 18 months to 2 years (younger or older, depending on individual development, of course), who are able to recognize that something has changed when an object has been removed from, or added to, a collection of objects. If the child sees two collections of marbles, one of which has six marbles and the other four marbles, he will know which collection contains more and will also know if some are later taken out or added. This is 'number sense', different from the child's ability to count.

Recent research at Duke University backs this up.[12] Seven-month-old babies demonstrated an ability to match the number of voices they heard to the number of faces they expected to see. In this study, babies listened to two women simultaneously saying the word 'look' and three women saying the same word. At the same time, the infants could choose between video images of two or of three women saying the word. As they had found in a previous experiment with monkeys, the researchers reported that the babies spent significantly more time looking at the video image that matched the number of women talking. "As a result of our experiments, we conclude that the babies are showing an internal representation of 'two-ness' or 'three-ness' that is separate from sensory modalities and thus reflects an abstract internal process," researcher Elizabeth Brannon wrote. Even before babies learn to talk, then, they seem to have an abstract sense of numerical concepts.

So babies have a sense of number. In a nutshell: number sense is not taught, whereas counting is.[13]

What we can see with children most probably reflects and demonstrates what happened with humans in prehistory. The ability to discern that there are *differences in quantities* of objects is something that was never taught, and this inherent ability should not be confused with *counting*, which is something that was developed later when mankind first began to use agriculture and to hunt.

So what have we discovered after all that? For one, the obvious point that zero meaning *nothing* (an absence) is different from zero used as a number. This was reflected in Latin, with its different words – *sefirum* and *sifra* respectively – for each of those zeroes. Returning to our analogy of the wheel, we can say that we have an inherent sense of number in the same way that we have an inherent sense of roundness. We also, as we have seen, have an inherent sense of absence – the absence of something that had been there, zero referring to *nothing* as an absence. Sense of number, then, is inherent within humans in the same way as is zero meaning *nothing*, while counting is a taught skill equivalent to the zero used in a mathematical system (counting).

Our examination of *nothing* has also brought up something else. Unlike what is often accepted – that abstract thought is based upon what is first perceived in the real world – we have seen the opposite in this particular case: that concrete facts can be based upon abstract concepts. The inherent sense of absence (*nothing*) and of number are the abstract concepts upon which mathematics is built.

This is all very well, but if we earlier showed that *nothing* as a concept was beyond what the Church could accept, how can we now claim that children understand or grasp it? They don't, of course. It's not *nothing* that they grasp, but rather the absence of something that was there before and has since disappeared.

There is, in fact, a big difference between *nothing* that is the **absence of *something***, and *nothing* that is the **absence of *everything***. A child who asks her father, "Where is Mummy?" is not delving into abstract thoughts about nothingness, and has no problem understanding the fact that her mother is absent. Jean-Paul Sartre, the French existentialist philosopher, made the same point when, arriving late for his appointment with Pierre at the cafe, saw the absence of Pierre but not the absence of the Duke of Wellington.[14] And what is the sad feeling of 'missing' a person, if not the awareness of absence of that person? It was his own absence that Elvis referred to in his rendering of *Are You Lonesome Tonight*:

> *Do the chairs in your parlor seem empty and bare*
> *Do you gaze at your doorstep and picture me there*[15]

The final absence is, of course, death. When someone dies, the chair he sat in every day reminds us strongly of that person; looking at the chair, all we can see is something that is not there. In a way, the absence is more real to us than anything else present.

This, then, is the third point that has been thrown up: the difference between absence and *nothing*, between an absence of something and the absence of everything. And that is the point: Zero is never *nothing*, but is, rather, an absence (of a number).

Absence may make the heart grow fonder, but *nothing* is more inclined to drive us crazy.

The world with nothing

Where would we be without zero, we asked. Certainly not where we are now. None of the things mentioned: computers, cell phones, electricity, etc. etc. would exist, **could** exist. It seems almost as if the birth of zero was inevitable, without which the world would not have been able to move forward.

It may, then, be not too much of an exaggeration, looking back from where we are in the 21st century, to state that the invention of zero as number was as momentous as the invention of the wheel, all of which makes the campaign against zero by the Church in the early 11th century – the period when zero was trying to get itself recognized in Christian Europe – really incredible.

But what seems clear in retrospect certainly didn't look so at the time. Or perhaps it did. After all, the mathematicians who worked on the new system and sought to get it accepted did so in the face of indifference at the least and downright hostility, even danger, at the most.

But why? Was the reason for the Church's objection to zero purely ideological – religion's objection to the concept of *nothing*? Given the circumstances at the time, it's unlikely. That is not to say that religion and defense of God on earth were not the Church's concern; they certainly were, but as a way of keeping temporal control. Politics and power was the name of the game – and what can be more lethal than a mixture of politics and religion? – with the Church in a constant struggle against the civil authorities symbolized by the Holy Roman Emperor and in the emerging national states such as England and France over the division of functions within 'the kingdom on earth', such as who was entitled to anoint priests. In sum, the struggle was over jurisdiction, and nowhere did the Church dig its heels in more than where the borders were blurred. A prime example was the new numeral system, which, on the face of it, had nothing to do with the Church. But it did, as we have seen. It had everything to do with the Church, and that everything was the *nothing* represented, as far as they were concerned, by the zero.

As for the Church's external struggles, it's uncanny how easy it is to draw parallel lines between what is happening today and what was going on a thousand years ago. In both we can discern a clash of civilizations, even though the roles of the players are somewhat different. If then the Christian world was on the defensive against encroachment – physical and cultural – by the Muslims, today we need only change 'Christian' for 'Western' to understand similarities. And there is also the opposite, with Muslims wary of a perceived Western threat to their values.

The fight against zero must, of course, be seen in the light of what was going on at that time. Zero was not the only one of the many seditious ideas that the Church was battling in the beginning of the second millennium, among them the idea that the earth was not the center of the universe. Like zero, this was an absolute no-no for the Church. Although the heliocentric – sun-centered – system, which claimed that all planets revolve around the sun, had periodically been suggested by natural philosophers as an alternative to the geocentric – earth-centered – model of the universe, it had been slammed down by the Church without even the possibility of discussion. And the Church did not exactly use polite arguments when it disagreed with a point of view different to its own. The best, most efficient way of getting its views across was the Inquisition and the threat of death (always the latter, but often both).

You would have had to be a brave man to challenge the Church in any way, especially as 'heresy' was such a wide term that could be applied to anything that challenged the Church's power. It was the Church who decided what constituted heresy, and so it was accuser, judge and, often, executioner.

In this climate of suspicion and fear, none found life more difficult than astronomers, mathematicians and philosophers, who were chaffing at the bit, no longer able to accept everything the Church espoused as true. Particularly frustrated were astronomers, gradually separating from astrologists to partake in a more scientific and measurable science, who were finding it ever more difficult to accept the official doctrine – set out by Claudius Ptolemy, an Egyptian from Alexandria, in about 150 AD – that the earth was a fixed, inert, immovable mass, located at the center of the universe, and all celestial bodies, including the sun and the fixed stars, revolved around it. It was a comfortable concept, so much so that it was accepted as true for 1400 years! Not only did it fit in with what people observed when looking up at the sky at night, it also appealed to human nature and fed man's ego, while at the same time being natural proof of the religious doctrine that the earth was the center of the universe. For astronomers, though, this is not what they understood when they looked up at the sky. For them, 'seeing is believing' meant something different from what the Church taught it should mean. For the Church, if you couldn't see it, then 'believing is believing' was just as good.

Belief was not supposed to be individual and independent, that is, in the eyes of the beholder, but, rather, what was officially sanctioned. Particularly problematic were beliefs that came from the fringes of the Church, such as Christian mysticism, that connected God with nothingness.

Of all the mystics at the time, none was as brilliant and genuinely religious as Meister Eckhart (1260-1327), a Dominican monk. In 1326 proceedings were begun against him for heresy, with his denunciation, luckily for him, announced a year after his death. Eckhart's theology about the possibility of man's unity with God enraged the Church; even without parallels between Christian mysticism and Eastern faiths that may have been noticed (so reinforcing the Church's opposition to the zero), there was no way the Church could allow an unmediated experience of, and union with, the divine, and so bypassing the Church's structures, sacraments, and, above all, its priests in all their hierarchies through which they exercised worldly power.

Climate of fear

The Church was in a bind. It felt it had no choice but to hold firm within that period of immense turmoil in which it – the Roman Catholic, 'established' Church in Europe – was battling opponents within and without. In Spain, the 'reconquista', the gradual armed regaining of the lands that the Muslims had conquered in 711 AD, was gathering momentum, at the same time that Crusades were making their way through Europe and into the Holy Land in order to crush the 'infidels' and heretics.

Despite these 'successes', carried out through the sword, the

Church had a much more invidious opposition: dissidents within Christianity, which they dealt with by branding them as heretics and adding to that the pious application of mass torture and death (often by burning alive). Take the anti-materialistic Cathars, whose home was in southern France but who existed in large numbers within sizeable pockets of Western Europe. They claimed in no uncertain terms that, among other things, the Catholic Church was not worshiping the true God and that it was corrupt, claims that the Church was particularly sensitive to.

Although the Cathars were possibly the largest, there were other sects in various parts of Europe that posed a real threat to the Catholic Church and so were persecuted in the cruelest and most horrific fashion. Crusades against dissidents and the ongoing Inquisition made sure that people acknowledged the primacy of the Catholic Church, saw the errors of their ways and understood that all was being done in God's name for their own good and for their salvation.

Yet despite winning many battles, it is not at all sure which war was being won. Not only did the Crusades not destroy the supposed-enemies, be they dissident Christians, heretical Muslims or any Jews who got in the way, they actually caused ever greater schisms within the church, while perpetuating and exacerbating the split between the Eastern and Western Church. The influence that the Church had for so long was weakening before its very eyes, and it was unable to do anything about it. Not only did it have to contend with religious wars, but with its very right to temporal, as opposed to spiritual, power that was being questioned. It was, in fact, part of a long struggle against attempts to restrict the popes to spiritual power only, while leaving the running of states to civil authorities.

So with all that was going on and the Church's attempt to suppress opposition (real and perceived), can we be surprised that people did not want to confront the Church that was becoming ever more vicious as threats to its hegemony increased from all directions?

Yet some did push the boundary, as we have seen with the early European discoverers of zero. In astronomy, as we move into the early modern period, there were a few brave souls who made noises in favor of the heliocentric system that displaced the earth as the center of the universe. Strangely, while the Church was stifling the use of zero, it didn't, at first, come out so forthrightly against these astronomers. Strangely, because on the face of it, the position of the earth within God's design was more overtly central to Church dogma than was zero.

It took a German priest, Nicholas of Cusa, to come out openly, from around 1440, on the side of what had up to then been quiet criticisms of Ptolemy's geocentric model of the universe. Why Nicholas wasn't branded as a heretic was very likely because he cleverly combined his mathematical and astronomical findings with emotional theological arguments. He put it all down to God. What he said, basically, was that since God could do anything, he could even have the earth circle round the sun. The Church swallowed it and Nicholas was left alone.

He was, actually, walking on thin ice, since he also stated that the universe was infinite and containing an infinite number of worlds, a point of view for which a later philosopher, mathematician and astronomer, Giordano Bruno, was burned alive in 1600. The spot is marked today by a bronze statue of Bruno in a friar's habit and cowl, arms crossed, looking down with great sorrow in Rome's Campo de' Fiori, a square bustling with restaurants, markets and enchanted tourists. A plaque says simply, "To Bruno, from the generation he foresaw, here, where the pyre burned."

Giordano Bruno was the unlucky victim of bad timing, because when he came along all hell had let loose, with the Roman Catholic Church acting like a wounded giant hitting out at everything that moved. Martin Luther had seriously split the church in 1517 and the new Protestant Church was questioning the very fundamentals of the mother Church. Nicholas of Cusa would not have been able to get away with what he had said a few years before, so that when Copernicus came out with his new, shocking astronomical theory, the gates were firmly shut.

A Polish canon of the church, a mathematician and physician, Copernicus (1473-1543) was the first to succeed in describing the movements of the planets using an astronomical theory that placed the sun at the center. When his book *De revolutionibus orbium coelestium* (*On the Revolutions of the Celestial Spheres*) was published in 1543, the Church cracked down on the whole idea and placed his book within the list of banned books, the Index (still very much alive, having recently added Dan Brown's fictional *The Da Vinci Code* to its notorious list). But they had closed the stable door after the horse had bolted, especially since the invention of printing allowed books to be disseminated easily.

There seems no doubt that fear of the unknown was part and parcel of the theological reason that drove the actions of the Church. A well-ordered universe, the earth at its center, surrounded by the sun and planets – that made sense. But to allow Copernicus and, later, Galileo Galilei to disseminate the idea of an infinite universe with an unknown number of worlds... that was unthinkable.

Copernicus' theory was not just about how the universe is physically; he brought about a complete shift in man's philosophical conception of the universe and his place within it. And it also implied that there was a place outside the universe, where man did not exist. Where there was *nothing*, in fact.

It didn't help that the French mathematician and philosopher Blaise Pascal (1623-1662) seemed to imply just that when he carried a mercury barometer to a mountaintop to prove that air was lighter the higher one went, so that eventually, he said, air would be weightless. The thought that past a certain point there would be nothing overhead, neither air nor light nor even God, went against the belief in a cosmos divinely created for humans. *Nothing* was a no-go area, as far as the religious authorities were concerned; it was too big an idea for the Church to contemplate, because to do so would be to implicitly question the very fact of God's existence. It goes without saying that questioning God's existence was heresy. And if there was such a thing as beyond heresy, this was it: a topic that could not be touched because even touching it raised an un-raise-able question.

The problem with *nothing* was just that – that it was *nothing*. If God existed there, then *nothing* would not be *nothing*, because it contained God. It would, in fact, be *something*. The Church had no intention of being trapped within a religious maze. The answer was to ban the maze. *Nothing* was out.

From the perspective of a democratic society today, where the Church deals with things holy and the state deals with all the rest, we can only look in horror at societies controlled by the purveyors of God's truth, where transgression against religious law can mean death. One has to be very brave – and foolhardy – to go against laws based on religious belief.

So who could blame Copernicus for being squarely in the camp of the non-brave? His heliocentric theory of the solar system was so revolutionary as to be the basis on which others, from Galileo to Newton, based their work. Yet he kept it quiet throughout his life, preferring to have it circulated anonymously. It is said that he saw his completed book only on his death bed, which was lucky for him, seeing as how things turned out for Giordano Bruno, that brave and possibly first martyr to science, who, for all his genius, turned out to be rather foolhardy, as we have seen.

Even Galileo couldn't get away with it. Despite his fame and academic positions in the leading universities of Pisa and Venice, not to mention the election of an admirer, Maffeo Barberini, as Pope Urban VIII, Galileo ended his days under house arrest for heresy. Had he waited a little longer – till 1992, 358 years, to be precise – he would have been gratified by his formal acquittal by Pope John Paul II. The wheels of justice can turn slowly, and presumably the outcome is better late than never. At the time, though, he had been given the choice at his trial by the Inquisition to either renounce his work and state that he had been wrong, or be put to death. He chose the former. It was a sensible choice but a sad end for a great man, the lesson not being missed by his contemporaries.

But in fact the Church didn't need laws as such; the laws were based on the Bible and the writings of the Church fathers. The role of the Church was to interpret for the people that which wasn't clear. Most often the Church's wishes were made known on the local level and percolated down through the hierarchy from the curia to the lowliest parish priests. Long before there was such a thing as 'mass communication' the wishes of the Church were widely known over large geographical areas.

Sometimes, when the message needed to be spelled out, special laws were enacted, such as in Florence in 1299, against the use of the new numeral system with its zero. In 1348, the ecclesiastical authorities of Padua prohibited the use of zero in price lists, arguing that prices had to be written in 'plain' letters. The need for special laws against it shows that zero was being used, often clandestinely; it was just easier to do calculations with it than without it.

So it wasn't just within the esoteric calculations of mathematicians and scientists. Zero was a godsend (!) to traders and salesmen – or at least it would have been if it hadn't been suppressed by the Church. The Medici Bank, for example, didn't use zeros until the sixteenth century. Now this was not just a bank. In the fifteenth century it was the most powerful financial institution in Europe, owned by the immensely influential Florentine Medici family from the 13th to 17th century. The family produced three popes, numerous rulers of Florence, and later members of the French royalty. In its heyday in the fifteenth century the Medici Bank was a veritable powerhouse, with headquarters in Florence, and branches in Rome, Venice, Geneva, Lyons, Bruges, London, and many other cities. The Medici family was intimately connected to the Church, to which the bank served as financial agent. Its influence was so great that it extended credit to monarchs, and was the leading institution for the facilitation of international trade in Europe. And all that without using the zero!

Whether by edict, by word of mouth or by an understanding of what the Church wanted through example, the reign of fear had lasted an inordinate period of time. For centuries, in fact. And throughout was the constant conflict between the advancement of knowledge and those that strove to suppress it. Although the Church had in the past eased up on various issues and absorbed them in a sort of sleight of hand so that they seemed to have always been part of Church canon,[16] it was now digging in, as people were only too aware. In fact, it was cracking down ever harder the more it felt threatened.

Some mathematicians tried the impossible: to progress while avoiding conflict with the church. Take Girolamo Cardano (1501-1546) of Milan, a brilliant mathematician and friend of Leonardo da Vinci. There was nothing meek about Cardano, an inveterate gambler, who was not loath to slash a face or two in the course of a life that was as much Mr. Jekyll as Dr. Hyde, losing and gaining fortunes in a life that was certainly different from the usual academic one. This was no meek English monk, but a hot-blooded Italian, who was not one to accept what was being dished out. He spoke his mind, was thoroughly disliked throughout a long career of successes and failures, of getting jobs and losing them.

Yet when it came to mathematics, his life's work, he behaved very differently. Cardano went through extraordinary calculations to solve cubic and quartic equations without using zero. He would have found his work so much easier if he had had a zero; but for him zero simply did not exist, despite zero being part of the numerical system that had already been widely known for over three hundred years! A wild character he may have been, but suicidal he certainly was not. Seeing how Copernicus was handling his own work, Cardano was not about to become a martyr to the cause of mathematics, or as we could say, to the cause of *nothing*.

Avoiding it, though, didn't make it disappear, and neither did pretending it didn't exist. Once something is out there, you can't make it go away. From Galileo onwards, *nothing* was out of the closet, in the form of zero. What Galileo had said in 1636 – and had angered the Church perhaps more than his actual astronomical theories – came to be accepted, and so led to modern science and unbridled advances in civilization. In a nutshell, he argued that the Bible had to be interpreted in the light of what science had shown to be true. In even a smaller nutshell: when science clashes with God, the truth lies with science.

All that was needed was to find out what the truth was!

And that is where we hit a paradox. Science – and we include everything that is not based on belief alone – may have expected, in the seventeenth century, to find the ultimate truth; but that is not the aim of science today. And we no longer expect it of science. What science is seeking is an explanation, or, rather, a theory to explain the phenomena it is examining.

Accounting for zero

Although zero had a slow, painful birth, its survival was inevitable, if only because once it was out it was too useful to have been allowed to disappear. Now although true, that is not really the whole story. The problem with inevitability in general is that it can only be seen as such in hindsight and so does not prove anything apart from the fact that something (whatever it is you are showing) happened. Fate is a wonderful theory because it always works – as long as you look back to what has already taken place. So it is with the struggle of zero to find its place in the world, where the inevitability of its success is now clear. Once we map out its past, the rest, as they say, is history.

Zero came to be universally used almost without anyone noticing. There is no line that can be pointed to as being the border between pre- and post-zero use. Zero was grasped only when it was thought of in its own right as a number and not as *nothing*. Zero was everything that *nothing* wasn't.

At what point did the Church stop its opposition to it? There was no such point, of course. The pressure that came from the realities of science and commerce played a part, but until the Church accepted the difference between zero and *nothing*, it did not let go.

So how did it happen? The accountants came in, that's how. Unnoticed, except by those who needed them, they worked to help the merchants in the trading states of Italy, particularly Venice, a huge trading power. It was a time long before accountants were the butt of jokes and sketches, such as in this extract from a Monty Python sketch:

Counselor (John Cleese):
Well I now have the results here of the interviews and the aptitude tests that you took last week, and from them we've built up a pretty clear picture of the sort of person that you are. And I think I can say, without fear of contradiction, that the ideal job for you is chartered accountancy.

Anchovy (Michael Palin):
But I am a chartered accountant.

Counselor:
Jolly good. Well back to the office with you then.

Anchovy:
No! No! No! You don't understand. I've been a chartered

accountant for the last twenty years. I want a new job. Something exciting that will let me live.

Counselor:
Well chartered accountancy is rather exciting isn't it?

Anchovy:
Exciting? No it's not. It's dull. Dull. Dull. My God it's dull, it's so desperately dull and tedious and stuffy and boring and des-per-ate-ly DULL.

Counselor:
Well, er, yes, Mr. Anchovy, but you see your report here says that you are an extremely dull person. You see, our experts describe you as an appallingly dull fellow, unimaginative, timid, lacking in initiative, spineless, easily dominated, no sense of humor, tedious company and irrepressibly drab and awful. And whereas in most professions these would be considerable drawbacks, in chartered accountancy they are a positive boon.[17]

Far, far from a joke, though, was the topic in the 15th century. In the same period that Nicholas of Cusa and Copernicus were making waves with their theories about the earth, the sun and the planets, and bringing the Church down on their heads, other mathematicians were working on figures that had more immediately practical uses. One of these was Luca Pacioli (1445-1520) in Venice, who set down in writing for the first time, in 1494 – and, this being only a few years after the invention of printing, the first printed textbook on accounting – a description of the double-entry system of accounting, which we still use today in much the same form. Pacioli, a rather dour, severe and largely mirthless Franciscan monk, was one of the most versatile mathematicians of his time, and was a close friend of Leonardo da Vinci, with whom he collaborated on many projects. It was

Pacioli who helped Leonardo lay out his painting, *The Last Supper*, with mathematical precision, while Leonardo reciprocated by illustrating Pacioli's books on mathematics and accounting.

And so it was that the great swirl of history surrounding the battles over zero came to its conclusion not with a bang but through double-entry bookkeeping. Zero just slipped naturally into the mainstream without anyone really noticing. Or perhaps Pacioli did realize it and put God into the equation just to make it all kosher. Neatly, in the trial balance (*summa summarium*) at the end of the accounting cycle in his book, he listed the debit amounts from the old ledger on the left side of the balance sheet and credits on the right, and demonstrated that if the two totals were equal, the old ledger was considered balanced. If not, "that would indicate a mistake in your Ledger, which mistake you will have to look for diligently with the industry and intelligence God gave you."[18] In other words, the absolute requirement is that those two columns sum to zero. To put it another way, the two columns are balanced when the difference between their sums is zero. As simple as that is, it is the basis for tracking all financial transactions today.

It was a matter of balance, with which the Church had no problem. In fact, keeping everything on an even keel was what the Church always wanted. The problem the Church had with zero was its association with *nothing*. When zero was the result of balance, it was perfectly acceptable.

Balance was something that Pacioli's friend, Leonardo da Vinci, understood very well. Without going into the conspiracy theories connected to da Vinci, his life and beliefs encoded in his paintings (around which a whole literary cottage industry has grown),[19] it seems that he did somehow tread a narrow path between his religiosity and other sides of his personality. This can be seen very nicely through his opinions of nothingness, which he expressed in a way that even the Church could accept. In his

Notebooks,[20] Leonardo strikes a neat balancing act by discussing nothingness in relationship to time and speech. Regarding time, he wrote that nothingness stands between the past and future and has no existence in the present; in speech, therefore, it is one of the things that we say are not, or are impossible. Cleverly, Leonardo was making his point about *nothing*, without saying that it was *nothing*.

But it was not Leonardo da Vinci who made *nothing* acceptable. His description was merely a play with words that meant nothing. *Nothing* became acceptable by default, when zero came into its own. In the end, it was a matter of checks and balances that slipped zero to legitimacy. Thanks to Pacioli and double-entry bookkeeping, zero was no longer *nothing*.

Because of nothing

Nothing may have come out of the closet a long time ago, but it is no less mysterious because of that – not to mention the cause for a headache or two. Take away a zero from someone's bank balance and what happens? There are so many stories of bank accounts that have had a zero or two deleted, and even some cases (rarer, strangely!) of great leaps of fortune through the addition of the extra zero or two. Here is a genuine example from The [British] Daily Telegraph of December 31, 2005:

> *British Greenpeace... donors who gave direct debit saw their bank accounts charged a hundred times the usual amount... "We are still trying to find out how this glitch happened... For some reason two noughts* [zeros] *seem to have been added... said [a Green peace spokesman, January 2006].*

In the meantime, while Greenpeace was trying to find out how it happened, people were out of pocket.

Here are a couple of questions: Was there a year 0? After all, we know that there was a year 1 BC and a year 1 AD. A second, and related, question is: Did the third millennium begin in 2000 or 2001?

Take the calendar. Julius Caesar did just that in 46 BC, when he replaced the Roman calendar with one he considered better. As megalomaniacal as that sounds, the new calendar was, in fact, better; it simplified everything, giving the year 365 days divided into 12 months, with a leap year added every four years. This gave an average Julian year of 365.25 days, the idea being to make it coincide with the solar year. But even that improvement to the calendar turned out to be not accurate enough, since it contained an error that accumulated over the years.

Now it didn't bother the average person in the street that as the centuries passed the Julian calendar became increasingly inaccurate and that the seasons were slipping, so to speak. But the Roman Catholic Church was becoming ever more troubled by what was happening to Easter – the Crucifixion seen as the single most significant event in the history of the human race – which, by the 16th Century, was well on the way to slipping into Summer. That was solved with the introduction of the Gregorian calendar in 1582, by Pope Gregory XIII.

But what has all this got to do with *nothing*, zero and the millennium? Before getting to it, let's take a look at what happened when the Gregorian calendar was actually introduced: ten days were omitted from the calendar to get it back to where it should be. They simply didn't exist. Popes can do that – certainly in those days. It was decreed that the day following Thursday, October 4, 1582 (which would have been October 5, 1582, in the old calendar) would thenceforth be known as Friday, October 15, 1582. It was a sign of the times that the rest of the world – the non-Roman Catholic world, that is – did not follow. After all, if there was one thing they would not do, it was to follow the pope! It was an example of cutting off their nose to spite their face, because the calendar eventually would have to be changed, and when it was, some two hundred years later when Britain and the American colonies adopted the Gregorian calendar after the rest of Europe – Protestant Germany and Denmark last in 1700 – in 1752, the old calendar had drifted off by one more day, requiring a correction of eleven days, rather than ten, so that Wednesday, September 2, 1752, was followed immediately by Thursday, September 14, 1752.

But the British were positively speedy compared to a slew of other counties, which stayed with the Julian calendar, and so drifted away on some sort of time raft. In the end, all paid with days that never existed, with the Russian empire paying the heaviest price of thirteen days after the Bolshevik Revolution in 1917, when it was decreed that the day following January 31, 1918 would become February 14, 1918. That is, by the way, why the 'October Revolution' is also known as the 'November Revolution'. It's the same revolution, which occurred on October 25, 1917 according to the Julian calendar then in use in Russia; for the rest of the world, that used the current Gregorian calendar, the date was November 7.

Quite a problem it all was. In a way it's like a rather extreme version of flying across time zones. What happens to the time that we have leaped over? What happened to those missing days in 1582, 1752 and 1918? Of course people didn't suddenly age by ten or eleven days (the common people, though, thought otherwise, and there are records of rioting in 1582 at the presumed loss of their missing days, although it wasn't so much that they didn't know where they were as that they had been cheated out of a week and a half's wages), just as we don't 'lose' (or 'gain') hours when crossing time zones. It is, after all, just playing with numbers. Yet for us landing in another time zone those hours simply never existed, just like those days didn't in 1582, 1752 and 1918. A question that begs to be asked, then, is whether something that doesn't exist (like those missing days) is nothing.

Getting back to our original question: Why was there no year 0? Actually, the question was: "Was there a year 0?" but since we know there wasn't, let's have a look at how the years were counted.

We mentioned that the Julian calendar was introduced in 46 BC. That is correct but also not correct. The point is that there was no such date as 46 BC at that time. Years then were numbered according to the whims of the Roman emperors, either *ab urbe condita*, 'from the founding of the city' (of Rome), or else named after the emperor, the number changing when the emperor did. It was not until the time of Charlemagne (Charles the Great), more than 800 years later, that it was officially decided to number the years of the Julian calendar from the supposed incarnation of Christ.

At last we are getting to our zero. Charlemagne (747-814), the first sovereign to be anointed over what was called the Holy Roman Empire, that included most of what is today France, Belgium, the Netherlands, Germany, Switzerland, Austria, and northern Italy, felt the world needed a conscious and daily reminder of Christ's arrival. What greater symbolic reminder could there be than counting the passing of time since that momentous event? Even the founding of Rome or – and this was a huge gesture – the crowning by the pope of Charlemagne himself were insignificant compared to God's manifestation on earth. And so Charlemagne adopted the years as AD (Anno Domini – 'the Year of Our Lord'), taking the idea from the Roman abbot Dionysius Exiguus, historically known as the father of the Christian calendar, who espoused it in around 572 AD.

Now while the initials AD stand for Anno Domini, they could just as easily stand for "Anno Dionysius" to commemorate the person who introduced the concept to the world. It would certainly be more accurate, since the signs are that the actual 'Year of our Lord' probably occurred at least five years earlier.[21]

For someone who changed the way the world counts its years,

Dionysius Exiguus was a decidedly retiring and self-effacing figure, to which even his name alluded ('Dionysius The Little', the latter appendage referring to his humble character, rather than to his physical size). The only journey he ever made was from his home in Dacia, in what is now Romania, to Rome, where he stayed for the rest of his life. No wandering around the countryside and sitting in taverns for him. Because of that, he could get on with what he was good at, translating important church documents from Greek to Latin.

He could have continued the life of anonymity as one of thousands of parchment scribblers, living out his days in the cold and flickering light within the recesses of the church. Where he left his mark for posterity, though, was supposedly working out the exact date of Christ's incarnation (and so introducing the Christian era). From that he compiled a table of subsequent dates of Easter, the most important date in the Christian calendar.

Dionysius worked out that Christ's incarnation, linked with the revelation to Mary that she would conceive the Son of God, occurred in 754 according to the then system of counting – on March 25! So that's how Christmas, the birth of Jesus, came to be December 25,[22] nine months later and designated by Dionysius as the year 1 AD (which originally, and in full, stood for *Anni Domini Nostri Jesu Christi "Years of our Lord Jesus Christ"*). And so momentous was it, that everything before had to lead up to it, like a slow countdown to The Event.

But it didn't happen like that. As romantic as is the story of the humble monk who gave us December 25 as the joyful and colorful festival of Christmas, there was, in fact, more to that date than meets the eye. Without going into the mistakes that Dionysius made in his calculations of Jesus' birth (with modern historians assigning 6 AD or 6 BC as more likely, depending on which historical events are used as evidence), the date of December 25 was not chosen by chance. In fact, there was considerable pressure to give that date a Christian aura, since it was the last day of Saturnalia, an important Roman pagan holiday celebrating the Winter Solstice. And not just any holiday. It was one of the highlights of the year, in which citizens let themselves go in a week of lawlessness, debauchery, rape and all-round drunken licentiousness, culminating in a great orgiastic and riotous merrymaking shriek on the last day, December 25.

There was no way that this momentous and eagerly-awaited festival could have been dispensed with, so in the 4th century, Christianity imported the Saturnalia festival, thereby succeeding in converting to Christianity large numbers of pagans by promising them that they could continue to celebrate the Saturnalia as Christians, with December 25 now cast as Christ's birth date and Charles Dickens largely responsible in the 19th century for its ubiquitous family-oriented ho-ho-ho glow.

Whatever the not so auspicious past of Christmas or the link of 1 AD with Jesus, from that point, the world was counting its years differently.

Now obviously during the BC years (designated as such by the Venerable Bede some 200 years later),[23] people didn't actually count the years backwards (towards something they didn't know was coming!), but it was a neat way of looking at the world afterwards, in retrospect. Yet even with this after-the-event backwards counting, one year was patently missing: the year after 1 BC was 1 AD. No year 0.

The missing year

Why was there no year 0? The most obvious reason, and the one given often, is that zero as a number had not yet been introduced into Europe at the time of Dionysius. In other words, it is said, the concept of zero did not exist yet. This, though, is not true, since zero was definitely around as a date marker in 572 AD, when Dionysius did his far-reaching calculations. For the purpose of dating documents, periods of time were then being measured in 19-year cycles (every 19 years being the closest the lunar and solar years get together), and had been for some 240 years; in his calculation for the exact date of Easter, Dionysius named as zero the age of the moon on 22 March of the first of each 19-year cycle. The Latin word he used, *nulla*, meant 'nothing', even though no Roman numeral for zero existed. The other Latin word meaning 'nothing' – *nihil* – referred to the year that ended each 19-year cycle.[24]

It is not true to say, then, that the concept of zero was unknown in Europe until it was introduced by the Arabs in the twelfth century. Although it was unknown as a numeral within mathematics, it was around as a marker, a starting point not representing a number. In fact, both uses of zero – *nulla* and *nihil* – continued to be used in the calculation of Easter by all those who came after Dionysius. This should come as no surprise, since we know that the concept of *absence* of something is inherently accepted by humans – and that is what, in fact, Dionysius was representing through *nulla* and *nihil*: the absence of number.

Now we can come back to our question as to why Dionysius did not determine the year of Christ's incarnation as year zero, rather than year 1 AD. After all, he had no problem with zero being the last year of the 19-year cycle.

He did, though, have a problem with calling *nihil* the year that is intimately connected to God; to do that would be to extend 'nothing' to a realm that opens a Pandora's box of theological questions and problems. For as already pointed out, *nothing* is seemingly impossible. For there to be *nothing* would mean a situation where there is no God, since it would mean an absence of everything (including God). And since God is eternal, there could never have been a situation before God. Furthermore, *nothing* cannot produce something; only God can. All this was deeply rooted within the Christian ethos, that we come across again and again.

Nowadays, of course, all of those considerations don't come into play when we count years. We do, though, have our own hang-ups. People were hardly less hysterical at the approach of the third millennium than they were a thousand years before, and although they didn't really believe that the end of 1999 would bring the end of the world, there were enough prophets of gloom regarding computers going haywire and a consequent collapse of everything functionable including the possibility of planes dropping out of the sky and other unimaginables.

It was a mass fear of the zero, while a thousand years previously it had been fear engendered by the end of 'The 1000 Year Reign of Christ'; more irrational then, we like to say, but in a period replete with alarming, earthly portents, including Vikings attacking Europe from the north, Hungarians from the east and Muslims from the south, it did really look like the end was nigh.

Each millennium was approached with trepidation, it seems. As for ours, once we realized that we had survived the year 2000, all we needed to do was to agree as to when the millennium had actually started; that is, whether the world was right to celebrate the start of the millennium on January 1st 2000, or whether it should have been on January 1st 2001, according to a few bothersome voices.

Unfortunately, logic, history and our conception of how numbers work point to the latter being more on the mark. How does our year start? – With the first day of the first month: 1/1. How did Humble Dionysius begin the Christian era? – He began it with the Coming of Christ, in the year 1. In Emperor Charlemagne's time, the numbering system began with I and ended with X (10). When he renumbered the Julian calendar, there was no number 0 and there could have been no year 0.

So does that make any difference to how we count our years today? Now that we do have the number 0, could we conceive of having a year 0, or a month 0 or a day 0? It doesn't seem so. We also begin counting with number 1; the first (1st) is always number 1.

We seem, then, to have a watertight case for the millennium

beginning in 2001 and ending in 3000. Does that mean that the celebrations at midnight December 31, 1999, to mark the beginning of the millennium, were a year too early? Not necessarily, because there is another side, a justification for those celebrations.

Again we can call on logic, history and our conception of how numbers work today.

When a child has her first birthday, she is one year old. But that child didn't begin her life at 1; the months before that birthday were in her first year and the first birthday marked the end of that first year. A day after that first birthday, the child begins her second year. In the same way, the millennium began its existence on January 1, 2000.

It all, of course, hangs on *nothing*, zero. Unlike at the time of Charlemagne, when there was no 0, we do have the 0 and it is deeply entrenched in our counting system. At the time the numbers were 1, 2, 3, 4, 5, 6, 7, 8, 9, 10, whereas we have, logically, to consider 0 as being the first number: 0, 1, 2, 3, 4, 5, 6, 7, 8, 9. The number written after 9 is '10' (one, zero): because the zero is a place marker to show that there are no units, the 1 indicates its status as one ten and that the number is in the second group of 10 numbers.

But don't we still start from 1 when we count? Actually, we don't – not necessarily when it comes to units of time, where it seems to be no more natural to start from 1 than it is to start from 0. So while the days of the month and the months of the year are still counted as they have been since ancient times, it is different for hours and seconds, which begin from 0, not from 1. A day begins at midnight, 12.00 (00:00:00 on the 24 hour clock), not at 1.00 am. 9:00:00 (9 hours, 0 minutes, 0 seconds) is considered the beginning of the hour, and not the end of the previous hour. And when it comes to the millennium, it does seem, somehow, 'natural', more satisfying, for it to begin in 2000.

And we do have the expression 'Year Zero'. A fairly new one

and in the main with political connotations, it is used for a year that was so momentous as to signal a watershed from which nothing coming afterwards will be the same as what was before. Year Zero is momentous in the eye of the beholder: it was applied by the Khmer Rouge to their takeover of Cambodia in 1975, and, for example, by Naomi Klein to the Bush policy in Iraq after the invasion of 2003.[25]

When new, car odometers read 00000 miles. When a car odometer passes 99999 miles, and again reaches 00000, we do not celebrate the end of a cycle, we celebrate the beginning of a new cycle. Presumably it is the change in the thousands column – the passing from no thousands to the countdown to one thousand, or one thousand and the start towards two thousand and those zeros – that does it. The same sense of 'naturalness' goes with decades as well; when we talk about 'the sixties', we see that period as 1960-1969 (not 1961-1970). Our perception – our gut feeling – is that the millennium began in 2000. And who says that our perception, the way we see the world, is wrong?

So do we now know whether the millennium should have started in 2000 or 2001? No, not really.

We haven't even yet agreed how we should call the first decade of the 21st century. After completing the nineties, what should we go for? The ohs? The double-ohs? The zeros? The zips? The nadas? The noughties? As non-satisfying as they all are, how about 'the aughts', that has gained some popularity? But 'aught' does not mean 'nothing', 'zero', or 'cipher', but rather 'anything' as used by writers down the centuries, including Shakespeare ("I never gave you aught," Hamlet says to Ophelia) and Milton ("To do aught good never will be our task / But ever to do ill our sole delight," Satan declares near the beginning of *Paradise Lost*, before sliding up to tempt Eve). And that is why 'aught' is so apt. Zero is not nothing, as we have seen, and nor are two zeroes. But two 'anythings'? We should be able live with that.

Apples, oranges, zero and nothing

It's time to breathe and take stock. With all this headlong rush into *nothing*, we have spent a lot of time on zero. Perhaps we were rash to connect zero and *nothing*, even though 'the man in the street' does connect them even while feeling that zero is not always *nothing*. He is right. Zero may feel like nothing when his bank account is empty, but it sure doesn't when the zeros add up otherwise.

So what is the connection? Let's take a basket and apples to illustrate the point. A basket that had contained apples but is now empty is considered 'to have nothing inside' (ignoring, for the moment, air, dust, particles, microbes, and much more, both living and dead).

Yet if we ask *how many* apples are in the basket, the answer is none, that is, no (zero) apples, where zero applies to the number: not 1, not 5, but zero. In other words: what is in the basket? – nothing; how many apples are in the basket? – none. The answer to how many apples are in the basket is not *nothing*, but *none* – zero apples.

The question is whether this helps in any way to distinguish between zero and *nothing*. We have said that if we ask what is in the basket, the answer is *nothing*. But is that correct? After all, if there are no apples in the basket, it does not mean that there is nothing there; it only means that there are no apples. But there are no oranges in the basket either, yet it would be strange to say, after the apples were removed, that there are no oranges in the basket (rather than that there are no apples). We consider the basket to be empty of apples, rather than of oranges, even though the basket is empty of both. Although the result is the same – there is nothing in the basket – our perception *of what there isn't* is different.

Instead of apples and oranges, let's try it with numbers. Is the result the same in both of the following cases?

$$\begin{array}{cc} 5 & 8 \\ -5 & -8 \\ \hline 0 & 0 \end{array}$$

Yes and no. The result is zero, as we can see. But the two zeros do not really have the same connotation: in one of them, the zero means that there are no fives, while in the other one, the zero means that there are no eights. To put it another way: in one case there is an absence of fives, while in the other case there is an absence of eights. Coming back to our baskets and fruit, a basket from which you take out all the apples and another basket from which you take out all the oranges will both be empty, but will be empty in a different way: one will have zero apples and one will have zero oranges (an absence of apples and an absence of oranges). Both, though, will have nothing in them.

This can be seen very clearly if we refer back to the examples of young children. A child will say that "Daddy is gone," and at another time that "Mummy is gone," and although in both cases something is gone, the child will think of **what** is gone in a different way in each case.

We have discovered something interesting, referred to earlier when we spoke about the farmer and his missing goats: Zero is not *nothing*; zero is an absence. Repeating what we stated previously, we can differentiate between an absence (the **absence of something**), and *nothing* (the **absence of *everything***).

Very interesting in this connection is the Latin word *nihil*, 'nothing', used by Dionysius Exiguus in the 6th century. The word was applied, as we saw, only to a specific 'nothing' – the result of 19 subtracted from 19 and was not extended to any other subtraction. A mummy that isn't there is not the same as a daddy that isn't there.

This may have seemed like a diversion – the so-called difference between zero and *nothing* – but it is, actually, important within the discussion of what *nothing* is. For a start, we can see that when we talk about *nothing*, we may be referring to *nothing* that, like zero, is an absence, or to *nothing* that is the absence of everything. The former is easy; it is the latter that is the mystery.

Separating nothing and zero

So where are we? Less muddled about *nothing*, hopefully. For a start, we know that *nothing* is not always nothing. If it is an absence, like zero, then it is something. That doesn't solve our problems of course, for all we can say at this point is that zero is something, whereas *nothing* is, well, nothing.

Let's try another tack. Perhaps the difference between zero and *nothing* is due to the grammatical parts of speech of the words themselves. Zero can be a noun ('He received a zero on his test') and an adjective ('a zero score'), whereas *nothing* is only a noun (apart from infrequent literary devices: "the utterly nothing role of a wealthy suitor" – Bosley Crowther).[26] So we can have 'zero numbers' but not 'nothing numbers'. We can, of course, have 'no numbers', but, as we have seen, 'no numbers' is not equivalent to nothing, in the same way that 'no apples' isn't *nothing*.

But surely there must be more to it than merely the difference between nouns and adjectives.

Perhaps the time has come to do what we should have done in the first place – to look up the meaning of *nothing* in a dictionary. After all, isn't that what dictionaries are for?

Here are a few random definitions:

> **pronoun** *not anything*
> *(Compact Oxford English Dictionary)*
> *Pronoun: no thing, not anything*
> *noun: something that has no existence*
> **not anything:** *an indefinite pronoun indicating that there is not*

> anything, not a single thing, or not a single part of a thing
> **zero amount:** *a zero quantity or zero*
> **state of nonexistence:** *a condition of nonexistence, or the absence of any perceptible qualities*
> (Encarta)
> **Nothing** *is the lack or absence of* **anything** *(including empty space).*
> (Wikipedia)

Not only doesn't that help, but it looks as though compilers of the dictionaries have no idea either. To label *nothing* a noun seems the least harmless – until we try it, that is. The moment we say that *nothing* is something (as in 'nothing is something that has no existence'), we are in trouble, as we have already pointed out: if *nothing* is something, then it can't be nothing. The White King in "The Lion and the Unicorn" in *Alice's Adventures in Wonderland* made a similar blunder when he reasoned that if Nobody had passed the messenger on the road, Nobody should have arrived first. With apologies to Lewis Carroll, let us make some changes and use 'nothing' instead of 'nobody':

> *"I see nothing on the road," said Alice.*
> *"I only wish I had such eyes," the King remarked in a fretful tone. "To be able to see Nothing! And at that distance too! Why, it's as much as I can do to see anything, by this light!"*
> . . .
> *"What did you pass on the road?" the King went on, holding out his hand to the Messenger for some more hay.*
> *"Nothing," said the Messenger.*
> *"Quite right," said the King: "this young lady saw it too. So of course Nothing walks slower than you."*
> *"I do my best," the Messenger said in a sullen tone. "I'm sure nothing walks much faster than I do!"*
> *"It can't do that," said the King, "or else it'd have been here first.*

However, now you've got your breath, you may tell us what's happened in the town."

So much for *nothing* being a noun. Even worse, though, is labeling *nothing* a pronoun, which muddies the issue even more. Why a pronoun? A pronoun (*he, she, it, who, which…*) supposedly replaces a noun. Which noun does 'nothing' replace? As far as can be seen, the only noun ('thing', according to the dictionaries) that *nothing* replaces is 'something'! But, just as with the 'no apples' example, if you don't have something, you are not left with *nothing*, but with an absence of what was there. And neither is *nothing* a noun in a normal sense, because if it is replaced by a pronoun, the meaning of the sentence is changed. So 'Nothing was there' does not have the same meaning as 'It was there' or even 'It wasn't there'. The best would be 'Everything wasn't there' – except for one thing: it isn't considered correct English.

Now the reason this is interesting is because it touches upon the mystery of *nothing* (and, in different ways, other negative entities). Because of the difficulty in defining *nothing*, it is also impossible to classify it, therefore giving the compilers of dictionaries a monumental headache.

For *nothing* to be a noun it would have to be something, while their definition is that it isn't something or anything. So by a sleight of hand, they call it a pronoun – and hope no one would notice. What dictionaries do, in fact, is sweep the problem under the carpet, leaving it to others to sort out.

Which brings us back to what happened in the Middle Ages, when *nothing* was so misunderstood. Strangely, it is because the Church **didn't** sweep the problem of zero and the concept of *nothing* under the carpet that the Arabic numbering system was stopped in its tracks. Had the Church let it go, had they accepted the separation between zero and *nothing*, the new numbering system would have come into general use, perhaps helping to herald the big Renaissance some four hundred years earlier than it actually came to pass.

It was Ibn Ezra, that eccentric wandering rabbi, who may have had the solution, and more is the pity that nobody saw it, or if they did, ignored it. By naming the character according to its shape – 'galgal', *circle* in Hebrew – he demystified it. No longer immediately associated with *nothing*, it was a physical object rather than an abstract philosophical concept. Ibn Ezra, in fact, changed *nothing* from an undefined – and indefinable – property that could not be grasped, to an article that could be seen: from the invisible *nothing* to the manageable zero.

Nothing in the eyes of the beholder

Zero has lost its clout. Having shed its aura of mystery and attendant danger, it has become an anemic, relative animal, tamed within expressions, such as *zero degrees* in temperature, *zero-degree longitude*, *Ground Zero*, *zero tolerance*, that have no connection to *nothing*.

We certainly think of 0°C (zero degrees centigrade) as cold, but we do not consider it to be no temperature. Even 'absolute zero' has a number (-273°C, below which the oscillations of molecules become as slow as they could possibly be, i.e. they stop moving); but it is not *nothing*.

Often, then, zero is used as a starting point, a marker. Take zero-degree latitude and zero-degree longitude. Ptolemy, the astronomer whose geocentric model of the universe was accepted as true for some 1400 years, was actually more successful as a cartographer. It was he, in 150 AD, who marked the equator as the latitude starting point (zero-degree latitude), the line he chose being a natural separation that marked the northern and southern boundaries of the sun's motion over the course of the year.

The longitude line, though, is not so easy to define, since there is nothing natural about where it lies. Ptolemy marked it as running through what are now the Canary and Madeira Islands, while later map makers moved the longitude line, until it was eventually universally accepted as running through Greenwich, London. Whether drawn 'by nature' or according to politics, then, the zero-degree latitude and longitude lines are merely a starting line of reference.[27]

The more recent adoptions of 'zero', in terms such as 'Ground Zero' and 'zero tolerance', also consider it as a marker – and not even an absolute marker – rather than *nothing*.

Now while in all these cases, 'zero' is not thought of as 'nothing', common perception still links them. Disassociating *nothing* from zero is still difficult, it seems.

In mathematics, because we can see it and use it, zero is easier to understand than *nothing*. However, we are as far from *nothing* as we ever were.

If we thought that by understanding zero, we would understand *nothing*, we were sadly mistaken. While there is so much we can do with zero, we can do nothing with *nothing*. With zero, in fact, we are master of our domain, king of the castle. Not so with *nothing*.

> *What does a man love more than life?*
> *Hate more than death or mortal strife?*
> *That which contented men desire,*
> *The poor have, the rich require,*
> *The miser spends, the spendthrift saves,*
> *And all men carry to their graves?*
>
> (Leeming, 1953, 201)

Two

Nothing in the Arts

Considering its history, you'd have thought that by now problems with *nothing* were a thing of the past, sorted out well before the end of the seventeenth century, and that thereafter *nothing* was nothing to talk about and certainly nothing to worry about.

Apparently not. Far from it, in fact. Not only does *nothing* remain a mystery, but (and possibly because of it) – *nothing* also keeps on making an appearance in virtually every walk of life, even when we don't notice.

But then how could we notice *nothing*? That, surely, is the point of *nothing*: it is... nothing. Yet there it is, alive and well, and still, obstinately, as far away as ever from being understood, despite our advances in science, technology, and most spectacularly our ability to garner information and knowledge. In some way, in fact, it is even more of a mystery, precisely because we know so much about everything else. Since it follows that the more we know, the less we don't know, we are left with one of those strange paradoxes that the more we know about everything, the less we know about *nothing*.

And let's face it: *nothing* just doesn't make sense, and because of that it's more than annoying – an affront to those who are endeavoring to understand the world.

If in the past the powers-that-be discouraged people to even think about it, today *nothing* is well out of the closet. Brought out from the recesses of forbidden thought to an honored place within the hallowed halls of philosophy and religion, and finally into the wide world, *nothing* has been taken on board big-time by the arts, almost to the point of obsession. Whether in film, television, music, literature, theatre or visual art, the search for *nothing* (and so to understand it) is there, sometimes on the surface, at other times below, as if *nothing* is the holy grail through which everything will be better understood.

For the arts, *nothing* seems to be the last frontier, the one windmill that blocks the way to depicting everything, the ultimate mystery that needs to be solved. With all and sundry trying to disprove King Lear's dark prediction that "nothing will come of nothing," *nothing* is thought about, laughed about, written about, sung about, painted and fashioned.

Laughing at nothing

In an interview for the Sunday Times, Robert Pirsig, the author of *Zen and the Art of Motorcycle Maintenance*, summed up *nothing* succinctly when he said: "If you talk about it you are always lying, and if you don't talk about it no one knows it is there."[28]

One way of talking about *nothing* is joking about it, for what can be more incongruous than the very concept of 'doing nothing', or of 'hearing nothing' or all the rest of the impossible *nothing* scenarios that form the inevitable butt of many a joke?

> *Seagoon: We can't stand around here doing nothing. People will think we're workmen!*
>
> (From the *Goon Show* – "Scarlet Capsule", broadcast 2/2/1959)

Or how about the following (also from the Goon Show), showing the absurdity of 'hearing nothing':

> *Announcer: For years we heard nothing from Neddie. And then, one day...*
> *Sellers: We heard nothing from him again.*
> *Announcer: We put a light in the window. Nothing much happened, except the house burnt down.*
>
> (From the *Goon Show* – "The Mighty Wurlitzer", broadcast 3/1/1956)

Humor at its best is when it gets us to see things in a different way to how we saw them before. And so it is with jokes about *nothing* that make us instantly conscious of the improbability of its non-existent characteristics. Oscar Wilde, who had something to say about everything, also had something to say about *nothing*: "I love talking about nothing. It is the only thing I know anything about."

But can we 'do nothing' or 'hear nothing'? And is it possible for us to 'see nothing' or 'say nothing'? Let's face it: as soon as we say something, that cannot be nothing.

> *Jerry: What are you saying?*
> *Elaine: I'm not saying anything.*
> *Jerry: You're saying something.*
> *Elaine: What could I be saying?*
> *Jerry: Well you're not saying nothing you must be saying something.*
> *Elaine: If I was saying something I would have said it.*
> *Jerry: Well why don't you say it?*
> *Elaine: I said it.*
> *Jerry: What did you say?*
> *Elaine: Nothing. [pause] It's exhausting being with you.*
> (from "The Red Dot" – *Seinfeld* Season 3, episode 12, 1991)

It is the very nature – the absurdity – of *nothing* that makes it such a useful prop for comedians. But seeing the absurdity of *nothing* goes only so far in our quest to understand it. It does, though, illuminate the paradox that *nothing* isn't nothing as soon as it is used; then, in fact, it is something, or, in Jerry's words: "[If] you're not saying nothing, you must be saying something."

Whether *nothing* is nothing and therefore cannot be referred to at all (because then, as we can see, it would be *something*), laughing at *nothing* at least shows up *nothing* for what it is (or, rather, isn't). There were immensely popular TV series in the

USA and Britain, with characters like Sgt Schultz ("I hear nothing, I see nothing, I know nothing!" – *Hogan's Heroes*, CBS 1965-1971) and Manuel ("I know nothing" – *Fawlty Towers*, BBC2 1975-1979), that used the audience's collusion in the impossibility of knowing nothing while, in fact, the heroes knew everything.

But if it isn't nothing, what is it? If we are laughing at it, isn't it *something*? That's a question that will keep on resurfacing as we look at how the arts deal with *nothing*.

Sometimes the problem is easier than it at first appears, such as the case of zero – a definite something, as we discovered in Chapter One – when nothing is an absence, so that, in the parallel case of laughing at *nothing*, there is no doubt that it too is the absence of something: of speech (saying nothing), of visuals (seeing nothing), of sound (hearing nothing), of action (doing nothing), of information (knowing nothing), and sometimes the absence of anything important:

> Tia: *This is the best sundae I've ever had.*
> Jerry: *Oh, man. You know what... they got the fudge on the bottom – y'see? That enables you to control your fudge distribution as you're eatin'*
> *your ice cream.*
> Tia: *I've never met a man who knew so much about nothing.*
> Jerry: *Thank you...*
> (from "The Airport" - *Seinfeld* Season 4, episode 12, 1992)

Jerry's *nothing* here is obviously not the absence of everything, but rather the absence of things important. The fact that Jerry took *knowing about nothing* as a compliment adds an interesting dimension to what can be epitomized as the nothing culture of relentless reality shows and the insatiable obsession with celebrities' lives.

Whether laughing at *nothing* gets us any closer to understanding it is a moot point. It would be nice to think that it does, so that we could fill up the rest of the book with jokes (which the philosopher Wittgenstein thought of doing, long before I did). Unfortunately, that won't work. What laughing about it has done, though, is to show up the absurdity that is the paradox of being able to do anything with *nothing*. Or we could take P.J. O'Rourke's advice: "A very quiet and tasteful way to be famous is to have a famous relative. Then you can not only be nothing, you can do nothing too."

Nothing but silence

Joking apart, we have a love-hate relationship with *nothing*. While many of us profess to like doing nothing, it is, of course, not nothing that we are doing. Actually, we don't like *nothing* at all. Nature, it is said, abhors a vacuum. And so do we, with a passion. We'll do anything to break the sudden silence that blights a social gathering, the silence that pops up uninvited on a date, the unbeckoned silence that descends on a hitherto meaningful conversation. Never at a loss for words, the Spanish even have a way of dealing with it, through the neat silence-filler 'pues nada' (*so nothing*), or the even more expressive 'bueno, pues nada' (*okay, so nothing*) – anything, in fact, to hold off the confession that we have nothing to say when that gap, *nada*, suddenly separates words from words in the silence that we can't bear.

Silence is a gap. The question is whether silence is *nothing*. There is no doubt that it is the absence of sound; but it is not necessarily the absence of everything else. Moreover, there is not only one sort of silence; silence can, in fact, have many functions.

Here is how Robert Bolt, in his *A Man for all Seasons*, shows different types of silences.

> *Cromwell*: Now, Sir Thomas, you stand on your silence.
> *Sir Thomas More*: I do.

Cromwell: But, gentlemen of the jury, there are many kinds of silence. Consider first the silence of a man who is dead. Let us suppose we go into the room where he is laid out, and we listen: what do we hear? Silence. What does it betoken, this silence? Nothing; this is silence pure and simple. But let us take another case. Suppose I were to take a dagger from my sleeve and make to kill the prisoner with it; and my lordships there, instead of crying out for me to stop, maintained their silence. That would betoken! It would betoken a willingness that I should do it, and under the law, they will be guilty with me. So silence can, according to the circumstances, speak! Let us consider now the circumstances of the prisoner's silence. The oath was put to loyal subjects up and down the country, and they all declared His Grace's title to be just and good. But when it came to the prisoner, he refused! He calls this silence. Yet is there a man in this court – is there a man in this country! – who does not know Sir Thomas More's opinion of this title?

Crowd in court gallery: No!

Cromwell: Yet how can this be? Because this silence betokened, nay, this silence was, not silence at all, but most eloquent denial!

Sir Thomas More: Not so. Not so, Master Secretary. The maxim is 'Qui tacet consentiret': the maxim of the law is 'Silence gives consent'. If therefore you wish to construe what my silence betokened, you must construe that I consented, not that I denied.

Cromwell: Is that in fact what the world construes from it? Do you pretend that is what you wish the world to construe from it?

Sir Thomas More: The world must construe according to its wits; this court must construe according to the law.

It was a valiant effort, but Sir Thomas More had very little chance of persuading the court that his silence meant the opposite to what they perceived it to mean (and what he had really meant by it). After all, it was More's silence – the silence that was taken as his refusal to repudiate the Pope – that infuriated Henry VIII so much in the first place. And as we can see, nobody was fooled by More's claim that his silence meant nothing.

Nowadays, he might have got away with it, for the legal system in Western countries does treat silence as if it were nothing. Saying nothing is neither a nay nor a yea. The legal right to silence is a recognized awareness that no legitimate inference may be drawn from that which does not exist. You cannot assume something from nothing, in other words. Of course that doesn't work in less enlightened societies, where silence is not accepted as nothing, so that when used, it always works to the detriment of the one who is silent.

Actually, outside a strictly legal setting, silent answers aren't a good idea in our part of the world either. When a woman asks a man if he likes what she is wearing, woe betide him if he answers with a silence. That silence is not *nothing*; it is a definite no, as far as she is concerned. And what does it mean when the question 'Do you love me?' is met with silence? The silence itself is a loud answer. Or, in a police investigation, silence as a reaction to the question, 'Did you kill that man?' is not taken as a denial, but the opposite. Silence is definitely charged, more often negatively.

Even when the understood answer is 'yes', the repercussions are negative more often than not, as, for example, the silence in answer to 'Did you see anything suspicious?' Or this notorious event: on TV, in January 1998, viewed by multitudes of the insatiably curious, US President Clinton asserted forcefully, "I did not have sexual relations with that woman, Monica Lewinsky." Shown around the world, and repeatedly for months after the event, the answer was unequivocal. Now imagine, instead, that Clinton's answer had been silence to the direct question, "Mr. President, did you have sexual relations with Monica Lewinsky?" Silence would have been understood as admitting to sexual relations. His silence would not have been a non-answer.

Is silence *nothing*, though? If silence can mean different things at different times and contexts, it is tempting to believe that silence is not *nothing*. And we would be right, but only partially. As we discovered, the *nothing* that changes according to context – the absence of something, in this case the absence of sound – is different from the mysterious *nothing* that is the absence of everything. Zero, we saw earlier, changes according to context. Silence, like zero, is *nothing* within boundaries. It is the space between.

The space between

Now while we do everything to avoid the gap, there is at the same time a certain fascination with *nothing*, the absence of everything. The lure of *nothing* is akin to the simultaneous fear and attraction that possesses us when we stand in front of a deep ravine. The pull towards the edge. The bottomless unknown.

It's an attraction that is more widespread than we at first realize. Anybody who's anybody, it seems, is looking towards *nothing*. In theater and film, it is silence – the absence of sound – that is the 'space between', not necessarily in the way alluded to by Stacy Chapman, whose silence, in *Telling Stories*, is filled with deception:

> There is fiction in the space between
> You and reality
> You will do and say anything
> To make your every day life
> Seem less mundane
> There is fiction in the space between
> You and me.

For Lynn Anderson, in *Nothing Between Us*, *nothing* too is a space that is filled:

> *Now nothing stands between us no wedding bands between us*
> *She set you free to come to me and now everyone has seen us*
> *Now nothing stands between us but there's nothing between us*

Her nothing here is a big something. It is everything, in fact, that separates her from her lover.

The notion of *nothing* as being a gap between somethings is a reasonable way of tackling it. It is, after all, a contrast between something that comes before and comes after. Indeed, how else could you show it? How else could you show silence, that absence of sound, if not by contrasting it to sound?

Until they discovered that secret, film makers found it impossible to produce absolute silence on the screen. They eventually succeeded by contrasting it with the sound of something that is removed. Mark Berger, sound director of the film *The English Patient*, put it this way:

> The sound of nothing is hard to convey by itself. It is best accomplished by contrasting it with the sounds of something that suddenly goes away. The more the contrast, either in volume, density, or variety of sounds that completely go away when you enter the room, the greater the sense of emptiness and isolation.

The sound designer Randy Thom of the movie *Contact*:

> We literally put no sound at all into certain parts of two scenes, and it seemed to work pretty well. We were a little concerned that people would think something had happened to the theater sound system, so in the opening sequence we gradually faded the sound out rather than

ending it abruptly.[29]

So silence is – and can only be – created through its contrast with what has been removed, something that is no longer there. To exemplify the point, let's take the adage 'It's always darkest before the dawn' as an analogy. It isn't, though, darker just before dawn than it was five minutes earlier, or, in fact, any time previously. Not at all. It is the introduction of light that gives an idea of how dark it had been. Since darkness and dawn do not occur simultaneously, they cannot be compared to each other at the same time. In fact, it is not the darkness that we refer to, but a **memory** of the darkness that we compare to the present light of dawn. And so it is with silence that we 'hear' so deeply after noise that has been taken away. It is the memory – the trace that we can still hear ringing in our ears – of the noise, that makes the silence so profound.

If silence can be profound in relation to a memory, it can be just as profound, perhaps more so, in reaction to what is still to come, as described so graphically by Rick Atkinson about the fighting in Sicily during WWII: "Perhaps only a battlefield before the battle is quieter than the same field after the shooting stops," he writes of the aftermath of the Salerno landings. "The former is silent with anticipation, the latter with a pure absence of noise."[30]

An illuminating example of effects being enhanced by memories of what came before was an exhibition by the Belgian artist Joëlle Tuerlinckx in 1994 that took place over 24 hours at the Provinciaal Museum in Hasselt. The light was manipulated so that visitors arriving at night would enter the gallery as if flooded by intense sunlight, while during the day the atmosphere was a ghostly half-light. What was interesting, though, was what happened when visitors left the gallery and entered 'the real world': at night, they attested that the darkness seemed blacker and the silence was more intense.

What makes *nothing* graspable – literally and figuratively – is having it wedged between somethings: comparing it to before and after. By giving *nothing* borders, it becomes something, so that artists can at least hold it still, use it and come to terms with it.

And artists do want to come to terms with *nothing*, either directly by trying to reproduce it, or indirectly by manipulating it to make a point.

Two playwrights who use silence spectacularly are Harold Pinter (1930-2008) and Samuel Beckett (1906-1989), both known particularly by the silences that permeate their plays. Part of what has been called the 'Theatre of the Absurd', that contained, among others, the playwrights Eugene Ionesco, Jean Genet and Arthur Adamov, they show their characters' sense of bewilderment and anxiety in a world they cannot understand. Life is absurd, their plays show, so that meaning cannot be found through logic or rational thinking, but rather through silences, stilted language and a sparse stage.

There were differences, though. The fact that Harold Pinter and Samuel Beckett had a bleak view of the world and used silence as part of the discourse in their plays did not mean that the two playwrights were similar. Apart from eventual fame (adoration, even) and the Nobel Prize for Literature (Beckett in 1969 and Pinter in 2005) they were very different people; what they did have in common, such as a lonely and unhappy childhood, only puts into sharp relief how differently they use silence in their works.

Beckett, known as 'the poet of nothingness', born near Dublin to a Protestant family, and Pinter, born in London to a Jewish family, were both brought up as part of minority groups. Whether that had any effect on them as individuals is a cause for speculation, but living under the shadow of war certainly had.

For Pinter it really was a shadow, since he was evacuated from London to Cornwall at the start of World War II in 1939 at the age of nine and stayed there until he was fourteen. The trauma of evacuation and separation from his parents influenced a long life of political activism and attendant pacifism, which began already in 1949, when he became a conscientious objector, was put on trial and fined for refusing to do national service.

For Beckett, war was more than a shadow. Although old enough to have a memory of the First World War, that did not stop him from joining the French Resistance in 1940 when the Germans occupied Paris, where he had been living on and off from 1928 and permanently from 1937.

While Pinter was living in the safety of a castle in Cornwall with other boys of his age, Beckett was typing and translating secret information for British Special Operations in conditions of deprivation and extreme danger. He and his wife, Suzanne, escaped arrest by the skin of their teeth (10 minutes or so) when his cell's cover was blown, with many of his comrades deported to concentration camps. The war had a lasting influence on his life, as his diaries attest.

Given their past, it is not surprising that the silences they use in their plays are different. Pinter's pregnant silences enhance the feeling of tension and underlying menace that has become known as 'Pinteresque' (but not by Pinter himself, who professed not to know what that meant). Awkward, embarrassing and threatening, they hit us hard, possibly because they are in some way 'familiar', those silences that we sometimes endure ourselves.

Not so Beckett's silences, which are not pauses as much as long, drawn out spaces that take over from speech. Struggling to create what he called, "a literature of the unword," he waged a lifelong war on words, trying to yield instead the silence that underlines them. *Waiting for Godot*, his most well-known play and famous as a play where 'nothing happens', premiered in Paris in 1953 to baffled audiences, who found it hard to accept the view that nothing is everything. (A widely quoted comment by the Irish critic and Beckett scholar, Vivian Mercier, that *Godot* is a play in which "nothing happens, twice," hurt Beckett at the time but was meant to be ironical and certainly not disparaging, as it is mistakenly understood to be.)

A very different silence, then, is Beckett's compared to Pinter's. Pinter's silences are gaps that enhance and give extra meaning to the words that surround them. They are indeed 'pregnant silences' and demonstrate Susan Sontag's apt statement that "Silence remains, inescapably, a form of speech."[31]

For Beckett, on the other hand, silence is an end in itself. Words are superfluous, as far as he is concerned ("every word is like an unnecessary stain on silence and nothingness") since they are necessary marks in a world that would be better silent, convinced as he was that there are some things that cannot be expressed in words, a sentiment expressed by the philosopher Ludwig Wittgenstein, in another context, as "Whereof one cannot speak, thereof one must be silent."

Not for nothing have Beckett's plays been called 'hymns to nothingness', which could very well be extended to his prose. His book *Stories and Texts for Nothing*[32] brings together three short stories and thirteen 'texts for nothing' in which, like his plays, he strips away all but the essential, paring language, character and narrative almost to vanishing point in order to arrive at the core of truth. For him, *nothing* is more than important; it is behind everything ("the night sky of nothingness behind the pyrotechnics of culture," according to his friend, E.M. Cioran, a writer even more pessimistic than Beckett, which was quite a feat). Picasso was of the same mind, and concluded succinctly that "Art is the elimination of the unnecessary."

The obsession with cutting down everything that could interfere with the message the artist is trying to purvey – most commonly associated with visual art, but alive and well in all the arts, as we have seen – is brought out in what is known collectively as minimalism, a catch-all term that sums up 'eliminating the unnecessary'.[33]

And it *is* an obsession, this search for the least in order to say the most. And of course the least is never enough, as we shall see. However far artists go and however much they eliminate, there is always something remaining, something that should be unnecessary but is still there, blocking the way to a 'true understanding'. We cannot but feel the frustration of minimalist creators of the arts, who, if only they knew how, would produce *nothing*.

Some are closet nothingers, wanting to tackle it, but not daring to, or, more likely, not knowing how. Take Gustave Flaubert (1821-1880), the celebrated French novelist, known for his rich detailed plots, who at some point expressed the desire to write "un livre sur rien," *a book about nothing*. Such a book, he maintained, would not be concerned with subject matter or plot and would hold up through sheer force of style and structure and thus be an ideal work. But however ideal he considered *nothing* to be, Flaubert was wise enough not to ever attempt it. Perhaps he realized that there was no money in *nothing*.

Whatever the reason, his style went as far from *nothing* as was possible, as illustrated in his most well-known work *Madame Bovary*. Heavily grounded in the daily realities of his native Normandy, the book is laden with detail of plot and descriptive writing.

Leaving Flaubert for a moment to move forward almost two hundred years, to Enrique Vila-Matas whose book, *Bartleby & Co*, consisted of no text as such, but footnotes only. It was, it can be said, a non-novel. The footnotes did weave a story though, about writers who stopped writing, and who, in fact, made nothingness the subject of their work. Words, according to the writers, were simply inadequate to describe the amazing quality of even the most ordinary things.

Anne Lydiat's *Lost For Words* went the final step. The only words in Lydiat's book of 75 empty pages are those on the cover, which quote philosopher Maurice Blanchot: "About this book I have promised myself to say nothing."

The irony of Lydiat's blank pages and the power of Vila-Matas' non-words are as far as possible from the power of Flaubert's highly detailed *Madame Bovary*. A story of adultery and the unhappy love affair of a provincial wife, Emma Bovary tried desperately to attain what was unattainable, and was crushed by a mediocre society. Not surprisingly, the real live inhabitants were not too happy with the many details of life in Normandy. Obviously far from 'nothing', the realistic depiction of adultery was condemned as offensive to morality and religion, and Flaubert was prosecuted (though he escaped conviction).

And speaking about nudity – which we weren't, but it's a good example of minimalism at its most literal – we can do no better than take a side road with this quote from Mark Twain: "Clothes make the man. Naked people have little or no influence on society." If that was at all true at the end of the nineteenth century, it is certainly not so today.

Little or no influence on society? It took the merest glimpse of a bare breast at the 2004 Super Bowl for the heavens to fall. A few seconds' exposure [accidental or otherwise] of Janet Jackson's right breast at the end of a song with pop star Justin Timberlake rocked the USA to its core, sending MTV, the network responsible for the half-time show, into a hysterical spasm of apoplectic apologies to the country, to its children, to the world and its mother. Federal Communications Commission Chairman Michael Powell, whose sensibilities were seriously and personally offended, ordered an investigation of the incident. Powell said he was watching the game Sunday evening with his two children and found the incident "outrageous." His fury knew no bounds and grew by the minute. "I knew immediately it would cause great outrage among the American people, which it did," he said, citing "thousands" of complaints received by Monday morning. "We have a very angry public on our hands," he announced. Working himself up to a moral frenzy, he added,

"We all as a society have a responsibility as to what the images and messages our children hear when they're likely to be watching television." Not physical violence shown daily on those same TV screens and in video games, not scantily clad actresses in simulated sex, nor models that have almost all exposed in order to advertise everything from cars to bottled drinks. But a bare breast. Not even that: had the nipple been covered, it would have been fine. The world went into shock over a nipple.

If an exposed nipple caused such ripples, what would one call 18,000 completely nude people? Answer: art. The American artist Spencer Tunick (b. 1967) uses large numbers of nude people posed in artistic formations to make his point: the nude form loses its individuality a result of sheer numbers. If Mark Twain talked about clothes making the man, Tunick says the same – but in reverse. For him, people without clothes show their essence, brought out by massing them together, so blurring differences of beauty, age and all the rest.

Spencer Tunick's endeavors to minimize the individual in order to maximize her humanity is the antithesis to what Brian is trying to instill in the crowd in the Monty Python movie *Life of Brian*:

> Brian: *You're all individuals!*
> Followers: *Yes, we're all individuals!*
> Brian: *You're all different!*
> Followers: *Yes, we are all different!*
> Dennis: *I'm not.*
> Arthur: *Shhhh.*
> Followers: *Shh. Shhhh. Shhh.*
> (Warner Bros. 1979)

For Tunick, more was definitely less. His oeuvre in Mexico City at 18,000 people on May 6, 2007 is a record to date, hugely topping the previous record of 7,000 people in Barcelona four years earlier and more modest ones in Sydney on March 1, 2010 with 5,200 people and 1,000 people in Manchester, England, later in that year. Although he did some fairly spectacular installations in the USA as well – his largest, 2,754 people on June 26, 2004, in Cleveland Ohio, followed only two months later by a slightly more moderate 1,800 nudes in Buffalo's old central train station – he was arrested only five times (all in New York), and only when his creation was outside.

Quite amazing, isn't it? One flash of a nipple versus thousands of completely nude men and women, the former giving rise to a veritable earthquake, while the latter causing ne'er a stir. What was it that made the breast incident not art in any way, yet confers the badge of art to a tableau of massed nude people? It could, surely, not have been merely the surprise. And we can assume – can't we? – that Michael Powell, who was so incensed by the peek his children had of Janet Jackson's breast, would not bar his children from visiting the National Gallery of Art in Washington DC to see Titian's *Venus with a Mirror*. In that work, painted in 1555, Venus has her right breast exposed also, for as long as we wish to linger and with much more of it bared. One cannot help wondering what those thousands of people traumatized for a couple of seconds' glimpse of Janet Jackson's breast would say when confronted with another Venus (*Venus of Urbino*) by Titian painted in 1558, if they were lucky enough to procure tickets for the Uffizi Gallery in Florence. Not only is this reclining Venus completely naked, but she has one of her hands resting between her legs. It is about this painting that Mark Twain wrote in *A Tramp Abroad* that it was "the foulest, the vilest, the most obscene picture the world possesses." No denying that it is art, though.

Nowadays there isn't much that doesn't come under the broad umbrella of 'art', and as we progress in our pursuit of *nothing*, we will find less and less that is not considered art by someone or other. Perhaps it has something to do with intention, which would account for Janet Jackson's bare breast not even being considered as art (although in different circumstances, it might be. But let's not give anyone any ideas).

As far as minimalism goes, Tunick would seem to have gone all the way. After all, what can be more minimalistic than the *nothing* with which he clothes his 'models', who come in the thousands to be part of Tunick's tapestry? (In case you're wondering, his models are volunteers, whose reward is a photo of the installation. Interestingly, there is a distinct majority of male models.) In some way, the huge scenes of packed-together nudes are reminiscent of the gigantic choreographed dance numbers that originated in the Far East, the Soviet Union and its satellites of yore.

The result is a feast of sameness, where the original simple idea is expanded in order to lose its individuality. Not only with human bodies, of course. Walter De Maria's *The Broken Kilometer* of 1979, consisted of a kilometer of brass rods cut into pieces on the ground in a gallery in Manhattan. As with Tunick's nudes, the result is an orchestrated balance, the fragility of the individual pieces counteracted by the sense of strength given by the sheer number – a case of more being less, and less being more.

Let's look more closely at the 'less is more, more is less' circle. Four striking examples come to mind, all effective as memorials. The first one is the Holocaust Memorial in Berlin, consisting of a sprawling field of 2,700 stone slabs near the Brandenburg Gate. Standing on 19,000 sq m, it is a vast featureless mass, the stones containing no plaques or names of any kind. "I fought to keep names off the stones, because having names on them would turn it into a graveyard," Peter Eisenman, the architect of the project said when the memorial was opened in May 2005 to commemorate 60 years since the end of WWII. As with Beckett's silence, words inscribed on the stones would be superfluous. One stone wouldn't have done it, neither would ten. It is the sheer mass of thousands that causes a numbness emanating from the enormity of it all.

The second example of a 'less is more' memorial is British artist Rachel Whiteread's *Memorial to the Victims of the Holocaust*, in Vienna, which also uses repeated forms in a structure that resembles an inside-out library, with rows of concrete books, spines facing in, lining the outer walls. Here again, the repeated sameness is meant to dull the senses while bringing out and reinforcing a sense of absence and loss.

And who cannot fail to be moved by the Vietnam Memorial Wall in Washington DC? Designed by American architect Maya Lin, the two black granite walls form a faceless monolith that is alive through a seemingly unending array of inscribed names of those killed or missing in action in the Vietnam War. The sheer number of names (58,256) conveys an inescapable feeling of individual loss that is all the more personal within the enveloping security of not being alone: a place where people can come and touch the individual names and feel the enormity of what they were part of. The reaction of all who come there is silence, for there is nothing to be said. As an example of less being more and more being less, the Memorial Wall is extraordinary.

If we think about it, memorials themselves are a strange phenomenon. Not only do they commemorate something that is not physically present – a memory, in fact – but, as far as the twentieth century is concerned, they do not depict a recognizable resemblance of the subject, as would be, for example, a general on a horse. Modern memorials are 'art': what they resemble is not what we immediately recognize from nature, but are, rather, abstract and symbolic. As Gerard Wajcman so cryptically observes: "…they essentially – each in its own way – put forward nothing to see."[34]

The fourth example, the proposed memorial for Ground Zero in New York, was considered in a different way from the outset, almost literally from when the dust had settled. The 'less is more' point of view, fine for other memorials, was felt by large numbers of people to be inappropriate, ineffective and inadequate to commemorate the loss of life in the dastardly destruction of the Twin Towers on 9/11, 2001.

The battle for how the memorial should look, carried out vociferously in the media, was between the supporters of *nothing* and the supporters of *something*. The initial gut feeling was that the memorial would be most effective as an empty space that would let the absence of what had been there speak for itself. It was a neat idea and an acknowledgement of the power of *nothing* that said everything; after all, whatever one said would be too little, so that *nothing* is all that there is left. The palpable absence, it was thought, would forever be present and thus certainly more effective than the materialism of actually building on that place.

The fact that the materialistic solution won out is not surprising; countries who see themselves as powerful have never gone in for minimalism to make national points. In fact, no country, however dire its lack of means or resources, subscribes to 'less is more' when it comes to demonstrating its national pride, constructing its government buildings or its capital. In any case, the effectiveness of a memorial comes down to taste. And let's face it: even if Ground Zero had been left empty, it would not have been *nothing*, nor would it have shown *nothing*. It turns out, then, that whatever the intention, 'nothing to see' would always have been 'something to see.'

Seeing nothing

Art in the twentieth and twenty-first centuries is like chalk compared to the cheese of what art had been previously. Think of the earlier great paintings and symbolic images compared with the abstract art of today. Gerard Wajcman, a Paris-based psycho-analyst and author of numerous philosophical studies in English and French, talks about art providing a more 'lateral' vision –

broader with more meaning than can be immediately seen – in contrast to what came earlier. Perhaps. Certainly lovers of modern art would agree with him. But whether we agree or not, it is the idea of *nothing* that has a big hand in that change of approach.

The possibility of actually coming to grips with *nothing*, and the excitement of trying to use it as a concept within the way artists set about their work, creates a particular awareness of objects and phenomena that is not visible at first sight. "Shut your eyes and see," as James Joyce writes in the first chapter of Ulysses, seems to be the ultimate aim of artists who urge us to see differently.

When Wajcman asked: "Would it be exaggerating to say that in the twentieth century we very often go from an art to be looked at to an art in which to a certain extent there is nothing to see?", he meant the question to be rhetorical – what Latinists call a *nonne* question, i.e. one that expects the answer 'Yes'. But it was not a rhetorical question; it would only have been so if we understood what 'nothing to see' meant, and it is not sure if Wajcman knew either. Did he mean that there is less to see and more to think about? But surely not '**nothing** to see'.

For a concrete example of 'nothing to see' definitely being 'something to see', we could have done no better than to visit the exhibition in Ando's Gallery, St. Louis, Missouri, held in 1994. Not concrete, though, but linen painted black, that took up the major part of two walls to which it was stapled, at right angles.

Titled *Pacific Judson Murphy*, by Richard Sierra, it looked like a gaping hole in the wall, or, to be more poetic, the feeling it conjured up was of a black hole within the infinity of space. On the opposite wall – with nothing else in the room – was Picasso's *Woman with Yellow Hair*. The juxtaposition was a shock, both startling and brilliant. Not only did the blackness of Sierra's painting take on an even greater starkness, but the Picasso with its continuous arched line and bright colors became stunningly more alive and vivid in return. It is a classic and rather wonderful example of nothingness affecting its surroundings and being affected itself at the same time. And more than that: the difference between nothingness and something leads us to perceiving it as the difference between not being and existence, between death and life.

And neither have we forgotten zero in all of this. Nothing and zero. Just as zero takes its value, its 'color' from the surrounding context – the zero in 202 having a different value to that in 220 – the nothingness of a black painting takes on 'meaning' from its surrounding context. To put it in different terms, zero and a black painting, each of which is 'meaningless' on its own, become visible and with character when juxtaposed with something else.

But is a black painting art? The question has to be asked. What is art, in fact? Compared to what was considered art in earlier times, we have come quite a distance. Not that long ago, in the mid-nineteenth century, Charles Baudelaire, the highly influential French poet, noted critic and acclaimed translator, defined great art as containing luxury, calm and sexual pleasure. An obviously luscious, opulent feast for the senses, in other words.

Whether we want to apply Baudelaire's criteria to Picasso's *Woman with Yellow Hair* is a matter of personal opinion. Yet Picasso's works are almost universally considered great art today. What, then, about two walls of black linen? Many people, if asked, would not call that art. So what, for them, makes a Picasso art and Sierra's black linen not art?

There is a widespread feeling that art is supposed to engage feelings, i.e. to bring out an emotional response. The common belief is that art needs to be 'enjoyed' in some way; if not, then it isn't art. Here is a typical reaction, from someone who reviewed Richard Wollheim's book *Art and its Objects* on amazon.com. The reviewer, D.S. Heersink, wrote, inter alia, that "I suspect he is trying so hard to be anglo-analytic in his approach that he forgot that art touches the heart as well as the mind. Wollheim focuses entirely on the mind, and the mind games that ensue do little to enlighten one's understanding of art and its objects, what and why they do what they do, and why they're important."

A legitimate opinion, that. But who is to say that art should not bring out only an intellectual response? In fact, why does art necessarily need to engage the heart at all? And how can we 'understand art' if not through the mind? We don't lay down the same critical faculties for literature, do we? We don't say that literature is only something that emotionally engages us, and that if we are stimulated intellectually, then it is not literature. So what is it about visual representations that allows us to admire a Rembrandt but scoff at so-called 'modern art'?

It would be nice to answer those questions at this point. But let's leave for the moment the question 'what is art?'; we will come back to it – because of *nothing* we will have to, in fact – as we look at the influence of *nothing* on artists and their work. And a huge influence it is, also on us, who are asking the questions. It's not only that *nothing* is getting us to ask questions about art, but also that the questions are making us wonder what *nothing* is (and that is the big question!), and whether *nothing* is what remains when everything has been taken away.

Going for nothing

Chasing nothing in art is one thing, but seeing *nothing* as art itself is another kettle of fish. In order to do that, artists (with a reminder that by art and artists that create it we are including visual art, music, literature, theater, television – in short, all the arts) need to stare *nothing* in the face. They need to create *nothing* – or, to put it more precisely, the concept of *nothing*. As impossible as that sounds, the challenge has not fazed them. After all, if art is supposed to reflect human emotions, aspirations and thoughts, the idea of *nothing* is definitely among them somewhere.

Nothing as art? Yves Klein (1928-1962) accomplished the ultimate in 1958 with an audacious exhibition in Paris that consisted of an entirely empty gallery. It was a sensation, and although Klein was not averse to provocative behavior, neither he nor anyone else could know that his empty gallery would, in retrospect, be considered one of the first examples of conceptual art, the term itself coming into use only some ten years later, in the late 60s.

What Klein's concept actually was it's not sure even he had completely worked out at the time. Or perhaps he did; after all, the exhibition was called *Le Vide* (The Void). The point he was making, it has been said, was that space can be art; but that seems to be an explanation volunteered much after the event in order to bestow historical proportion to what not many people understood. After all, few had gone that far before, even in a period when artists were delighting in pushing the boundaries of the acceptable. The 'swinging sixties' were about to happen in Europe and the USA, and Yves Klein was a true prophet, prefiguring much of what was to occur in the 60s and 70s, including minimalism, earth art, installation, pop art, and the rest. Unfortunately, fate was such that he saw virtually none of it.

If not the first, Yves Klein's empty gallery exhibition was arguably the most publicized statement that art can consist of ideas or concepts, rather than being concerned with traditional aestheticism. For Klein it was the supremacy of the spirit over matter, while for the wider world he affected a change in the concept of what art is (or can be): art can concern the mind, not necessarily the heart – thought rather than 'beauty'.

For Klein it was a natural culmination of what he had been doing for some eight years in his attempt to get to the basics, from the material to a spiritual balance. In around 1950 he was experimenting with monochrome strips of 'pure' colors, eventually settling on a brilliant, electric ultramarine (later patented as International Klein Blue) as his representative color. He had found a way to represent the blue of space, the sky, infinity – in short, nothing less than the spiritual dimension of the universe.

Yves Klein was a driven individual (a not-uncommon trait among artists, it turns out) and so it should come as no surprise that for him whatever he did was not enough. He was looking for more – actually, less. The paint and surfaces themselves were becoming a drag, a dead end, too 'real'. What he wanted was for his colors to become invisible, to achieve the 'immateriality of art' – to become *nothing*, in fact – and he got it with the *The Void*, the empty exhibition that the French art critic Iris Clert hosted in her gallery. "Having rejected nothingness," Klein said, rather enigmatically, "I have discovered the void."

If life didn't turn out to be any more content after that for Yves Klein, Iris Clert, on the other hand, was well and truly on the avant-garde map that enabled her fifteen minutes of fame, to paraphrase Andy Warhol's statement, ten years before he made it.[35]

Having accomplished a brilliant publicity campaign and sending out invitations replete with faux postage stamps in Klein's signature blue,[36] she was delighted at the packed opening of *The Void* exhibition (fronted by two Republican Guards!) containing the avant-garde of the Parisian art scene downing blue cocktails she had supplied. Perhaps her invitation – which some said showed more art than what was in the gallery – had something to do with the big turn out:

> *Iris Clert invites you to honor, with all your affective presence, the lucid and positive advent of a certain reign of the sensitive. This manifestation of perceptive synthesis confirms Yves Klein's pictorial quest for an ecstatic and immediately communicable emotion.*

Whether an empty gallery can be considered art is not something we will dwell on at the moment.

For Yves Klein it was his way of getting to the nitty-gritty of life, the 'what's it all about'. His ongoing experiments with color and space as effective realities in themselves led him to the concept of what the exhibition represented: the void as being the underlying reality of all phenomena. He was not the only one who saw *nothing* in this light, as we shall see.

There is not much further you can go after exhibiting an empty gallery, as Klein himself must have felt, since his career (and his life soon after) ended with ever more bizarre and frenetic artistic stunts. On November 27, 1960 a one-day newspaper disguised as the Sunday edition of *France Soir* showed a photograph – actually a photomontage – of Klein leaping from the roof of a suburban house, under the headline, "A man in Space" and the caption, "The Painter of Space casts Himself into the Void."

He had now gone as far as he could, by connecting *nothing* with death, a theme we will return to. His remaining artistic efforts went in a different direction: experimenting on painting canvases using nude models covered with paint. A particularly interesting work of art, *Anthropométries*, was executed live in 1960, in front of a serious, well-dressed audience, in which nude female models were covered in blue paint and dragged across the canvas to the sounds of an equally serious orchestra. It was a return from *nothing*: from an attempt at showing what cannot be seen, to a definite something.

Yves Klein died of a sudden heart attack in Paris at the tragically young age of 34, and we will never know if he had anything more to give the art world. *Nothing*, though, was on the map, more openly than before.

What Yves Klein attempted in visual art, other artists did in their own fields. If in the visual arts the aim was to show what cannot be seen, in music the aim was to listen to what cannot be heard.

John Cage (1912-1992) had longer than Yves Klein to give the world the benefits of his artistic achievements, and became a seminal figure of the American avant-garde scene. He experimented with prepared pianos, unusual percussion instruments, electronics, weird notation, as well as introducing the element of chance into the performance of his music. As a composer, his most notorious work, 4′33″, composed in 1952, consists of four minutes and thirty-three seconds of silence. The performance itself had the pianist sitting at the piano and staring into space for the allotted time, after which he bowed at the audience and left the stage.

"I have nothing to say and I am saying it," wrote John Cage in his "Lecture On Nothing", included in his book *Silence*.

Is silence 'music'? Certainly not according to Victor Hugo, whose opinion was that "music expresses that which cannot be spoken and cannot be kept silent." For John Cage, though, silence was as much music as that which was made to be heard. Silence, he felt, allows us to hear what we wouldn't normally hear. This is how he puts it:

> For in this new music nothing takes place but sounds: those that are notated and those that are not. Those that are not notated appear in the written music as silences, opening the doors of the music to the sounds that happen to be in the environment.[37]

Cage was in a bind. Impressed by the series of 'white paintings' produced in 1951 by the artist Robert Rauschenberg when they both taught at Black Mountain College in North Carolina, he wanted desperately to produce *nothing* in music in the same way that Rauschenberg was able to make *nothing* the subject of a painting.

But by the time he composed 4′33″ a year later, he had come

to realize that there was no such thing as absolute silence, having visited a room designed to be absolutely sound proof at Harvard University a year earlier. In that room (the 'anechoic chamber') he was astounded to hear sounds where there should have been none. As he wrote later: "I heard two sounds, one high and one low. When I described them to the engineer in charge, he informed me that the high one was my nervous system in operation, the low one my blood in circulation," reminiscent of Ingmar Bergman's movie *Wild Strawberries* in which the silence at one point is so profound that Isak becomes aware of his own massive heartbeat. Whether the engineer's explanation is accurate, or was even given, there seems very little doubt that silence is impossible to attain.[38] The writer Jenny Diski, describing a boat trip in New Zealand, stated that "unfortunately, there was the sound of listening" instead of "the sound of silence" that she was urged to hear by the captain.[39] We have all heard 'the roar of silence' and the hum of *nothing*, have we not?

With the realization that *nothing* didn't exist, John Cage proved it through the sounds from the audience and the sounds that seeped in from outside to fill in the four minutes and thirty-three seconds of his piece. He let us hear 'the sound of silence', literally.

As avant-garde as the enterprise seemed at the time, the art world had a short memory, and Cage didn't jog that memory (if he knew what had happened some thirty-three years earlier, that is). In 1919, a completely silent piece "In Futurum", one of the movements in *Fünf Pittoresken* for piano, was composed by the Czech composer Erwin Schulhoff. Silent it may have been, but the idea behind it was different to Cage's. For a start, Schulhoff was not looking for the impossibility of *nothing*, but, in the way that Beckett and Pinter would do in their plays a generation later, he used silence as part of his music. For Schulhoff, the silent movement was an integral part of the whole piece, that was meant to be listened to as such. Not for him the experimental idea of having the audience as part of the 'art'.

In retrospect, the silence in "In Futurum" was a sad and eerie portent for what was to happen to the composer. Hounded by the Nazis in the 1930s for his 'degenerate' work, Schulhoff's life became unbearable in 1939 when the Germans invaded Czechoslovakia. Suffering for a sin even greater than being degenerate, that of being Jewish, he was thrown into the Wülzburg concentration camp, near Weissenburg, Bavaria, in 1941, where he died on August 18, 1942 from tuberculosis.

Perhaps art is a matter of timing more than what it is in itself. John Cage, just a generation later, was venerated as a seminal 60s artist, and died in 1992, only weeks before his eightieth birthday, while Erwin Schulhoff, a brilliant pianist and composer, died in misery, pain and filth, degraded as a human being as the Germans had degraded his art. That his career, like so many others at the time, was tragically cut short is no doubt. But whether his experimental works, such as the silent "In Futurum" would have been accepted, is another question. Perhaps it was just too early. Perhaps it needed a period like the 60s that was open enough to break down all previous boundaries.

But that is precisely the problem with *nothing*, whose boundaries move as soon as you get to them, as Yves Klein and others after him discovered.

Although it would seem that one can't have anything more empty than an empty gallery, Michael Asher (b. 1943), a Los Angeles-based conceptual sculptor, didn't agree and went a step further. For him, even paint on the walls themselves was an impediment to what he was looking for. In the Galleria Toselli in Milan in 1973 he asked for all the layers of white paint to be removed from the walls and ceiling of the gallery, right down to the original structure of the building as it was before being converted into an art gallery. This resulting transformation was his 'exhibition'. One can't help thinking that Asher would only really have been content if he had had the gallery knocked down completely, although presumably Franco Toselli, the owner, would have put his foot down at that, even if it meant the thwarting of pure art.

If Asher thought that his stripped gallery was as far as one could go, other artists proved him wrong in their own way. The Spanish artist Dora Garcia (b. 1965) did not allow people to access her work at all! Her *Locked Room* consisted of just that: a locked room in the Galerie Jan Mot, Brussels, in 2002 where nobody but her could enter. In this way, the artist created an area in the museum that was to function as a mental space, accessible only to one's imagination. Unfortunately, though, even this was not original; something similar had been done already in 1969 by the American artist Robert Barry (b. 1936) in his *Closed Gallery* at the Art & Project Gallery in Amsterdam, which consisted of a locked gallery that had nailed to the door an announcement reading: "For the exhibition the gallery will be closed."

Taking a different approach to the empty gallery idea, Karin Sander, a German artist (b. 1957), in her piece *Zeigen* (*Showing*), in 2006, got rid of the art object itself (at least she allowed people in!) and left in its stead the title labels of the paintings that weren't there. She didn't leave it at that, though. She added recordings of the artists describing their paintings, the idea being that instead of seeing the art works, visitors would be able to 'feel' art through their imaginations.

Whether *Zeigen* was a step towards fundamentals and *nothing* is debatable. If Sander's aim was to release the 'viewer' from the concrete, so enabling him/her to confront the abstract, the result seems to be merely the replacement of one noise for another, one sense for another. Listening to a description is, surely, not more abstract than seeing the object. Not only that, but the idea was far from original. Giving the title and having someone describe the painting does allow for the imagination, but not more than the imagination at work when reading a book or listening to an audio book. And why imagination should bring one nearer the basics is also not clear. As John Cage demonstrates so dramatically in his silent piece *4'33"*, where the audience provides the noise, taking away all the elements of one's art leaves more than only imagination.

It's one thing showing nothing, but is quite another for an artist to destroy everything he owns in the name of art, which was what the British conceptual artist Michael Landy did in a prime location in London's Oxford Street in 2009. Calling it *Break Down*, he threw everything he had ever created and, in fact, all his worldly possessions into his 'art bin', while shoppers watched him do exactly the opposite of what they had come to Oxford Street to do – acquire things. As an act of destruction to demonstrate that a person is more than merely his possessions it didn't really work, since Landy accrued wealth and possessions soon after as a result of his conceptual stunt.

The impossibility of *nothing* is illustrated nicely by the French philosopher Jean Baudrillard in his observations of America, who gives a visual dimension to 'the sound of silence'. "The silence of the desert," he writes, "is a visual thing, too... There can be no silence up in the mountains, since their very contours roar." In his travels through California, he was struck by the desert as "a product of the gaze that stares out and finds nothing to reflect it."[40]

Yet there are artists for whom the impossible is merely a challenge – as far as they are concerned, if a concept is thought to exist, art should be able to represent it. And that, of necessity, can mean going very far. Robert Barry, before his *Closed Gallery* shut people out altogether, pushed his horizons to the limit in an attempt to seriously show *nothing*. At first his art moved from what was visible but could not be seen (pieces made of extended wire so thin and high above the ground that they were virtually impossible to see or photograph) to things that could be neither seen nor perceived in any way (energy and inert gases).

Inevitably, that was not far enough for Barry, and his next

efforts ran through radio waves and radioactive isotopes that had a half-life of a millionth of a second, until his art involved energy without an object-source of energy at all. In his *Telepathic Piece* for Seth Siegelaub's exhibition (1969) at Simon Fraser University in Vancouver, the catalog stated that "During the exhibition I shall try to communicate telepathically a work of art, the nature of which is a series of thoughts; they are not applicable to language or image."

There is no doubt that Robert Barry saw his *Telepathic Piece* as art. Whether he expected it to be accepted as such is something else. A piece that does not even have a place in which it can be photographed is either truly a specimen of *nothing* or the work of a desperate artist who has gone too far. It is perhaps not surprising that Barry later came down to earth, with a room that no one was allowed to enter.

Leaving nothing

Vincenzo Peruggia, an Italian housepainter, had his fifteen minutes of fame in 1913 when he was arrested for stealing the Mona Lisa from the Louvre two years earlier. I personally am prepared to grant him an extra fifteen minutes for making the world interested in *nothing* and causing thousands of people to stand in line to see it.

Amazingly, more people rushed to look at the empty space after the Mona Lisa was stolen in 1911 than had previously gone to look at the actual painting. The psychoanalyst Darian Leader sees this phenomenon as the search for what we have lost.[41] It was not only that people who had seen the Mona Lisa previously went to see where it had been, but that many of them had never seen the painting or, in fact, had ever been to the Louvre. Was it merely a spectacular case of 'absence making the heart grow fonder' that attracted them as, indeed, attracted Franz Kafka and his friend Max Brod three weeks later to stare at the empty spot? There must be more to it than that, for, in some unfathomable way, the space where the painting had been was more exciting than the painting itself. So while that may account for some of the hysteria, there are aspects that make us wonder what that empty space meant for the people who gawped at it.

If the thought of people flocking to see an empty space is mind boggling, it becomes less so when we think of a similar phenomenon half a century later: Yves Klein's *The Void* exhibition. The only real difference was that the space left by the Mona Lisa ignited a spontaneous reaction, while Yves Klein's void was attended by an 'arty' crowd that had been subjected to some crafty PR work.

And is what happened so different to the attendance of an audience at John Cage's silent 4'33"? Now while the space left by the absent Mona Lisa in 1911 would obviously not have been considered art in any way, later similar (but planned) works that showed *nothing* were considered 'conceptual art'. (In that light, Vincenzo Peruggia in 1911 could be said to have been the artist!)

So what were the crowds looking at in 1911? More or less the same as what people would look at in Yves Klein's *The Void*: nothing. Not the same *nothing*, of course; in one it was the absence of the Mona Lisa, while in the other it was the absence of exhibitions in a gallery.

Obviously, it wasn't what people were seeing that was important, but what the Mona Lisa had become when it was gone. The painting had taken on a new life – had, in fact, become more real – due to the space that it had left. It seemed to be a case of "the glory [lying] not in the act of removal, but in the experience of what is left," as British architect John Pawson put it when discussing minimalism.[42]

But what experience were people having? What was that empty space doing for them? The question – and it's a big question – is whether the less there is for the eye to see, the more the viewer moves within himself in order to see what he wants to see. By looking at 'nothing', do we make our own art? This, surely, is the principle behind John Cage's 4'33", where the audience, left to their own devices, hear sounds and think thoughts that come to the fore in the silence that is the performance. It makes sense, since we all have our 'best thoughts' when we don't have to concentrate on something, say when we are walking, driving, or washing the car.

In fact, going a little further, we could make the point that anything we are forced to look at stops us seeing something else; or, as Darian Leader so provocatively asks: "What it is that art stops us from seeing?" In the light of our discussion, the answer could well be "nothing": it is art that stops us from seeing *nothing*.

Which is where we started this section: the space left where the Mona Lisa had been before Vincenzo Peruggia stole it. And with that I have kept my promise of giving an extra fifteen minutes to that Italian gentleman, who, by the way, stole the painting in order to return it to its native Italy, where he believed it belonged. A hot-blooded Italian patriot Peruggia may have been, but knowledgeable he certainly was not. The Mona Lisa was not stolen by Napoleon as Peruggia believed, but was actually given as a gift by Leonardo da Vinci to King Francois I, a great patron of the arts, when da Vinci was invited to France and became a painter at his court.

And while we are on the subject of art theft, another one that reverberated around the world was that of the Danish artist Edvard Munch's *The Scream* of 1893, stolen in August 2004 and recovered, damaged, a few months later. It wasn't the first time, and somehow it was a picture begging to disappear: another version (there were four versions altogether) had been stolen in 1994 from the Norwegian National Gallery as the Winter Olympic Games began in Lillehammer, Norway. Although it was just one of a number of high profile art thefts in the 20th century (included paintings by Picasso, Renoir, Monet, Van Gogh, Vermeer, Rembrandt, Goya, Raphael, Manet, Degas, da Vinci), and certainly did not carry the greatest monetary value, the theft of *The Scream* garnished the biggest headlines and captured the world's imagination.

The iconic image of that wild-eyed figure on a bridge, hands clapped to his head, mouth contorted in a silent shriek of nameless terror is as instantly recognized as today's idiotically contented Smiley face. Used in everything that was designed for its shock appeal, schematic versions of *The Scream* stare out at us from political adverts to horror movies, most famously, of course, on the Halloween mask worn by the teen slasher in Wes Craven's movie *Scream*.

It's obvious that Munch's *The Scream* has an effect beyond what is visible. That tormented face of one man's despair and alienation seems to touch a core of anxiety and unknowing fear within anyone who looks at it. When the American artist Spence Finch asked in 2007, one hundred and fourteen years later, whether it was possible to see oneself thinking, he need only have looked at *The Scream* to solve the "paradox inherent in vision, an impossible desire to see yourself seeing," as Finch put it.[43]

And what has *The Scream* to do with *nothing*? For that we can do no better than to take a look to another Scandinavian, the Danish philosopher and religious poet Søren Kierkegaard (1813-1855), who viewed anguish as the foreboding anticipation of nothingness. Anguish, he maintained, is the most basic of human feelings, causing the individual to face the inevitability of his/her own death.

It was yet another Scandinavian, the Swedish film director Ingmar Bergman, who also used the face in a number of his works as a way of demonstrating the feeling of despair and fear when confronted with a complete void, that which Edvard Munch captured pictorially in *The Scream*: the horror-filled individual who lets out a scream that no one hears – the most primeval expression of understanding, in a flash of terror, being the one thing that we all know but don't want to think about, the only thing that we know for sure. The scream that no one hears is our biggest nightmare, for in the end we are ultimately alone. Face to face with nothingness, we know everything – we understand our mortality.

It was the German philosopher Arthur Schopenhauer (1788-1860 – a similarly cheerful soul, whose pessimistic philosophy espoused the inevitable suffering of man) who had claimed that because real dread can only come from within, works of art were limited through their inability to reproduce a scream. Munch proved him wrong on that count.

The Scream was eventually returned, but not to the public. It continued to be absent from Munch's later exhibitions: on March 17, 2007, the largest exhibition of Munch's works outside Norway took place in Milan, Italy, without his most famous work. The Symbolist painter would not have failed to miss the symbolism of the post-Scream exhibition; it's as if the presentiment of nothingness was self-fulfilled – *The Scream* announcing its own pending real disappearance. Minimalism had been given ultimate expression, for there wasn't even a space where *The Scream* had been.

Since we are in Scandinavia, let's linger a little longer in the awe-inspiring beauty of the lands of extremes, the midnight sun of summer and the relentless total darkness of winter.

Norway's major, and most well-known, literary figure, Henrik Ibsen (1828-1906), like Kierkegaard through philosophy and Munch through visual art, was fascinated (obsessed would be more like it) with nothingness as the core to man's existence. In the play *Peer Gynt*, the aging Peer, on his way back to his Norwegian roots, is forced to come to terms with himself. As he looks back upon his wasted life, he peels an onion, letting each layer represent a different role he has played. But he finds no core. He has to face the fact that he has become 'no one', that he has no 'self'.

So unspeakably poor, then, a soul can go back to nothingness, in the misty grey. You beautiful earth, don't be annoyed that I left no sign when I walked your grass. You beautiful sun, in vain you've shed your glorious light on an empty house. There was no one within to cheer and warm; – The owner, they tell me, was never at home.

Ibsen is not recommended as an elixir for pessimism. It is a bit of a bummer to look for yourself and find nothing there.

Let's wander away from the gloom and doom of Scandinavia and make our way south to some light as we follow those looking for *nothing*.

The problems that artists have as they approach *nothing* are understandable, since they can 'show' it only by contrasting it with something else, particularly by contrasting it with something that has been removed.

Martin Creed (b. 1965) did it simply by having lights go on and off, which is not way out for the British artist, who has taken minimalism to extremes (both in his private life by living on one of the remotest of islands off Sicily and through his own band, owada, a punk outfit, whose numbers like *Nothing* can go on for a whole five seconds!).

Creed's work, *The Lights Going On and Off*, an empty room in which the lights did just that, might have remained a curiosity in relative anonymity had it not been blessed with official recognition. To the vociferous protests of those who did not consider it art at all, *The Lights Going On and Off* – let's face it, a flashing re-look at Yves Klein's *The Void* of forty years previously – won the prestigious Turner prize in Britain in 2001, the most minimal work ever to win the £20,000 prize, and proving that the modern art world (or at least those who hold the purse strings) has not ended its love affair with minimalism and all that it entails.

Creed, in line with his fascination with nothingness, has no studio and sees no reason to explain his work, even if he could. To him it is obvious that any search for *nothing* can only be spontaneous and unplanned, since that is what *nothing* is. "I try every time to make something afresh as if I'd never made anything before, from zero, from the point at which nothing has been made." But even that statement goes against his grain, when he says: "I feel I've been talking too much about the work because sometimes I hear myself saying things I've said before and I don't like that."

Be that as it may, he did not fail to turn up to receive the prize ("just a stupid prize," as he had earlier called it) and share the limelight with Madonna, who presented it. *Nothing*, it turned out, had become a big something for him.

Subtracting on the way

In our meanderings in and out of *nothing*, we have asked, so far tentatively, the question that is becoming ever more difficult to answer: what is art? Empty rooms, closed rooms, black squares, white squares, invisible gases, flashing lights, human feces (still to come), lines, squiggles, blobs, thousands of naked people, silent music... We will ask it again and yet again as we come across the sometimes-weird offerings that go under the label of 'art'. So far, though, when we ask the question, "What is art?" we have asked it from our point of view, we as consumers/ customers/clients. The answer is much easier when we refer to what the artists themselves consider as art; in other words, what it is that they are producing and why.

Through their work, artists describe the world as they see it – not necessarily visual seeing, of course, but also their feeling and thinking about it. Perhaps 'describing the world' is too bold a statement, so let's put it another way: artists show us something that they see in the way that they understand it. If it was once a scene from nature, say, or a biblical scene, nowadays it might be a concept, like 'loneliness' or 'fear' or whatever. The change from art as a visual description of the world to a cerebral one is summed up nicely by Picasso, who said, "I paint objects as I think them, not as I see them."

No different in that sense from authors and musicians, the visual artist attempts to explain what he feels and what he thinks; and no different from the philosopher, the artist attempts to show in his or her way 'what it's all about'.

With the arts and philosophy dealing with similar questions, it is not surprising that art is sometimes difficult to 'understand' immediately. How much more so when it looks towards *nothing*; if we have not yet found the words to describe it (and what a mess dictionaries have made with 'nothing', as we have seen), we shouldn't be surprised that artists are still struggling with it. And if modern art is sometimes far from what we recognize from nature, it helps to again recall Picasso who made the point that "art is a lie that makes us realize truth."

Why should modern artists (and not only artists, of course) be so obsessed with *nothing*? More so than with sex (in their art, it should be said), even though, most famously due to Freud, sexuality is thought of as being at the center of human nature. But let's face it, sex is not that much of a mystery any more, certainly not for artists, who have shown it in every way imaginable. It is over *nothing*, though, that artists get themselves into a cold sweat.

For a start... Exactly – for a start. Since scientists, mathematicians and philosophers are so concerned about how it all began, we would expect the same of artists in what they depict through their work. In their different ways, each asks a similar question: If everything started from something, can we assume that before something there was *nothing*? If so, then *nothing* is the basis for our very existence, and it is no wonder that artists try to represent it. Graphically put, "Nothing is the background on which everything happens."[44]

It is a captivating notion that everything comes from *nothing*. As the fount of all things, it is as shrouded in mysticism as are earlier symbolic representations in art. Pure and unsullied is *nothing*, parallel in the secular world of art to the purity represented by the Virgin Mary in Renaissance art. Whether or not they consciously connect it to the universal search for innocence and purity, how could artists not meet the challenge of capturing *nothing* in their work?

In our questions about *nothing*, we can willingly dispense with the assorted *isms* that usually accompany overviews of artists and their works (the ones that include, Expressionism, Impressionism, Fauvism, Constructivism, Cubism, Dadaism, Surrealism), which are in any case flexible, largely arbitrary and often subjective.

It doesn't matter what we call works of art, but rather what they do – or try to do, to be more precise – that is important. In the broadest sense, we are looking at 'abstract art', that does not depict objects as they are in the natural world, but instead uses color and form to represent them in different – non-representational – ways.

But if we stop to think about that for a moment, we realize that *nothing* does not strictly fit within that description, since *nothing* is not an object in the natural world, and neither is it an idea, concept or emotion that we can even imagine, as we can, say, happiness, jealousy, pride, love, or any of the myriad concepts that come to mind. It is no wonder, then, that art is having a hard time depicting *nothing*. The most art can do is to show the **search for** *nothing*, with that search consisting of a stripping down and simplifying of objects in nature. It is that stripping down that I lump under 'minimalism', virtually my only *ism* (although I do plead guilty to throwing in the term 'conceptual art' and sneaking in a couple of *isms* from time to time).

If we dwell on minimalism – which we are bound to do if we look at the trend towards less and less – it is not for the purpose of classification, but as a broad context into which we can see the common denominator of what many artists are striving for. And let's not get confused by the term 'conceptual art' ('art for art's sake'), which we can lump in as part of minimalism without feeling too guilty.

'Art for art's sake' was not an invention of the 1960s or even of the twentieth century. Théophile Gautier (1811-1872), French poet, dramatist, novelist, journalist, literary and art critic, was a vocal proponent of 'art for art's sake' long before it became chic (and way before a Latin version "ars gratia artis" appeared in the oval around the roaring head of the lion in the Metro-Goldwyn-Mayer movie logo), so adding to his reputation for eccentricity. An intellectual giant of the breed that was common in Europe in the nineteenth century, Gautier's eccentricities were accepted as part of what made him tick.

In music also, there were early proponents of 'art for art's sake', such as the French composer Camille Saint-Saens (1835-1921), whose views on expression and passion in art conflicted with the Romantic aesthetic sense that was all the rage at the time. In his memoirs he stated that music need not be only about pleasure and emotion, but that it could also consist of "a simple series of well-constructed chords, beautiful only in their arrangement." That was, of course, long before 'art for art's sake' ceased to have any connection to beauty; but it was the principle that led to what is presented today.

It was James McNeill Whistler (born in America but living mostly in Paris, London and Venice), who took a significant step down that slippery slope. He did so by reducing detail within all white when he painted *Symphony in White No. 1: the White Girl* in 1862 – a portrait of a model wearing a simple white dress standing against a white background and holding a white lily in one hand. Whistler's life, incidentally, was anything but white and pure: he loved the good life, colorful clothes, relished controversy, had a reputation for violence, and was constantly in debt –

hardly an artist whose art reflected his outward personality.

When it was first shown (in London and then in Paris) the painting was a sensation, and although a number of artists and critics praised *Symphony in White No. 1: the White Girl*, understanding what Whistler was doing, it was met with severe public derision, due to the elimination as far as possible of all traces of expression from the model's face and pose. In fact the painting was consistently misread, variously described as a ghostly apparition, a vision, a medium, or a bride on her wedding night.

That a picture did not convey any literary or moral ideas and that there was, in fact, nothing to look at apart from an expressionless model (actually, Whistler's mistress Joanna Heffernan) posing in an artist's studio, was, to put it mildly, alien at that time.

Whistler, going against the trend of realism, was far more interested in creating an abstract design than in capturing an exact likeness of the model. He believed that painting should exist for its own sake, to be seen for what it is, rather than what it copies, and he often gave his pictures musical titles to suggest an analogy with the abstract art of music: "Art should be independent of all claptrap. It should stand alone, and appeal to the artistic sense of eye or ear, without confounding this with emotions entirely foreign to it, as devotion, pity, love, patriotism, and the like. All these have no kind of concern with it, and that is why I insist on calling my works 'arrangements' and 'harmonies'."

His creation of 'art for art's sake' became a virtual rallying cry of modernism. In particular it was a small step into what would eventually become minimalism in the sense that we refer to it here.

And it is precisely the reason it is better not to classify works of art, for by doing so we would miss the connection between Whistler's *Symphony in White No. 1: the White Girl* and the Russian artist Kasimir Malevich's abstract white-on-white compositions in 1917-18, his black squares and Ad Reinhardt's black squares, all of which we will be delving into shortly.

Not all art critics would agree with Whistler's painting being classified as minimalistic. Yet on the road toward *nothing*, where there always remains more that can be stripped away, Malevich's white on white paintings and Yves Klein's *Void* are no closer to *nothing* than Whistler's white girl is.

Hard as it is to imagine today, Whistler was subject to similar disdain at the time as was to be shown later to abstract art, his work described by many as 'art that is just paint thrown at the canvas'. In fact, Whistler became so incensed by such comments that in 1878 he sued John Ruskin for libel after the critic accused him of conning the public by selling *Nocturne in Black and Gold: The Falling Rocket* – "flinging a pot of paint in the public's face," in Ruskin's words – for two hundred guineas. Whistler won a pyrrhic victory – he was awarded a farthing in nominal costs – with the enormous actual legal costs bringing him to bankruptcy. With all that, it is rather doubtful he would have found consolation in the fact that he was a precursor of modern art.

In any case, he did not feel the need to sue anyone when he painted the sequels *Symphony in White, No. 2: The Little White Girl* in 1864, and *Symphony in White, No. 3* in 1865-67, for by then he was accepted by all and sundry within a trend that he had begun. 'Art for art's sake' was in, and so was the notion that it is possible to see more when less is shown.

From Whistler to modern memorials to present-day store display window arrangements, the idea that the less shown the more we see is so natural as to be part of our lives.

Nothing from something

That there is more to life than meets the eye is not a particularly original or new thought. From earliest times it was understood that what is really important is often hidden, with the ancient Greek philosophers writing about it extensively. And now, particularly since Freud's theories of psychoanalysis hit the world, 'the subconscious' has become part of popular language and culture, so that the idea of every person having hidden layers is self-understood by the proverbial man in the street.

Which brings us to Ad Reinhardt and his black squares, that attempt to show us what we can't see. The culmination of a life searching for a way to get to the very basics of art, Reinhardt's black painted canvases can be seen as either a brilliant way of making his point, or just meaningless black squares. They have also, at various times, been called 'the end of art', although Reinhardt was not alone in having that hurled at him.

Ad Reinhardt (1913-1967) was not the only artist to produce monochrome paintings, but he was arguably the most obsessive. Even Yves Klein, not the steadiest of personalities, as we have seen, moved on from his blue monochrome paintings, albeit not very far and for not very long. Reinhardt, though, stuck to his philosophy of painting: "The more stuff in it, the busier the work of art, the worse it is. More is less. Less is more. The eye is a menace to clear sight. Art begins with the getting rid of nature."

In words almost identical to those of John Cage, Ad Reinhart wrote that "an artist-as-artist has always nothing to say, and he must say this over and over again." He continued in a sort of cri de coeur that at once summed up conceptual art – 'art for art's sake' – as well as his own frustration:

What else is there to say? In work or words what in hell, on earth, or in heaven, is an artist up to when he says he has something to say? All artists-as artists say the same thing. The…artist-as-artist… is aware of himself as artist, aware of art-as-art, aware of everything that is not art in art, inside or outside art. The only way to say what an artist-as-artist is is to say what an artist-as-artist is not.

And obviously, if art is just art, then it would have nothing to do with commercialism nor have any practical use whatsoever:

> A fine artist by definition is not a commercial or industrial or fashion or applied or useful artist. A fine, free or liberal or abstract artist is by definition not a servile or professional or meaningful artist. A fine artist has no use for use, no meaning for meaning, no need for any need. A fine artist has nothing to use, has no need for any meaning, and would not use himself or his work for anything. A fine artist by definition does not use or need any ideas or images, does not use or need any help, cannot use or help anyone or anything.
>
> Only a bad artist thinks he has a good idea.
>
> A good artist does not need anything.[45]

For Reinhardt, then, being an artist meant doing art; not talking about art, but just doing it. And not just visual art, as the American poet Archibald MacLeish made clear: "A poem should not mean / But be." The British-born poet W.H. Auden went further, when he said that "Poetry makes nothing happen." Not only that, but it isn't meant to, Auden implies. Poetry, he would say, is just what it is, and must be judged for what it is and nothing else.

For Reinhardt art for art's sake became an obsession, a desperate attempt to get to the bottom of what life is, to reduce everything to its barest essentials and then to reduce it even further. Again and again he got to blackness as his answer; the blackness that represented *nothing*, the *nothing* that represented the potential for everything.

Starting in 1960, he painted his "Black Pictures" for five years. He kept making the 'last picture', an empty repetition of the same square black painting, in an attempt to take out of art its 'meaning' and be left with a representation of art itself. It was, in effect, an attempt to show that in the end there was nothing, in which lay the potential for a beginning, reminiscent of how John Donne declaimed it in 1633, some 300 years earlier:

> For his art did express
> A quintessence even from nothingness.[46]

For Ad Reinhardt in the 1960s, the 'last picture' was as close as he could get to painting *nothing*, and as such, a representation of art itself. In that sense 'the last picture' was not really a painting at all, but was a picture which only stood for painting, a sort of surrogate, a proxy for any other possible picture.

To be fair to Ad Reinhardt, we can say that he did keep to his non-commercialism credo, since 'the last picture' was literally that for him. We can hardly blame him for what happened after his death: the high prices for his works and their jostling for position in museums and galleries throughout the world. Few and far between are artists today who are able to resist the fame and fortune that come with the astronomical prices paid for modern art.

One of the few who did was Sol LeWitt (1928-2007), a founder of minimal and conceptual art styles and as such one of the most influential American artists of the 20th century. He hated being photographed and rarely gave interviews, eschewing most media attention. As art is about the art itself, he refused to connect it to the personality of the person who made it. "It's not about the star power but about the art," as he put it.

But the notion 'art' is not clear cut, and even less so is that of 'pure art'. If Reinhardt's black square does indeed represent art, which he characterized as "breathless, timeless, styleless, lifeless, deathless, endless," there would be nowhere further to go, and, in fact, is a fair description of *nothing*.

Apparently, though, life is not that simple, because there are, it seems, black squares and there are black squares. Take Russian painter Kasimir Malevich (1878-1935), who had done it earlier with his *Black Square* of 1913 (the year Ad Reinhart was born) and long pre-dated minimalism proper with his 'less is more' theories.

Black squares they may have been, but the artists' intentions could not have been more different. Now while both had the intent of stripping art of all meaning and so getting down to art at its purest, for Ad Reinhart it had to be devoid of feeling, of everything. Not so Malevich: his *Black Square* was for him the ultimate expression of feeling, "the supremacy of pure feeling," as he put it. His aim was to get rid of visual images, all images in fact, that could interfere with pure feeling. Unlike Reinhart, Malevich did not express an idea – art as art and nothing else – but rather, feeling, which, for him, was the only thing that was real. He himself expressed it with breathless excitement: "Even I was gripped by a kind of timidity bordering on fear when it came to leaving 'the world of will and idea', in which I had lived and worked and in the reality of which I had believed." Any object that we can see, then, takes away from pure feeling, which comes from our non-visual senses. In consequence, his Black Square "was no 'empty square'," he wrote, "but rather the feeling of non-objectivity... The black square on the white field was the first form in which non-objective feeling came to be expressed. The square = feeling, the white field = the void beyond this feeling."[47]

Yet unknowingly (or perhaps subconsciously), and despite his strong proclamations, Malevich reached beyond feeling, making what is outside of it more fundamental, with his white frame taking on a significance at least as important as that of the black square. Nothing is beyond feeling, he said. Taken literally, he was right: Beyond feeling is *nothing*. Unlike Reinhardt, who tried to show where *nothing* is, Malevich indicated that *nothing* is beyond what we can envisage.

A quick jump in time and space to Swedish artist Peter Frie (b. 1947) half a century later will demonstrate that there's nothing under the sun that can't be expanded. A Frie landscape is instantly recognizable because it is always set into a large white painted surrounding frame, a device that separates the image from its immediate physical surroundings. These vast white spaces, often larger even than the actual landscape element of the work, is the artist's way of reminding us of the ultimate negative space, or void, a physical reminder of the nothingness that would exist without landscape.

Unlike Frie's landscapes and Ad Reinhart's black squares, greeted with understanding nods by art pundits, Malevich's work fifty years earlier in Russia had been met with howls of fury. For Malevich, art was a way to express the brave new world brought on by the Revolution, and his austere paintings were among the most radical paintings of the day. For the Soviets, though, *nothing* was certainly not what the new order was about. It was about everything, in which *nothing* played no part.[48]

But politics generally has a problem with *nothing*; parties who say they know nothing simply do not exist. One notable exception, at least in name, was the Know-Nothing party of the 1850s in the USA, a right-wing, anti-immigrant, anti-Roman Catholic political movement, that was surprisingly influential for two years or so but disappeared within the impossibility of supposedly knowing nothing while being so doggedly anti everything. .

With that aside, let's get back to black. Not just black, though. Like Whistler before him, Malevich also used white as a way of reducing 'real' elements from outside. His *White on White* in 1918, in which a white square floats within a white background, was meant to create a feeling of infinity, and signified a realm of higher feeling, of purity, of moving away from objectivity. But not for the general public, and even less so the authorities, who slammed Malevich's works as not being art at all.

Malevich was unfortunate to have been born when he was. Interestingly, though, there is a wavering link between him, John Cage, and Robert Rauschenberg. We met Robert Rauschenberg a few pages back, when we showed how his 'white paintings' in 1951 influenced John Cage to write his silent piece *4'33"*. Just 33 years before that, though, Malevich had painted his *White on White* and five years after came his *Black Square*. Just as Cage did not acknowledge the earlier silent composition by Schulhoff, neither did his friend Robert Rauschenberg acknowledge the earlier works of Kazimir Malevich, even though the connection is clear.[49]

And since we are into white squares, it would be impossible not to mention another American artist, well known for using white in his art: Robert Ryman (b. 1930). Ryman, though, was not concerned with the essence of painting, since he didn't believe there was such an essence. Rather, he believed that painting constantly needed to be changed and experimented with. Using different shades of white in order to emphasize properties of the paint itself, such as translucency or reflectivity, while making visible even minute variations in tone, texture and brush stroke, he was most definitely into *something*, rather than *nothing*, which perhaps saved him from the despair and early death of other artists, like Kazimir Malevich and Ad Reinhardt.

Look at what happened to the Italian artist Piero Manzoni (1933-1963), who also tackled all-white painting in his *Achrome* 1961 (achrome = non-color). Made with kaolin (a light clay used to make porcelain) on canvas, the crumpled white surface hovers between the pure and the impure. He saw it as "a single uninterrupted and continuous surface from which anything superfluous and all interpretative possibilities are excluded."

Whether or not he thought he had achieved his aim of getting to virginal nothingness, Manzoni drank himself to death in 1963 at the age of 30, but not before he had filled 90 cans with his own excrement, labeling them *Merda d'artista*, which could be a reflection either of what he thought of himself or what he thought of art. He might have kept off the booze had he known that not only would his feces be sold, but that they would be literally worth their weight in gold, with one of the cans recently sold to the Tate in London for £22,300. Those who are interested in seeing it can do so at Tate Modern, where it is ensconced in all its glory behind plastic protection.

But it is black that is pulling us back to where we were before being sidetracked, not surprisingly, by white.[50] As strange as it is – after all, black is the *absence* of all color, while white is the *inclusion* of all colors – white is as descriptive as black in the movement towards less and less, as we saw from Whistler's white portraits and Malevich's white frame. Intuitively, though, if we think about 'nothing', we see it as black.

Lest we imagine that the search for *nothing*, with its monochrome paintings, empty studios and all the rest, was a product of a period around the 1960s and remained so, we need only look at what is going on in the arts today to realize that the idea of ultimate reduction to blankness and *nothing* is alive and well. Wherever we turn, be it photography, architecture, choreography, fashion or cooking, the search for the purity in the basics is well and truly still on.

It is visual art, though, that goes to the extremes that shock us most. Although it seems unlikely that artists could get away with black painted squares any more, that doesn't stop them from playing the same theme in its modern reincarnation. Take Stefan Bruggemann's video *A Production of Nothing* that formed part of the exhibition *Clearly Invisible – An (invisible) Archive*, shown at the Consulta, Centre d'Art Santa Monica, Barcelona, from March to June 2007. It consisted of 4 minutes 47 seconds of blackness; apart from the fact that it is a video presentation, it is a case of *plus ça change*.

If producing blackness doesn't get artists further in their relentless move towards *nothing*, the use of spaces and illusion are more modern attempts. Creating spaces where we don't see anything is impressive. The British sculptor Antony Gormley (b.

1950) unveiled his first London solo exhibition, *Blind Light*, in May 14, 2007, featuring a glass chamber which made visitors disappear in the mist.

Participants, 25 at a time, who stepped inside the 8.5 x 10 meter (28ft x 33ft) box were enveloped in a cloud of damp fog so dense they could see only a few inches in front of their faces. The mist, which was bright white, thanks to the bank of fluorescent lighting overhead, brought out a wide range of reactions ranging from anxiety to euphoria, but mainly the former. Losing all sense of location – left/right, front/back – visitors immediately were lost in space, making them anxious in the chamber that had only one small exit which was impossible to spot until they were inches away from it. (A possible, but unreported, by-product would have been a dose of claustrophobia for those who had never suffered from it before.)

The fear of losing oneself, of not being part of the world, of facing nothingness, in fact, is a timely reminder of Edvard Munch's *The Scream* and Søren Kierkegaard's connection between fear and nothingness, mentioned earlier.

But losing oneself is not always a bad experience, it seems. In fact, people go back often to try and feel *nothing* in the 'sensory deprivation tanks' located in the Lincoln Park area in Chicago. Floating effortlessly in a sound- and light-proofed tank on salt-filled water at a controlled skin temperature of around 93.5 degrees Fahrenheit, it is nearly impossible to feel the difference between your own body and the water you are submerged in and so are freed from all stimuli. After forty-five minutes, an attendant knocks on the door of the tank to let you know that your session is up and you are expected to knock back. Not surprisingly, it is far from nothing that floaters feel; some have referred to an 'out of body experience', while others have reported being in a dream-like state with very vivid dreams. If the idea is to get rid of external noise, it works, even though the result is to replace external noise with internal noise, which is 'almost deafening' according to some floaters.

The use of mist, fog and clouds is a common theme when referring to *nothing*. In M. Swiezynski's web page/blog "The Art of Memory", April 29, 2007, dedicated to minimalism, photos showing hills shrouded in fog are entitled "being an eye for nothing."[51] The quote under the photos is: "To be a cinematographer of nothing, to express its own impossibility? To imagine one being an eye for nothing, an eye for the impossibility demand such vulnerability at times. Maybe cursed and blessed at the same time." Perhaps Swiezynski has hit the nail on the head, since the attempt 'to express its own impossibility' sums up the problem that all artists have when they tackle *nothing*. Or as Jonas Mekas, the American avant-garde film maker put it: "The deeper you go, the more you get lost."

But of course even getting lost doesn't get us to *nothing* or even closer to it. Being lost or not seeing anything still leaves us with ourselves, or as Ringo Starr sang: "What do you see when you turn out the light? I can't tell you but I know it's mine."[52] And neither does hallucinating get us to *nothing*. All these are experiences – not a place where *nothing* can be.

Questions from nothing

So where does all that leave us? With plenty of questions, for sure. Not only about *nothing*, but, just as interestingly, about what *nothing* signifies. Take, for example, Ad Reinhardt's black squares, which adorn the walls of many major museums: *nothing* they are not, but their recognition as art is clear.

Having said that, a whole lot of questions bubble up. If Ad Reinhardt's black squares are accepted as art, are all black squares art? I can say without a shadow of doubt that if I paint a black canvas like that today, it won't make it to any gallery; I may just have a chance of getting it affixed to the wall of my study.

This proves that the value of that style is only relevant in its historical context, and devoid of that it loses its meaning, which presents a problem: viewers don't always recognize what an artist wants to convey without an explanation. When we see a painting of a field of flowers, say, or of a church in a village, we don't need a caption to describe what we are looking at. A black square, though? We certainly don't look at it and understand that we are looking at 'Nothing', or 'The Eternity of Feeling' or whatever. A black square can mean anything the artist wants it to mean (which the viewer may or may not 'accept').

Or not to mean. Ad Reinhardt didn't want art to mean anything. "Art is Art. Everything else is everything else," was how he put it, and expected us to see that.

But not everyone does or necessarily wants to. Why would we need to read up on the artists or go through a series of lectures before we walk into a museum or art gallery? Shouldn't it be possible just to enjoy art without requiring a background in the theory of abstract art?

It is a question that has a reach far beyond art, since we can ask it of any discipline. It applies just as well to music and to literature, to architecture and to renaissance churches, to wine and to coffee.

Those of us who are pleased to drink wine without knowing much more than whether it tastes okay – something like "I don't know anything about wine but I know what I like" – are aware that there are others who get more from wine than we do. That doesn't mean that it isn't perfectly all right to be content with what we know or feel. Of course it is. The question is whether we want more from, say, cooking, plants, herbs, architecture, quantum mechanics, whatever. We certainly can't appreciate quantum physics without knowing at least something about it.

But surely there are things that we can enjoy simply by enjoying them. What does one need to know when watching a sunset, for example? What indeed when facing a sea turning slowly red as, above the horizon is the sun, changing from fiery yellow to orange to a dark red sphere that hovers between heaven and earth, cut by the very horizon that slowly swallows it up.

It's true: When it comes to 'feelings' we need not know anything, in the same way that we can enjoy a glass of wine or drink a cup of coffee without knowing anything about them. And when we see a painting of a sunset, we can enjoy that as well (if we do), even though it cannot, of necessity, be absolutely faithful to an actual sunset. A different enjoyment, but enjoyment nevertheless, even when the painting becomes more abstract; as long, that is, as we can still identify it as a sunset.

But a painting of a sunset is not merely a copy of the real McCoy; if we can see real sunsets, why would we want to see a painted version? The reason is, of course, that an artistic rendering of a sunset adds an extra dimension, gives different elements, and makes us see or think – indeed, feel – about it in a different way.

John Constable (1776-1837), whose naturalistic landscape paintings were so mainstream that they became synonymous with English romantic art, wrote in 1821 that "Painting is but another word for feeling." Yet, far from photo-like copies of nature, Constable's paintings were an idealistic stretch – in a way an enhancement of nature – that came from within the painter's inner feelings. "It is the business of a painter," he said in 1824, "not to contend with nature, but to make something out of nothing, in attempting which, he must almost of necessity become poetical," which was his own poetical way of saying that he stretched the imagination somewhat. His *Autumnal Sunset* of around 1812 depicts a peaceful scene in which the undulating landscape is touched by the glow of the waning sun; yet the actual painting is more an abstraction of the scene, rather than a photographic copy of actual details.

Stretching abstraction further was J.M.W. Turner (1775-1851), another English painter of the same period, whose *The Scarlet Sunset* from around 1830-40 shows the sunset through vaporous, swirling atmospheric effects. Way more abstract than the

Constable sunset, but no less effective for that, it is not difficult to lose oneself within the powerful image even when confronting the painting in the sterile environs of Tate Britain in London.

As hard as it is to imagine today, Turner was not appreciated in the beginning. His paintings were looked at in horror for their indistinct style, in a way reminiscent of modern reactions to abstract art. William Hazlitt, the English literary critic, blasted Turner's style in 1816, stating that "...[Turner's] pictures are... too much abstractions of aerial perspective, and representations not properly of the objects of nature as of the medium through which they are seen..."[53] In a particularly sharp rap on Turner's knuckles, Hazlitt concluded by stating: "All is without form and void. Someone said of his landscapes that they were pictures of nothing, and very like." For Hazlitt, *nothing* applied to anything that did not conform to what one actually sees, to whatever doesn't 'exist', in fact.

Not everybody would agree with calling Constable and Turner minimalist artists. But they were. Admittedly, along the minimalism scale they were pretty far from the 1960s lines, squiggles and monochromes; but they definitely began the slide in that direction. And what is abstract art if not subtractions from 'reality'? Abstraction rarely adds – it almost always subtracts. And once we accept that art can be other than a copy of nature, we are on the way towards less and less.

Almost two hundred years have passed since Hazlitt's anti-abstraction harangue, and we are now able to accept a sizable amount of abstraction without batting much of an eyelid. We are able, in other words, to 'see' more than those that came before us; in many ways it's a matter of getting used to something that was unacceptable earlier.

One example is the cubism of Picasso; we have been 'trained' over the years to accept that Picasso has something to 'tell' us through his art. A century after Picasso painted his enigmatic and mysterious *Les Demoiselles d'Avignon*, the museum-going public has not only grown accustomed to looking at non-representational paintings, but hardly even considers many of them as being non-representational.

It was Picasso who stated what should have been obvious but is not acknowledged by those for whom only traditional art is art. Traditional artists, Picasso claimed, were striving for the perfect stroke of the brush, or blend of color to produce the perfect image, one which encompasses the world as they saw it, without realizing that everyone perceives the world differently. That being the case, there could be no perfect realism, since the rules of perception change with every viewer. "I don't paint pictures in the hope that people will understand them. They understand or not, according to their capacity," he said.

Picasso's views, that paintings were a tool to imaginative freedom, the end result of artistic expression that allowed every person who saw their work to participate in the works' completion, were reflected by every thinking artist and can be considered the credo of modern art.

It is amazing how much of what is today mainstream and loved for its simplicity and beauty was once shunned as being too modern. One of the most popular operas, *The Barber of Seville* by Rossini, was hated when first performed on February 20, 1816, and was met with hissing and booing. Even the most comfortable and most loved staples of our current repertoire, including Brahms, Chopin, Debussy and Tchaikovsky, had been condemned by contemporary critics in the very same way. Even Beethoven's *Fifth Symphony*, possibly the most popular classical work of all, was damned as "odious meowing", and not music, decades after its premiere.[54] As unlikely as the thought is today, it is possible that Stockhausen's electronic abstractions will one day be played as mainstream classics, as is, more and more, the dissonant-laden Stravinsky's *Rite of Spring*. As impossible as it is to imagine now, the first few listenings of the Beatles' record *I Want to Hold Your Hand* in 1963 fell on incredulous ears until we got used to it. Society was just not ready for the Beatles. Here is a *Newsweek*'s 1964 cover story on the arrival in the USA of the Beatles:

> Visually they are a nightmare: tight, dandified, Edwardian-Beatnik suits and great pudding bowls of hair. Musically they are a near-disaster: guitars and drums slamming out a merciless beat that does away with secondary rhythms, harmony, and melody. Their lyrics (punctuated by nutty shouts of "yeah, yeah, yeah!") are a catastrophe, a preposterous farrago of Valentine-card romantic sentiments.

There was nothing unusual about those sentiments in 1964. That same year, in the movie *Goldfinger*, James Bond compares drinking unchilled champagne with listening to the Beatles without earmuffs.

It's not only a matter of getting used to new things, of course. Part of the process is experiencing them over and over, so that what seems strange at first, becomes gradually normal. But part is also education, the furthering of knowledge that changes a baroque church, for example, from 'nice' to spectacular. Kunal Sen puts it very well: "Knowing how to read does not prepare one to appreciate modern poetry, or having a pair of ears is not enough to enjoy classical music. Some art forms," he says, "may be more accessible than others, but without adequate exposure one cannot learn the 'language' or the basic grammar of that art form. This 'training' need not necessarily involve a 'tutor', but requires the exposure to a large variety of examples of that art form."[55] This is what we call 'an acquired taste'.

During the period that Picasso's *Les Demoiselles d'Avignon* was exhibited in 2007 at the Museum of Modern Art, New York, to celebrate the one-hundredth anniversary of the painting's creation, guides were spending close to an hour at a time describing the work to rapt groups, one of which I joined. I had seen that painting countless times previously, but I can testify that because of the insights I was exposed to on that occasion I will never look at it again in the same way.

Without prior instruction and education, then, how far can we stretch abstraction before it loses us and we cease to 'see' anything? Until the dripped paint on a Jackson Pollock is just squiggly lines, not *Lavender Mist*, as he named that painting of 1950? Or until Ad Reinhardt's black square is just a black square? Many people, without the necessary prior knowledge, would have no hesitation in calling them 'nothing' (putting it politely) as did Hazlitt about Turner's paintings.

Indeed, for those who recognize only the great classical pieces as art, art just isn't art any more once it is no longer understood. Here is the concluding paragraph of an article against modern art written by Claudio Lombardo,[56] which will strike a cord with many:

> Since modern art is no more than 'a high sounding nothing', to use Metternich's famous expression, this nothing needs a perpetual choir of apologists and elucidators, the noisier the better, to ensure that the crowds of pretentious fools that visit modern art exhibitions, and buy the ridiculously expensive catalogues, keep doing so. On the other hand it must be said that this whole farcical structure rests on solid foundations: the unbearable stupidity of the snobbish Western middle-class nitwit that would die before admitting he does not understand a word of what is said in that useless art book he, or she, has just purchased and that would end on the coffee table, to the sheer delight of like-minded visitors (isn't it magnificent...?).

In a similar vein, one could ask what makes those "pretentious fools" feel that they are right in their taste? What, in other words, created the bon ton in the first place? For those who don't see abstract art as art at all, it is clever PR and market forces that have been at work to build up something from nothing.

Of course, it's not just visual art that comes under attack. Similar withering criticism has been made of modern literature and ideas. Reflecting, as it were, the point of view of 'the man in the street', Alan Sokal and Jean Bricmont wrote about the French philosopher Jean Baudrillard in their 1998 book *Fashionable Nonsense: Postmodern Intellectuals' Abuse of Science* that "if the texts seem incomprehensible, it is for the excellent reason that they mean precisely nothing."

Now while that point of view is still widespread, things are getting better. In the newspapers, modern art is presented in a better light than it used to be, partly because art has largely lost its ability to shock but also because it is now so 'in'. Irony can still be a weapon, though, as summed up in the title, "What a great idea. Doing nothing and calling it art", of an article by Grayson Perry in The Times of November 22, 2006.

Within the spectrum of minimalism, though, strange things may happen, with abstract shapes suddenly coming alive, forming themselves – returning, in fact – into what we do recognize. Mark Rothko's (1903-1970) style of horizontal form not so much expresses nature as to allow us to appreciate nature in a different way than we had before; it was what Rothko meant when he stated (with, possibly, a tinge of conceit) that his paintings were an improvement of nature. He objected to being labeled an abstract painter. "I am not interested in the relationship between form and color," he said. "The only thing I care about is the expression of man's basic emotions: tragedy, ecstasy, destiny." Rothko wanted us to discover for ourselves what we see, and so labelled his paintings only according to numbers or colors – *Light Red Over Black*, for example – and refrained from explaining the meaning of his work. Somewhat similar to Beckett, he said that "Silence is so accurate," fearing that words would only paralyze the viewer's mind and imagination.

It seems to work, as attested to by Camille Gizzarelli in her art appreciation website,[57] who sees Rothko's work as an example of biomorphic surrealism, defined as "abstract shapes that have come alive or threaten to come alive." She describes how she saw a Rothko painting come alive ('biomorphism'), when, a few years previously, "I saw the most incredible sunrise. The colors were maroon, yellow, and orange. I smiled and knew that artists like Rothko had indeed captured nature on canvas and interpreted it in a way that could be understood by humankind." It was what Rothko wanted: "Certain people always say we should go back to nature. I notice they never say we should go forward to nature." By showing less, Rothko meant, we can see more of nature.

It's a nice thought, that art can make us see the world differently, and having seen the world in that way, we can go back and see art differently.

Arthur Danto, art critic and philosopher, describes something similar, calling "a ready-made Rothko," the sunset he sees while flying 33,000 feet over Iceland – a heavy purple at the bottom, separated from the upper band of light blue by a band of rose and orange. But Danto is disappointed for the very reason Gizzarelli is excited, since he believes art to be more than just a reflection of the visual. Disillusioned, he comes to the conclusion that Rothko's paintings are all surface, merely about beauty.[58] For Danto, then, Rothko is not abstract enough!

As a footnote, Rothko, joining those other artists whose art did not help them to overcome depression, committed suicide, although in his case, it was when his career had really taken off. Just how successful his work would become can be seen in a recent sale of one of his paintings, *White Center (Yellow, Pink and Lavender on Rose)*, for $72.8 million, a record for contemporary art, that will no doubt be constantly be broken.

Perhaps, though, a certain amount of skepticism is not out of place. And how can we not be skeptical, if not downright cynical, when we see signs of artists playing God? A notorious example is of Robert Rauschenberg (he of the white paintings that influenced John Cage's 4'33"), who, in 1961, was invited to participate in an exhibition at the Galerie Iris Clert (the same gallery that had put on *The Void*, Yves Klein's empty gallery), in which artists were invited to create and display a portrait of the owner, Iris Clert. Rauschenberg's submission consisted of a telegram sent to the gallery, declaring "This is a portrait of Iris Clert if I say so."

As an example of sheer laziness plus contempt for art and for art lovers, it is hard to beat. And as an example of haughty conceit, it is likely to give minimalism a bad name, even though we could be charitable in a back-handed way by citing it as an example of a work of art being reduced to nothing. I do wonder, though, how many people could get away with such an open display of hubris and obvious disdain for 'the people'.

There is, of course, nothing wrong with a strong dose of cynicism, which art sometimes deserves. In fact, abstract art was mocked even before it actually made its appearance. Some twenty-four years before Malevich came up with his monochrome paintings, the celebrated French poet and humorist Alphonse Allais (1854-1905) and a group of inveterate cynics who called themselves "Les Incohérents" exhibited, in 1889, a dark blue piece of fabric entitled *Total Eclipse of the Sun in Darkest Africa*. It was but one of a series of exhibits they set up in Paris in the Salon des Arts Incohérentes as a parody of the strait-laced exhibitions held in the official Salon.

Les incohérentes started their visual mockery in 1883 with a pure white sheet of paper which, with suitable gravitas, was entitled *First Communion of Anemic Young Girls in Snowy Weather*, and continued, in the following year, with a piece of red fabric that was known as *A Harvest of Tomatoes on the Edge of the Red Sea Harvested by Apoplectic Cardinals*. Some hundred years before

Monty Python, this group of satirical anarchists let their cannons loose on the establishment while unknowingly foreshadowing abstract art of the future, and indeed the future movement of minimalism in general.

And not only in visual art. Long before John Cage – some sixty years, in fact – Allais and les Incohérentes published, in 1897, a blank set of musical bars, a completely silent musical composition: *Funeral March for the Obsequies of a Deaf Man*.

If art was fun before it became serious, then we can at least say that "There is nothing new under the sun."[59] It is, indeed, with absolute seriousness that the detractors of abstract art refer to many of its works as nothing.

Representing nothing

At the end of our spectrum of minimalism, where everything has been taken away, is the blankness (visual, oral or aural), where presumably *nothing* is, or where it is supposed to be. The problem is that while artists have been able to reproduce forms of blankness, they haven't actually been able to reproduce *nothing*. There is, as we have seen, an inherent absurdity in trying to express the concept of *nothing*, and it took artists a while to understand that. Those that did, either stopped trying to find it or committed suicide (or both), or took it in their stride and then made it their business to convey the idea that *nothing* cannot be represented.

John Baldessari, one of the most influential avant-garde artists of the 1960s and 70s, showed up the contradiction of art and what it is supposed to represent by creating a work in Nova Scotia in 1971 in which he asked students to write the phrase, "I will not make any more boring art" on the gallery walls. Baldessari completed the work by filling a videotape with himself writing the phrase over and over again, so deliberately contradicting the point – to refrain from creating boring art. Boring it certainly was, but it was also an interesting exercise in producing something that created its own opposite, and goes some way to demonstrating a point about *nothing*: that the moment an artist begins a representation of *nothing*, *something* is being created.

But let's stop for a moment and ask whether artists aren't being too hard on themselves. Why isn't a black square, for example, a representation of *nothing*, in the same way that a painting of a house is a representation of a house? (Naturally, a painting of a house is not a house, but merely a representation of a house.)

After all, is that not, basically, what art is? – a representation of something; it could be something from nature, from what we recognize. Or it could be extended to represent, as in 'modern art', an idea or a feeling, or anything that the artist wants to represent. And it doesn't matter whether we 'see' what the artist is representing (or trying to), for a representation is basically in the eyes of the beholder.

A picture of *nothing*, accordingly, is no different from a picture of a house; they are both representative of what the artist wants to show.

But is that correct? After all, we are able to compare a picture of a house to what we know houses look like in reality, whereas we do not know what *nothing* looks like and so cannot compare it to a picture of *nothing*. And neither can we compare *nothing* to ideas or feelings, because we have in our minds what those ideas or feelings are.

But how can we imagine *nothing*, the absence of everything? There is more to it than that, though. Let us imagine a picture of a square (any color will do) that is labeled "A House", which is the way the artist conveys his perception of a house, reminiscent of the song *Little Boxes*, written by Malvina Reynolds in 1962.[60]

> *Little boxes on the hillside,*
> *Little boxes made of ticky-tacky,*

Little boxes, little boxes,
Little boxes, all the same.
There's a green one and a pink one
And a blue one and a yellow one
And they're all made out of ticky-tacky
And they all look just the same.

Although it is clear that the lyrics refer to houses, if we were to see a painting of a box, or a painting of a number of boxes, we would need a plaque next to the picture to tell us what the artist was representing. Not so in the lyrics, even though the word 'houses' is not mentioned. The second verse, though, spells it out:

And the people in the houses
All go to the university,
And they all get put in boxes,
Little boxes, all the same.
And there's doctors and there's lawyers
And business executives,
And they're all made out of ticky-tacky
And they all look just the same.

Now let's get back to *nothing* and why it is different from other representations in art. Taking again a painting of a house, let's take it a step further. If, instead of painting a two-dimensional house, our artist paints a 3-D version, realistic enough to give the illusion of being able to get inside, would it be a house or only a representation of a house? Of course, it would still be a representation. Now let's say that our artist builds a life-size model of a house. Would that now be a house? At this stage we can no longer say with certainty that it isn't a house (which it may be, depending on our definition of a house), especially if it were big enough to live in.

Buster Keaton, the king of vaudeville, in his 1920 film *One Week* tells the story of an unfortunate pair of newlyweds and their attempt to build a house from a kit. After receiving crates containing their house, they proceed to assemble it by following numbers written on each of the boxes, unaware that the husband's rival has reordered them. The result, with a front door opening into mid-air and windows askew, looks nothing like a normal house, and cannot be used as a house. But imagine if they had used the crates, instead of their contents, to build a construction in which they could live, cutting out windows and a door. Would that not have been a house, certainly more so than the completed nonfunctional one?

We could do the same exercise with any piece of art, even ideas, by making them more and more concrete. If, for example, we did it with an artist's concept of 'happiness', we might get weird results, as we did with some of the representations of 'house', but we would still have some idea in our minds of what happiness is.

Yet if we try the same exercise with a representation of *nothing* – a black painted square, for example – it won't work. If titled *Nothing* or the artist has indicated that 'nothing' is the idea behind it, then, at first glance, it is a representation of *nothing* (or as we can imagine *nothing* to look like) in the same way that a painting of a house is a representation of a house. It is when we try to expand the concept of *nothing*, as we did with bigger and bigger models of houses, that the comparison breaks down. It doesn't matter how we extend the concept, we will not arrive at *nothing*.

We shouldn't be surprised, though, should we? *Nothing* cannot be represented, because as soon as it is, it is no longer nothing. As soon as *nothing* is enclosed, it becomes visible and no longer nothing: zero within its circle and a black painting within its frame (or surrounded by walls, whatever). This is what is remarkable about *nothing*; if we didn't know it before, it is art that shows up the uniqueness of *nothing*, which cannot be represented because it cannot be imagined without it becoming something.

Simplification

There is an appealing logic to the idea behind minimalist art, that a way of understanding the world, all of nature, in fact, is to take away what is unnecessary and leave the essence – 'less is more'.

The notion in general is that we can understand anything by examining ever smaller pieces of it, and that when they are reassembled, the small pieces would explain the whole. Marvin Minsky, one of the pioneers of artificial intelligence, puts it like this: "Once we split each old mystery into parts, we will have replaced each old, big problem with several new and smaller ones – each of which may still be hard but no longer will seem unsolvable." [61]

But where does one stop? At what point do we say that we have gone far enough and that we now understand everything? The inevitable logic seems to be, does it not, that, since there is always something smaller, we will eventually arrive at *nothing*.

That, though, doesn't happen. For a start, *nothing* is not the inevitable final point. Rather, reducing something to ever smaller pieces goes on and on and on to infinity, but never arrives at *nothing*. That may be why artists have not succeeded in getting to *nothing*; there is always something, even if it is a layer of black paint, a background, an inert gas, whatever. In any case, *nothing* cannot be the end result of reduction, since if *nothing* is truly nothing, then there will not remain anything that can be reassembled.

Reduction is not, then, the answer. There is, though, another way – in theory – of getting to *nothing*. Instead of **splitting** something into its constituent elements, it is emptied by **subtracting** elements. This seemingly makes sense, because taking elements away does not present a problem as such. At first glance, it has the makings of a neat solution, since when, eventually, everything is taken away, what is left is, supposedly, *nothing*.

Subtracting elements to get to *nothing* is demonstrated nicely in *How the World Was Saved* by Stanislaw Lem in his science fiction story, in which there was an argument about whether a machine was actually creating nothing as had been claimed: Was the machine doing nothing, which was exactly what was asked of it, or was it in fact not doing anything? Within the bickering, the machine interfered to say that he was, in fact, creating nothing by gradually removing things that are. Within a short time it was clear that there would be "no words, no people… only Nothing will remain…"

The Beatles' cartoon movie *Yellow Submarine* shows a similar idea, when the vacuum cleaner-type creatures suck up everything around them including the walls, the floors, everything, and end up sucking up themselves into themselves, leaving nothing.

For there to be *nothing*, then, everything has to be gone – including ourselves. A hard concept to show, since, at the end, there would be no one to see it!

Yet the urge for simplification is a universal one. The idea is that by getting to the basis of art (and, by extension, of life) we will understand it. But it is a fallacy. The deeper we get into an organism, the more complex it turns out to be; we need only look at the complexity of atoms and the building blocks of life to see how true that is. The more closely atoms are examined through ever more powerful atom smashers, the more particles are discovered, seemingly without end; not to mention quarks – the particles that make up the particles. The fictional inhabitants of the great coral of the Cosmos, in Umberto Eco's *The Island of the Day Before*, after first believing that the atom is the basis of everything, eventually understand it to have "infinite extension that is identified with absolute Nothingness," that gives "the illusion of everything."

The notion that we simplify things by looking at them more closely is, to put it mildly, suspect. There seems to be no limit to how far we can go and no way of simplifying each stage. And so it is with abstract art, which Kirk Varnedoe likens to hypertext, where the move towards *nothing* is not a gradual reduction of feature, but that the directions turn out to be numerous and complex, with each stop on the way opening up a window to an entire universe.[62] Louis MacNeice's lines, in the poem *Snow*, sum it up it up nicely: "World is crazier and more of it than we think, / Incorrigibly plural."

And let's face it: complexity and simplicity are almost impossible to define. The austerity of a Cistercian monastery or the simplicity of a Zen garden are both results of the same urge to reduce, to make clear, to unburden. But are they simple? Whether something appears simple or complex is usually a matter of where we are when we are looking at it. Complexity changes when we zoom in or pull back; only from where we are does simplicity seem to hold, and it is, like so many other things that we take for granted, a delusion. At any other magnification, the simple world vanishes and other rules come into play. If we look very closely at a monochrome painting, it turns out to have nuances and bumps, as inscribed on the gallery label for an Ad Reinhardt black square at MoMa, 2007:

> *At first glance this painting presents a flat black surface. But longer viewing reveals more than one shade of black and an underlying geometric structure. Reinhardt has divided the canvas into a three-by-three grid of squares. The black in each corner square has a reddish tone; the shape between them formed by the center squares is bluish-black in its vertical bar and greenish-black in its horizontal bar. Reinhardt tried to produce what he described as "a pure, abstract, non-objective, timeless, spaceless, changeless, relationless, disinterested painting – an*

object that is self-conscious (not unconsciousness), ideal, transcendent, aware of no thing but art."

Conceptual art – dealing with concepts and ideas rather than with material and aesthetic considerations – does not, it seems, necessarily help in understanding the world that we see around us. So when Sol LeWitt stated that "obviously a drawing of a person is not a real person, but a drawing of a line is a real line," he was quite simply wrong.

Whatever a "real line" is, as soon as we draw one, it becomes a representation of a line; it only needs us to zoom in closely to that representation to shake our complacent understanding of what we see as a line, for we will see that it really is a series of wavy lines and dots.

Now while it is true that we don't need the material world to prove the existence of a line, which is a geometric entity linking one point to another, we can, nevertheless, represent it by, for example, drawing it. This cannot be done with *nothing*, because to draw *nothing* would be to draw *something*; we cannot represent that which we can't imagine, in other words. We know what a house is and we understand what a line is, and so both a house and a line can be represented by an artist. But *nothing*? How could that be represented? Art can, and does, attempt to show *nothing*, but it fails. Or seems to.

Which *nothing*, though, are we referring to? We saw in Chapter One that there are two types of *nothing*: **the absence of something** (as is zero, the absence of something that had been there before) and **the absence of everything**. These are clearly different, and it's about time that we distinguish how we refer to them. Let's call *the absence of something* (such as zero) **NOTHINGNESS**, while *the absence of everything* we will refer to as **NOTHING**.

Artists have, in fact, little problem getting to nothingness, just as we all can handle the zero, because it is graspable. A painting of blackness is exactly that: black paint on canvas (or wherever); the painting is the absence of color (apart from black or whatever is there), and it is perfectly legitimate for the artist to present it as the concept nothingness. Conceptual art, then, has no greater problem with the concept of nothingness than it has with the representation of other concepts, such as eternity, happiness, marriage, whatever.

Since nothingness is the absence of something, it is not absolute, can change according to context and is – has to be – relative (being compared to its absence). Silence is an example of nothingness: it is the absence of sound, and is demonstrated in comparison to sound when it is taken away. And there are different kinds of silence, as we saw. Silence can be nothingness, but it is not *nothing*: it is the absence of sound but not the absence of everything else.

The problem is with *nothing*, which is what artists are trying to convey. In their movement towards less and less, minimalist artists are pursuing *nothing*; the reason they are unsuccessful is that they can never get far enough, i.e. it is not, and cannot *be*, *nothing*. As we have already seen, blankness – however it is shown – is not *nothing*.

Showing *nothing* is like doing nothing or talking about nothing: impossible. The fact that artists (and everyone else, with me having been just as guilty until now) freely interchange the terms *nothing* and *nothingness* and make no distinction between them adds to the frustration of what they are trying to achieve. It would be nice to think that a distinction is made by Madam Flora in Gian Carlo Menotti's opera *The Medium*: "If there is nothing to be afraid of, then why am I afraid of this nothingness?" but, as merely a play on words, she doesn't.

That this fact of life is not understood leads to the undying frustration of artists who go to ever more extremes in their attempts to illustrate something that by its very nature is unrenderable. (And, of course, it is not **something** that they are going for, but **nothing**.) The fact that Reinhardt painted so many "Black Pictures", each of which was always the 'last picture', exemplifies the Sisyphean task they are attempting.

Nothing limited

Does it matter? Who cares that artists are incapable of illustrating *nothing*? For a start, it may make us aware that there is a limit to what art can do. Swiss artist Paul Klee's contention that "Art does not reproduce what is visible but makes it visible" was, to put it mildly, overly optimistic, if not downright inaccurate. What he was saying was that we do not see all that is around us (or within us) until the artist shows it to us. Yet art, as we have seen, cannot represent everything, since it cannot show *nothing*, and so fails to make visible all of our thoughts, ideas, concepts and imagination. Because it cannot include *nothing*, art, then, does not reflect everything.

But why would we expect it to? Art is limited, true. But so is the human mind, which, as we have already noticed, has a hard time understanding the concept of *nothing*. Artists are merely human, are they not?, so why would we expect them to create something that is beyond what they can grasp? In that sense, then, art does reflect life, for just as aspects of art can be beyond the artist, so are aspects of life beyond the human.

As we have seen, though, art can represent the concept of *nothingness*, and it can do so through using something. It cannot, though, show **nothing** because in order to do so there would be nothing for it to show; art itself would be *nothing*. The circularity – the absurdity, if you wish – of that notion perhaps demonstrates dramatically why we are incapable of understanding *nothing*, and it is the limitation of art that shows us our own limitation. In the same way that art would cease to be art (or, in fact, anything) if it were to show *nothing*, so we cannot be present where there is *nothing*, since being conscious means always being aware of *something.*[63]

All is not lost, though. On the contrary, we have everything to gain from the continual search for *nothing* that artists are engaged in. Humankind, it can be argued, has made its advances through the hope that what is not understood will become understood and that what is still unknown will eventually become known. *Nothing* fits both those bills, but in a strange way: we feel we know what *nothing* is and only when we really think about it do we realize that we don't understand it and that it is, in fact, unknowable. And once we have separated it from nothingness – the 'nothing' that is the absence of something – understanding *nothing* becomes even more of a challenge.

Is there any point pursuing *nothing*? Is it 'real' in any sense, or is the very idea an illusion? Picasso said, "Everything you can imagine is real." The point is whether *nothing* can be imagined. If it cannot be, then it isn't real for us as humans, which is, presumably, why it cannot be represented.

It is not always clear how artists imagine the subjects of their conceptual art, or whether it has any connection to reality. But that is not only in conceptual art: all art is, to a smaller or greater extent, an illusion of the senses. As humans, we have the remarkable ability to see objects in the paint with which a surface is marked – which Richard Wollheim calls "seeing in" – rather than simply seeing the marks; it is exercised when we see faces in clouds, for example, or a face on the surface of the moon. And it is this ability that allows us to see in a painting what was intended by the artist. The more abstract (the less like nature) the art, the more we have to use our own interpretation of what we see and also the intention of the artist, which, according to Wollheim includes "desires, beliefs, emotions, commitments, wishes."

Illusion, reality, truth, fact, topics typically discussed among philosophers, are brought up as well through art, where *nothing* is a particularly good way of examining them. Attempts to show the illusion of reality through tricks of perception are illuminating.

James Turrell (b. 1943), an American artist whose years of solitude in prison gave him a particular sensitivity to light and space, has proven the unreliability of perceived reality on a number of occasions. At an exhibition in New York in 2006, several people were so convinced by the illusions of light that they tripped over his 'beams' and fell to the floor. Following that same exhibition, Turrell was sued by a woman who sustained a broken wrist by leaning against a blue wall that was, in fact, made of light. Touching something that turns out to be nothing can be very disconcerting, as attested to by visitors to his installations.

And since we are on about suing for *nothing*, it is illuminating to mention the court case in 2002, in which John Cage's publishers sued composer Mike Batt for plagiarism for crediting his track *A Minute's Silence* as being written by "Batt/Cage". Batt's intention was to merely separate some acoustic arrangements from rockier material on *Classical Graffiti*, the debut album by his newest group The Planets. "I thought for my own amusement it would be funny to call it something so I called it *A Minute's Silence* and credited it as track 13 and put my name as Batt/Cage, as a tongue-in-cheek dig at the John Cage piece." [64]

Unfortunately for him, Cage's publishers did not consider that silence to be either nothing or amusing, and Batt agreed to pay an undisclosed six-figure sum to the John Cage Trust by way of an out-of-court settlement in September 2002.

Presumably Batt will never hear silence in the same way, or think of it as nothing; stung and surprised by the verdict, he said that he considered his track "a much better silent piece. I have been able to say in one minute what Cage could only say in four minutes and 33 seconds." Batt told the London Independent that "My silence is original silence, not a quotation from his silence." Batt was right: we have seen enough to venture that one silence (the absence of sound) is not necessarily like another silence (the absence of another sound).

The fact that absences are different according to context is rather interestingly encapsulated in this event some forty years earlier, also involving John Cage, who went to see Robert Morris's untitled slab (an eight-foot-square plywood platform that sat a few inches off the floor), in 1963, at his first solo show. Cage's memorable comment was that he "only saw a platform with nothing on it."[65] One would have thought that if anyone would appreciate *nothing*, it would be John Cage.

Why nothing

It should not really be so surprising that modern artists are fascinated with *nothing*. It is a very human attribute to be beguiled by what we do NOT have, often more than what we do have. In the world of exploration, *nothing* would be the ultimate unknown area: across the frontier from where we are to where we and everything else disappears. To where we cannot be!

And here comes the problem. As hard as we try, we cannot make ourselves unaware of our own existence. And if that is not bad enough, we have to face the fact that we cannot conceive of our non-existence either. We don't worry too much about the former, because we just 'are' and get on with it. But the other thing really bothers us.

It is our ultimate fascination with the frustratingly unknown and unknowable: our own personal non-existence – death. The final challenge, the ultimate frontier, then, is to be able to see where we are not. Or, more accurately, where we will not be. Let's be clear: We know that it will happen; what we don't know is what it will be like to actually be dead, to not exist. (That is, of course, where religions come in, as we will see in the next chapter.)

It is *nothing* that is the ultimate mystery, not nothingness. Nothingness (the absence of something) as we have seen, is easier to cope with than *nothing* (the absence of everything). As difficult as the notion of death is, it makes sense if we think of it as the absence of life, and goes some way to explaining why artists are able to render nothingness but not *nothing*.

Artists, by subtracting more and more from their art, are endeavoring to move towards *nothing* as a way of understanding death, the ultimate mystery. They can't get far enough, though, and get stuck at nothingness. Nothingness is the point that is conceivable: the absence of something, even of life itself, the *concept* of mortality. What artists are incapable of showing is *nothing*, the *state* of mortality; as demonstrated by the vacuum cleaner-creatures in the Beatles' *Yellow Submarine*, it is what happens when there is nothing left and nobody to see it.

This brings us back to silence and to why it is or is not *nothing*. As John Cage discovered, silence can never be absolute. This was demonstrated nicely in his piece 4'33", where the absence of notes from the piano did not mean absence of other sounds, of non-intended sounds. It is the equivalent of nothingness. Absolute silence, on the other hand, is impossible to achieve; it is a border that cannot be crossed, the equivalent of *nothing*. It is impossible to imagine a situation where there will be no sounds, not from outside or from within ourselves. Silence as *nothing* is unachievable: until we die, there will be sounds.

All in all, it's not surprising that people who dwell on *nothing* and nothingness are none too cheerful individuals and that some of them come to premature ends. Artists may be particularly prone to expressing those thoughts; as Tolstoy said, whatever artists are thinking of, they are always thinking of their death. The Polish poet Zbigniew Herbert (1924-1998), who spent most of his life battling the authorities – in his youth (like Beckett in Paris) fighting for the resistance against the Germans in WWII, and later voicing strong opposition to Communism in Poland – wrote: "Now as I watch the death of the words, I know there is no limit to decay. All that will be left after us in the black earth will be scattered syllables. Accents over nothingness and dust."[66]

Tchaikovsky's obsession with death is expressed in the first and last movements of his Sixth Symphony, given the name *Pathetique* by his brother Modest and claimed by Tchaikovsky to be his greatest love. In the symphony's surprising finale, the pathos of muted sobbings and wild outcries gradually dissolves into a silence that signifies nothingness. He died nine days after the premiere, on November 6, 1893, most likely, it is thought, by suicide.

Luckily, most of us do not dwell on death if we can help it, since our minds are otherwise occupied. But take away all the objects that do keep our minds busy, and what we are left with is ourselves and the anxiety of nothingness (death). It's as disconcerting (well, more so, but you get the point) as what happens to a couple who are left alone to face their relationship when the children have left home.

Just as unsettling is getting *nothing* when we expect to find something. The eagerly awaited final episode of *The Sopranos* on 11/6/07 stunned fans of this incredibly popular TV series. With Tony and his family sitting in a diner, and tension rising with the expectation of his bloody assassination, the screen simply went black. That was it. It ended like everything ends: in nothingness. (David Chase, the show's creator and executive producer, wanted it to end there, with no credits, but the network's executives objected.)

Disconcerting – and for many people, unacceptable – it certainly was, and for good reason. Rather than seeing Tony Soprano die, i.e. seeing death from outside, as through the paintings of yore, with death depicted as some sort of beauty in its horror, we actually experience death as Tony did. If that was the idea, it was the most genuine way of showing *nothing* than of all the ways we have looked at so far. Did it work, though? Did we at last see *nothing*? No, not really, for what we saw was blackness, once more reminiscent of the monochrome paintings of modern art. A blank screen is not *nothing*. If it was shocking and disappointing, it was because we expected more. In the end, though, what we saw was how we imagine death was for Tony. For Tony death was *nothing*, but for those who saw it, death – the blank screen – was nothingness.

Making it

There is an old joke about a man who was finding it too expensive to feed his horse. So every day he fed it a little less, with no apparent change to the horse. The day after not being fed at all, the horse died. The man was really angry. "Now he had to die? Just when he was getting used to eating nothing?" The ultimate minimalistic joke.

Franz Kafka's 1922 story *A Hunger Artist*[67] has a similar plot, except that there is no horse and the protagonist, the hunger artist, is the one who is starving. As a fictional version of what was actually happening at the time, when real 'hunger artists' made money by starving themselves to near death, it brings us full circle to what art can do as well as what it is.

In a cage and watched at all times, the 'artist' fasts, even while the spectators are sure that the art is in the way he is somehow cheating, that they are witnessing an act in one sense or another.

As a spectacle, it is bizarre, with the audience growing as time goes on and the unseen ravages increase. There is something mysteriously artistic about fasting, with part of the 'art' consisting of nothing happening and letting viewers make what sense of it they will. Kafka, in fact, is less interested in what art actually is than in what it causes. For him, like Yves Klein with his empty gallery and John Cage with his silent music, he lets the audience make of art what they want, so that art comes from within themselves.

In the end, Kafka's hunger artist died alone, since people had by then lost interest and so he had been forgotten. If the end was *nothing*, no one saw it, nor in fact, could have seen it. The spectators had gone on with their lives because the artist's inevitable end would be nothingness, as normal as everyone else's.

An updated and very live version of a hunger artist was enacted in 2003, when the New York magician David Blaine was suspended for 44 days over London's River Thames in a transparent glass box, with only drinking water to keep him alive. If ever spectators were more interesting than what the artist was doing, it was in this case. Constantly taunting Blaine, the crowds swelled as time went on, disturbing his sleep (at one point by a man banging on an Indian bhangra drum) and tempting him by pelting him with food, one joker even using a remote-controlled toy helicopter to fly a cheeseburger inches from his face.

While on the whole friendly, the crowd had its ugly side, with Braine an irresistible target for people trying to get him to break his vow to fast for 44 days. Certainly part of the anger was directed at a man who was about to make money (a reported $8 million) for seemingly doing nothing. Another part of the anger could have been at someone who was somehow tricking them into believing that he was cheating death.

It is not new to think about art being a relationship between the artist and the audience, and we can appreciate that it does not have to be a one-way street. We can be sure that each one looking up at David Blaine in his glass box was looking at him in a different way, just as we all 'see' different things when we look at modern art. We are, in a sense, 'making our own art', as well as being part of the art itself.

Were not the enormous crowds that came in 1911 to see the space where the Mona Lisa had been making their own art and were they not also part of the art itself? Not to mention Yves Klein's empty space, *The Void*: was that the art or was it the crowds who crammed into the space and drank their blue cocktails? Would the empty gallery have been art if nobody had turned up to view it?

With this in mind, it is not at all strange that each performance of John Cage's *4'33"* is different. The shuffles of the audience, the sounds from inside the hall and from those drifting in from outside, all are a result of what is happening outside of the piece itself.

The idea that art is not only what it tries to show but what it **does** is becoming more important in a world where the focus is on 'communication' and 'interaction'. If, then, an artist does not succeed in communicating his/her intention to the audience but instead causes a reaction (puzzlement, say, or anger), is the work art? Chuck Klosterman, considered one of America's top music journalists, sums it up from his point of view:

> As a fan, I am interested in what music sounds like. As a writer, I am more interested in the audience for art and what a record (or film, or TV show, or a book) suggests about the culture at large.[68]

The sketch that the American comedian Andy Kaufman (1949-84) – a fairly morose character the rest of the time – was most proud of was when his performance consisted of nothing. Kaufman simply came out on stage and did nothing. He just stood there, looking at the audience, without doing or saying anything. The audience obviously started laughing straight away and laughed louder the longer he stood and did nothing. Art, it seems, is not just what there is, but also what there is not.

So perhaps there really is something to one of Shakespeare's most repeated quotes, from *As You Like It*: "All the world's a stage, and all the men and women merely players..." Perhaps it really is us who are the performance: we are art.

But if we are art, we are getting dangerously close to saying that everything is art. After all, whatever that we have looked at (and much that we haven't, due to restraints of space) in our forays into *nothing* has been called art by someone: monochrome paintings, empty galleries, closed galleries, light and sound, silent music, air, telepathy, human excrement... whatever the artist has called art. And then we have the Italian artist Piero Manzoni (he of the canned feces) turning the whole globe into a total work, and signing anything that moved, including human bodies, and designating them works of art. We may even agree with Stephen Farthing, who, in his book *1001 Paintings You Should See before You Die*, asks, "What is painting," and answers: "Who cares?"

In an article in the *American Spectator* entitled "Art, Beauty, and Judgment", Roger Scruton says that "if anything can count as art, then art ceases to have a point. All that is left is the curious but unfounded fact that some people like looking at some things, others like looking at others."[69]

It's not as simple as that, though, since there is no connection between whether we enjoy, say, Reinhardt's black square and whether it is a work of art. Obviously the weather-beaten expression 'I don't know what art is but I know what I like' is not relevant, since 'beauty' is in any case too subjective to be taken seriously. And neither, in our discussion as to what is art, is it relevant whether we consider a particular piece better than another piece, or even whether something is 'good' or 'bad' art, nor whether it has anything to do with 'good taste' or 'bad taste'.

It gets worse. A question we wouldn't have thought of asking before *nothing* brought 'modern art' into our line of fire is whether there is a difference between art and nature. After all, it is clear that a tree is nature and that a painting of a tree is art. If that is easy, how about the difference between a row of Brillo boxes on a supermarket shelf and Andy Warhol's plywood Brillo boxes? It was the American art philosopher and critic Arthur Danto who asked the question when he saw Warhol's exhibition at the Stable Gallery in New York in 1964. "Has the whole distinction between art and reality broken down?" he wondered.[70]

Perhaps it *has* broken down. If anything can be a work of art, then anything also has the potential to be a work of art. Also John Carey, the eminent British art critic and academic, thinks so. "A work of art," he says, "is anything that anyone has ever considered a work of art, though it may be a work of art only for that one person."[71] Is this not what Robert Rauschenberg's famous telegram, "This is a portrait of Iris Clert if I say so," meant?

If everything can be art if someone says it is, what is left? What, in other words, is not art? Nothing remains, it would seem. And that's it, of course: *nothing* is not art. It's the conclusion we are forced to come to after looking at how the arts deal with *nothing* and realizing that artists are unable to represent *nothing*. Of course *nothing* can't be shown; we can never see or experience *nothing* in any way, since *nothing* is where we are not. Putting it another way, if everything can be art and *nothing* is the absence of everything, then *nothing* is where there is no art.

Have we solved anything? Well, for a start, it isn't necessarily outrageous to claim that everything can be art. Making that claim does not imply that art does not exist, that nothing is art. On the contrary, we said: *nothing* is not art. It is, in fact, *nothing* that makes art possible. For there to be art, there has to be something that is not-art. And what is not art? *Nothing*.

Art and *nothing* are in many ways like an unrequited love affair, with artists chasing what they can never reach. While art, as we have seen, can represent nothingness; it cannot show what is not: *nothing*.

"And what if you feel nothing in front of his canvases?" Rachel Campbell-Johnston asks her readers after an enthusiastic description of a forthcoming exhibition of Rothko at Tate Modern. "Well, that's not nothing because to feel nothing is one of the strongest feelings you can have."[72]

So what better way of ending this chapter than to quote the TV character Ally McBeal: "Sometimes...when you hold out for everything, you walk away with **nothing**."

Three

Believing in Nothing

Even if we consider religion to be of interest only historically as an explanation of how humans attempted to find reasons for phenomena that they sought to understand, we are faced with the fact that the world in which we live contains hundreds of thousands of religions, beliefs and faiths. If we include cults, we will reach a truly astronomical figure of active beliefs.

That they share some common aspects is reasonable to suppose, as much as it is to claim that they have differences. If they didn't, there would be only one, a universal religion to satisfy everyone, whereas the sheer number of religions, faiths, sects and cults is so vast that at times there seem to be almost as many religions as there are believers.

Just those groups that call themselves Christian, of which there are arguably eight meta-groups (Roman Catholicism, Eastern Orthodoxy, Oriental Orthodox and Assyrian Churches, Protestantism, Restorationists, Anglican Communion, Pentecostals, and others consisting of hundreds of church groups that do not fit into other groupings) can be counted at over 1,200, each of which has innumerable offshoots, in the USA alone, with around 30,000 elsewhere. And that is just Christianity!

Just as numerous and not less fractured are the other religions and faiths that include, among others, Judaism, Islam, Buddhism, Hinduism, Sikhism, Taoism, Jainism, Confucianism, Baha'i, Voodoo and the myriad Neopagan, satanic, doomsday faiths and sects, too many to numerate even if each were not split into yet further strands.

Yet within the myriad beliefs and the subtleties of their differences, we are able to discern a common denominator, the one thread that each and every belief has to deal with in one way or another: *Nothing*. So if we say that they have *nothing* in common, we mean it absolutely literally.

Whether the beliefs are monotheistic, polytheistic or non-theistic, *nothing* is there in all its glory (or, if you wish, non-glory); mainstream religions, mysticism, Eastern faiths, Wiccans, Druids, New Age, wherever there is faith, *nothing* is there in one way or another: to be avoided, to be embraced, sometimes prominently, at other times less so, but somewhere there nonetheless. For many faiths, *nothing* is from where everything began; for others, *nothing* is in the here and now. And all of them – every single one – do not accept that life ends in *nothing*.

Having *nothing* in common does not, of course, mean that beliefs deal with it in the same way. In fact, despite the enormous variety, religions of the world can, interestingly, be divided rather roughly as to how they perceive *nothing*: those, in the West, that are ambivalent towards *nothing*, or those, in the East, that embrace *nothing*.

In the beginning

Pope Pius XII, opening a scientific conference at the Vatican in 1951, declared solemnly that the Big Bang theory bore witness "to that primordial *fiat lux* ['Let there be light'] uttered at the moment when, along with matter, there burst forth from nothing a sea of light and radiation... Hence, Creation took place in time; therefore there is a creator, therefore God exists!"

Only the pause at the end of that statement, and the pope's momentary glance through his round, thin wire-framed spectacles from the pages in front of him to the attentive audience seated in the ornate hall, gave any sense of drama to the words that had been delivered in the high, quavering voice of God's Vicar on earth. Letting his eyes fall to the written text on the lectern, the pope continued, but the rest of the speech was lost in the echo of what had just been said, the significance of which was not lost to the scientists present.

It would not be an exaggeration to state that not everyone at that conference was convinced by the pope's words, and most certainly not by the logic behind them. In fact, considering that it was a scientific conference, the pope's conclusion would have been received with more than a large dose of skepticism by a majority of the participants. The pope's words, of course, highlighted many more problems than the one that was supposedly solved. One doesn't stand up and argue with the pope, though, so his address was met with polite clapping from all present.

It's the pope's "therefore", (two of them, in fact) that pokes us in the eye when we realize that it represents a leap of faith across a bedrock of logic. In order to get to any sort of 'therefore' here, we need to check whether what led to it adds up. From his assumptions that from nothing there was a burst of light together with matter and that this took place in time, the pope came to two conclusions: that there is a creator and that this creator is God.

These particular conclusions work only if one first assumes that God exists. Otherwise why would one assume a creator if the world was formed in time?

There is another problem: If the Creation took place in time, as the pope proclaimed, then time already existed before the Big Bang (or at least the pope's version of it). Yet if there was time, then things had actually been happening beforehand, so that Creation, did not actually "burst forth from nothing".

And it would not be less problematic to claim that time was created along with everything else: for God to have existed before time, there would have been no past, no 'before'.

And worse: if God was around before the world was created (which, being eternal, he would have had to be), there could not have been *nothing*; after all, if God was there, there was something. There could never have been *nothing*, surely.

Yet it is axiomatic in the three monotheistic religions that the world was created from nothing. And although life would be easier for religions if they didn't have to worry about *nothing* and a universe springing therefrom, it is an article of faith as part and parcel of belief in God.

Creation from nothing, though, is not mentioned in Genesis I, which Christianity and Judaism take as the authoritative source for the Creation and which the Quran paraphrases for Islam. "In the beginning," says Genesis I, God created the world from *tohu vavohu*, which is variously translated from Hebrew as 'chaos' or 'unformed and void'. But *nothing* it certainly was not, not least because the second sentence tells us that everything consisted of water before the actual Creation began: "The spirit of God hovered over the face of the waters." *Nothing*, in fact, does not feature in the story at all.[73]

So why the Creation story? If *nothing* is such a problem, why do religions make a point of mentioning it as being at the start of the universe? Why is it that we are left with the general feeling – and, are, in fact, told – that the world was created from nothing, when that is simply not stated in most Creation texts and mythologies? We have already come across Pope Pius XII, who spoke about everything "burst[ing] forth from nothing", and way back in the ninth century, there was Abbot Fridugisus of Tours, who stated: "This nothing is a very important something, since it is that out of which God created everything."[74] We can surely assume that those gentlemen were not ignorant of what was actually written in the Bible.

In fact, we have to look far and wide to find *nothing* mentioned within Creation stories. One of the very few that mentions *nothing* specifically is the Baha'i, one of the youngest of the world's religions, founded in Iran in 1863, that believes in progressive revelation and unity for the common good of humanity. In the Writings of Bahá'u'lláh ('Glory of God' in Arabic), considered the latest Manifestation of God, it is stated:

"All praise to the unity of God, and all honor to Him, the sovereign Lord, the incomparable and all-glorious Ruler of the universe, Who, out of utter nothingness, hath created the reality of all."[75]

So why? If, apart from the Baha'i, *nothing* is almost universally not found in the basic religious texts, those that are considered sacred, why mention it at all?[76] Why shoot oneself in the foot by introducing a concept that is so impossible to grasp (and which for hundreds of years in Medieval Europe contained the unmentionable *nothing*, as we saw)?

There is a reason, and a very good one. *Nothing* **has to be** part of the Creation story. Without *nothing*, Creation is not such big a deal. But with *nothing* as the first ingredient (or more pertinently, a non-ingredient) the Creation process is really something to write home about; creating something from nothing is certainly more impressive than creating something from chaos or water. Not just something, of course: everything – the world and the universe that it is part of. *Nothing* is as important to the Creation as what was created.

Nothing is even more important than that. It is the connection between *nothing* and Creation that makes God what he is. For God to be all-powerful, he would have had to create the universe from *nothing*. If there was something already there, then we are forced to ask who put it there, since God supposedly created everything. Belief in God has to be contingent on there having been *nothing*.

One of the big questions is why didn't the holy-cum-mythological texts just come out and state that God created the world from nothing? A speculative answer as to why *nothing* was avoided in the earliest texts is that the concept of *nothing* would have been a hard sell and too much of a leap from the pagan religions that were around at the time. Just as the monotheistic religions took on board and adapted existing pagan festivals, so they would have absorbed current Creation stories, most of which were similar, as we have seen. Far easier it was to accept God's spirit hovering over a sea that was as deep as it was wide, a sea that covered the whole world. Later interpretations of the written text set out to prove what it 'really' meant.

A prominent exception to the belief of *creatio ex nihilo* is that of The Church of Jesus Christ of Latter-day Saints (Mormonism), which proclaims that creation *ex nihilo* is not to be found in the Bible and is therefore untrue: According to Mormons, God created the universe out of matter that had always existed, and *ex nihilo* Creation is a late invention of the church. As honestly forthright as that seems to be, it does not help the impasse: If matter is eternal, and so is God, where did it all begin? Placing Creation in a 'pre-existing life', as Mormonism does, does not solve the problem, but rather seems to be replacing it with others, such as an attempt to reconcile the eternal existence of matter with the question of when God created matter that had always existed.

So whichever way one looks at it, and however one tries to deal with it, *nothing* presents a quandary. For monotheistic religions, *nothing* is something that they would prefer not to live with but at the same time can't live without and therefore can't ignore. Once it is introduced into the equation of Creation, *nothing* has to be reconciled with an eternal God while not acknowledging the paradox of the existence of both.

Paradoxes and difficulties within faith are not only accepted but expected as part of the necessary 'mysteries' that are part of belief. It is the job of priests to smooth them over and for theologians to explain them rationally within the definition of the religion. One who endeavored to reconcile God with the very notion of *nothing* was the Church of England prelate William Temple, Archbishop of Canterbury until his death in 1944. Temple tried to turn the tables by using *nothing* as a way of capturing a basic truth about God in the famous pair of equations he propounded:

God minus the world equals God; the world minus God equals nothing.

Simply put, God would still exist if there was no world, but the world could not exist without God. Without God, then, there would be nothing. There is a problem, though. The eminent bishop unknowingly intimated that where there is nothing, there is no God. Whether he would have liked it or not, it does make sense, since, as we already pointed out, nothing is not nothing when God is present. But since nothing is from what God created the universe, it would seem, according to William Temple's logic, that God was not there before the Creation. Did God, then, create himself as well?

It goes without saying, does it not, that even if someone had pointed out the provocative conclusions brought out by creation from nothing, there would have been no effect on Temple's faith, nor on the pope's, had he been made aware of the far-from-solvable problems brought up by his speech in 1951.

An interesting postscript to Pius XII's 1951 speech was occasioned by another pope, John Paul II, fifty-five years later, also at a scientific conference at the Vatican, who told the delegates, according to the world-renowned astrophysicist Stephen Hawking who was present, that they "should not study the beginning of the universe because it was the work of God." Unlike his predecessor, who obviously felt that 'if you can't beat them, join them', Pope John Paul II, realizing that mixing God and science was a hard nut and an even more difficult sell, went for 'if you can't beat them, keep them away'. This was the pope, who, while four years earlier had exonerated Galileo of heresy, 350 years after his death now showed, unwittingly but unfortunately, that attitudes of the Church concerning the fundamentals of belief hadn't really changed.

Yet how could they change when *nothing* is in the mix? And while it would be nice to ignore *nothing*, as was tried in Medieval times in the Church's relationship with zero, there is simply no way that could now be done. Not for Christianity, nor for Judaism or Islam as well. *Nothing* is an integral part of Creation. Without *nothing*, Creation is not a miracle. And because of that, monotheistic religions have a sort of love-hate relationship with *nothing* – drawn to it and repelled by it.

Why something, not nothing?

It is not only the three monotheistic religions that don't have *nothing* in their original Creation stories. With very few exceptions, the world's faiths and mythologies do not specifically claim that the world was created from nothing.

Not only is Genesis I not the first account of the Creation, it is also not particularly original. Before it came the Sumerian, Babylonian, Chinese, Egyptian accounts, among others – not to mention the Greek mythological tales. Common to them all is the recurring idea of darkness, shapelessness, chaos and a nothingness (often with water) that is by no stretch of the imagination nothing. Take the Chinese myth (one of the few, incidentally, that does not mention water), which depicts the concept of nothingness as a dark swirling confusion, over and under, round and round, and where only chaos exists, "unformed and unillumined."[77] In the Babylonians' version of the beginning, similar to the Chinese myth, nothing existed on Earth except a great deep of water, which was vast, undivided, and bottomless.

So if it is so clearly stated that there was a beginning, what came before then? Obviously no believer would ask, since faith is faith. From the Maya gods Tepeu and Gucumatz who made the earth and everything on it by thinking about them, to Gisoolg, an Aboriginal god who created everything, to Odin, the Norse god, who created the earth, there is no indication, obviously, as to what was there before the gods themselves. In Greek mythology, Chaos, the fathomless place from which everything came, is sometimes conceptualized as the void, sometimes as a chaotic place without meaning: it is a place in which time and space, as necessary organizing principles of the mind, cannot operate. Even in Hindu mythology, where life is part of an everlasting circle, the potentiality of time and space are contained within the first golden embryo. Yes, but… if it is first, we can't help speculating about what brought it about and from where.

A meander through Creation stories among peoples and civilizations, from Africa to Asia to Europe to the Americas, shows up stories that may change in their details but not in the underlying theme of a powerful being (or beings) who was around to do the creating. Whether the great god Bumba of the Boshongo tribe of Central Africa, who one day, in pain from a stomach ache, vomited up the sun, dried up some of the water, leaving land, and then, still in pain, vomited up the moon, the stars, and then some animals, and finally, some men; or the Bushman's Kaang, who brought to the surface all the people and animals who had been living peacefully below the earth; or the two gods, Obassi Osaw and Obassi Nsi, of the Ekoi, a tribe in southern Nigeria, who created everything together; or the Fans, a Bantu tribe in Africa, whose god, Nzame, was three, and so an early example of the trinity – the Creation stories are numerous but are merely variations of a theme. From outside its own circle of believers, each is as [un]believable as the next, not any more or less so than the God of the monotheistic religions, for example. Or as Richard Dawkins puts it in his blunt way in his book, *The Blind Watchmaker*: If we are going to say that God created the universe, why not then give equal weight to the Nigerian tribe who believe the world was created from the excrements of ants?

Be that as it may, whichever story believers choose as theirs, there is one unavoidable thought that pushes its way up and lies there in its niggling persistency: the possibility that the whole thing might not have taken place at all, that the universe might simply not have been created by whatever god or gods we do or don't believe in, that there would have been *nothing* instead.

It is a question with which a cynic might confront a religious believer: the possibility that God could just have easily decided not to create the universe, so that *nothing* could simply have continued (whatever 'continued' could mean in the non-state of no time and no space). Or not decided anything, with the same result. After all, since God necessarily has free will and is not bound to any particular course of action, the universe was not an inevitability.

Now posing a question about the inevitability of the universe is one thing. For believers, though, there certainly is no such doubt about God. For them, God was an inevitability. Not only did he have to exist, but his very nature hinges on the fact that he has never not existed, and has never not existed through an infinite timescale. That being so, he would have been doing nothing for a very long time – an infinite length of time, in fact – and then chose one particular moment to create the universe. But why at that particular moment? Was he bored? What had he been doing until then? It cannot have been the result of a developing thought process as God is – has to be, if he is God – omniscient and perfect, therefore requiring no thought processes that are increasingly perfected. Now while that question may bring a smile of glee to the faces of atheists, for believers it does not present an insurmountable problem, since, they say, we, as imperfect beings, cannot know why God did something when he did. Attributing 'thought processes' to God is a useless exercise, for God is God.

The big question, then, as to why the universe exists at all – rather than the alternative, *nothing* – is easily answered by believers in God: Because God wanted it. They do not have to answer the other question – Why did he create it? – because the answer is simply that God decided to.

They are, then, let off the hook when it comes to answering what the British philosopher of language and metaphysics, Bede Rundle, calls "philosophy's central, and most perplexing, question": Why is there something rather than nothing?[78] For believers, the answer is simply that God wanted it that way. Even better, they can actually turn everything round and use the question as an answer to prove the existence of God: the fact that there is something rather than nothing proves that there is a God; if there were no God, there would be nothing (and nobody to know that there was nothing). And obviously, as far as they are concerned, they are also excused from asking themselves what would be the non-believer's follow-up question: Why is there God rather than nothing? But of course that is not even a question for believers; God just is – there is no 'if' when it comes to God's existence.

In the eleventh century, Saint Anselm of Canterbury made his way through this maze by elaborating the points into an ingenious argument for the existence of God. It is clearly greater and more perfect to exist than not to exist, Anselm reasoned, for a real being is greater than a merely fictitious one. "So truly, therefore, dost thou exist, O Lord, My God, that thou canst not be conceived not to exist," concluded Anselm's invocation.

Some six hundred years later, in the seventeenth century, René Descartes, arguably the first great philosopher of the modern era, also purportedly proved God's existence in a not dissimilar way, but through the theory of innate ideas and the notion that whatever one clearly and distinctly perceives or understands is true. God is so naturally clear to us, Descartes argues, that he must exist. Not only that, but God is the only thing that can be naturally perceived by us. God cannot be an invention, but is, rather, something native to the mind. Unlike other things that we can think of and are dependent on us, God is independent of us thinking about him, which is proof of his unique existence.

The emphasis on things that are dependent on us and the difference between them and God, who exists whether we think about him or not, is important, for it deals with things that exist, things that might exist and things that exist only in our minds. It is possible to know what a lion is, for example, before knowing whether it exists. In the same way, we can define what a unicorn is, even though we are fairly sure that it doesn't 'exist'. Lions and unicorns are dependent on us in a way that God is not.

Descartes' second argument for the existence of God is based on the supposition that there isn't anything, not even knowledge, that can be created out of nothing. Everything has a cause, he stated. Not only does something have to come out of something, the first something (cause, the creator) has to be more perfect than the second something (effect, the created). Hence, we, imperfect beings, could not have invented God (a perfect being); this notion of perfection, Descartes said, must have been put in our minds by something external to us which has to be perfect by itself. Hence, the notion of a perfect being – God – in our minds proves that he exists.

Now apart from the problems inherent in Descartes' idea that what exists in the mind, might or must necessarily exist in the real world (unicorns, spaghetti monsters, fairies, and teleporting are just a few that come to mind, not to mention God himself), there was a more specific problematic by-product of Descartes' good intentions. While ostensibly proving that God exists, Descartes, by stating that *something* can only come from *something*, in effect went against accepted Christian dogma that God created the universe from *nothing*. What he did, in fact, was to highlight the puzzle about *nothing*.

In the seventeenth century, though, puzzles about God were not what the church encouraged, and despite Descartes' rational proof of God's existence that he hoped would appeal to the mind rather than to blind faith, he lost many of his brownie points.

Rather than risk landing in jail, Descartes left France for the more liberal Holland and later to Sweden at the invitation of Queen Christina. Interestingly, the idea, accepted for more than three and a half centuries, that he died in Stockholm due to the rigors of the cold Swedish climate, has recently been questioned following the discovery of new evidence. According to Theodor Ebert, from the University of Erlangen, Descartes, whose 'heresies' had not been forgotten and were still deemed highly suspect, was poisoned through an arsenic-laced communion wafer administered by Jacques Viogué, a Catholic priest.

For Descartes, as with believers in God today, the question of why there is something rather than nothing is not a puzzle. That anything exists at all is an ultimate and unfathomable mystery only to non-believers, who cannot invoke God as the answer. For 'the man in the street', it isn't even a question worth asking, for the answer is simply 'because there is'. Not a bad answer at all.

Apart from anything else, it is a relief that there is something rather than nothing, or as the German philosopher Max Scheler put is so graphically: "He who has not, as it were, looked into the abyss of the absolute Nothing will completely overlook the eminently positive content of the realization that there is something rather than nothing." In a nutshell, it's better to be alive than to consider the alternative.

Let's stop for a moment. It may be that the arguments using God as proof of why there is *something* rather than *nothing* are not valid.

Perhaps our discussion about God should not be taking place at all. Faith in God is an indestructible belief that does not need justification or explanation (even though attempts have been made throughout the history of Christianity to reconcile faith and reason – provided that faith itself was not questioned).

For many theologians and men of faith, it is axiomatic that if we are going to talk about God at all, then God is not part of the natural order and should not be expected either to conform to the laws of physics or to feature as another entity in scientific accounts of life or the cosmos. It is no wonder, then, that theologians, whose task it is to explain and disassemble the inner workings of regions, are not universally keen on Creationism and its claim to be a scientific anti-evolution explanation of Creation and the universe. Creationists' view that God created humans and everything else exactly as they are now is often an embarrassment for theologians, since it places God into a position where he can be argued over through science and logic. God, theologians say, is beyond the scope of humans to understand, and the fact that he created the universe is just that: a fact, and that we are wasting our time trying to get him to conform to the scientific rules or logic that we know.

As a way of avoiding confrontation, it works. The questions, though, remain.

Something from nothing

We are stuck at a general impasse regarding the universe coming from nothing, with non-believers finding the whole business of *nothing* just as difficult as believers. More difficult, in fact, since they don't have the luxury of falling back on God and the attendant 'we aren't capable of understanding his ways' argument. And if we are tempted to think that science has a satisfying answer through the Big Bang theory as to how the universe began, then we may be in for a disappointment. In fact, science finds it so much of an embarrassment that John Wheeler, the American physicist who coined the term 'Black Hole', described the Big Bang as confronting us "with the greatest crisis in physics."[79]

The question as to what happened before the Big Bang some 13.7 billion years ago is somewhat similar to a question as to what happened before God. They are equally unanswerable, since for monotheistic believers and also for science, the concept of 'before' within those contexts is meaningless. Just as it is nonsensical for believers to consider the possibility of there being anything 'before God', for scientists, if both space and time were created together at the moment of the Big Bang, concepts like 'before' have no meaning when time didn't exist.

Unfortunately that doesn't really help. For a start, a cynic would suggest that not asking the question about a scientific explanation such as the Big Bang because the question purportedly has 'no meaning' is in some ways equivalent to not asking questions about the nature of God because 'we do not have the language that can cope with matters to do with God'.

Yet we can, and should, question scientific explanations, since, unlike those pertaining to God, they are not a matter of faith.

So let's ask a fundamental question about energy and the beginning of the universe. According to the First Law of Thermodynamics, energy cannot be created or destroyed. This would mean, surely, that energy was always in existence, also at the occurrence of the Big Bang. In any case, the Big Bang theory cannot claim that the world started from nothing, since it posits that at the point of the Big Bang, everything we now see in the universe existed in an infinitely small point with infinite density and at a huge temperature. Variations in energy at a sub-micro-scopic level were suddenly magnified by an enormous factor to make the universe expand, as it still is.

The point is, though, that energy was already present! Einstein's famous equation, $E=mc^2$, tells us that energy (E) and mass (m) are essentially interchangeable – i.e. energy can convert into 'things' and vice versa – and this is what happened in that early era. The high temperature radiation converted into subatomic particles, which eventually started clumping together into larger particles, giving, under the action of gravity in eons of time, the galaxies, stars, planets, dust and gas we see today.

It's clear, then, that we can, legitimately, ask about what was present before time began, and we cannot help doing so when we are faced with energy always having been present. The fact that it was always there, according to the First Law of Thermodynamics, adds another question mark: the concept of infinity. If energy cannot be created, then it has been around for an infinite amount of time – not merely for a long time, but for an infinite amount of time. So can we talk about infinity when there was no time? Infinity does not begin. And what does 'always' mean if time began only with the Big Bang? And if, as the Big Bang theory claims, time began with the big Bang, it would mean that energy also began with the Big Bang, so violating the basis of the laws of physics, that energy cannot be created or destroyed.

So did energy exist at the point of the Big Bang? If it did, then something – energy – was in existence. If it didn't, then energy was created and that would mean that the universe did somehow begin from nothing, with science being in the hot seat regarding how the universe did begin and what was there before.

For science, then, as with a God theory, *nothing* is a problem, with *ex nihilo* (something from nothing) as difficult for non-believers as it is for believers.

It seems that one doesn't have to be a theist to believe in eternal existence, with scientists believing that matter, in some form or another, has always existed. Alvin Plantinga, the American philosopher of religion, makes just this point to justify the theists' belief in an eternal God: that it is not more unreasonable to believe in an eternal God as it is to believe in eternal matter.

It's not that scientists aren't aware of the problem of energy having had to be present for the Big Bang to take place and the impossibility of the universe arising from *nothing*. A lot of thought and work has been expended on the huge puzzle that 'the beginning' presents.

One way of getting round the problem of *nothing* before the beginning is to propose that the total energy of the universe was zero, with the positive energy of matter balanced by the negative potential energy of gravity. Since the total energy is zero, no energy was needed to produce the universe and the First Law of Thermodynamics was not violated.

Is this a satisfactory explanation or is it mere fluff? Either energy was there or it wasn't. Whatever we call the total energy, zero energy consists of a positive energy of matter, which, even if it counterbalances the negative energy, was still there at the start of the Big Bang. No amount of words can disguise the fact that *nothing* it was not.

Quantum theory, which deals with the small-scale world of atoms, goes for another explanation. Instead of a balance of positive and negative energy, it posits speed as the answer to energy appearing out of nothing. It claims that the vacuum is not empty at all, but is seething with ultra-short microscopic particles. Energy is permitted to appear out of nothing, as long as it pops into existence and disappears again so quickly that the law of conservation of energy does not notice. Marcus Chown puts it in terms of a teenager borrowing their father's car overnight, with that being all right as long as the car is back in the garage before he notices it's gone.[80]

As serious as that theory takes itself to be, it does still not solve the problem. However fast energy pops in and out of existence, it still pops out of somewhere and not out of nothing. Just because it does so super fast does not change that fact.

There's simply no way of getting away from it. The problems of advocating a universe that arose from nothing are mind-boggling and a huge stumbling block to the acceptance of any theory that would be satisfactory.

Neil Turok, professor of applied mathematics and theoretical physics at Cambridge University, was yet another eminent scientist to tackle the problem of the universe beginning from a point – the Big Bang – that inevitably always leaves open what was there before. His calculations – worked on in Cambridge to figure out whether Stephen Hawking's theory of the start of the universe was viable – had the unfortunate result of predicting an empty universe. This should not have been so surprising; after all, if one starts with nothing, one should expect an empty universe, not a full one. Nothing comes from nothing, in other words.

And it does underline a basic scientific rule, one that is funda-mental to all others: causality, the principle that every state of affairs must be the result of some earlier state of affairs. As Michael Frayn puts it: "This is the bedrock on which all scientific (and historical) investigation rests."[81]

Turok's way out of the conundrum was the cyclic universe, with the Big Bang as one of a series of Big Bangs that occurred whenever two universes collided. Neatly (once one has accepted the theoretical reality of more than one universe), the problem of time having a beginning has been solved through the notion of cyclic time, with no point of beginning and no need to deal with the impossible concept of *nothing*.

Now while the notion of Big Bangs stretching back infinitely may be a satisfying description to scientists that seemingly solves any need to deal with 'the beginning', it still leaves in place the problem of eternity, a concept not less problematic than *nothing*. And is eternity within scientific explanations really so different to the notion within religion of an eternal God with no beginning, even with some nifty mathematical underpinnings? From the outside, it looks suspiciously like swapping one eternity that is God for another eternity that is a theory in cosmology.

Cycling round eternity

Science has come late into the game of tackling the problem of 'the beginning'. It could only begin to do so, and in fact, became science as we know it, when it separated itself from myth and religion and could ask the questions that religion didn't have to, and didn't dare to.

In the East, on the other hand, 'Creation' has never been a problem, since the concept 'Creation' simply doesn't exist. For Hinduism and Buddhism, among other faiths, the universe is accepted for what it is as part of an everlasting cycle within which the universe is created from itself, of which all nature is a part. In other words, God (in any way you wish to think of him/her/it/them as a higher force) is within everything, so that the universe is not a **creation** by God but a manifestation as part of God. God is part of the cycle that is everything. It is neatly expressed in Buddhism's cycle from and to the unworld, – "the Unborn, Unoriginated, Uncreated, Unformed."

Cycles are a very ancient mystical notion, represented in the shape of the zero in a large number of counting systems where the other numerals may be different from language to language. Circles – in almost all cases representing the unbroken cycle of life-death-life – have been used, among others, in the Celtic rites, the Ancient Egyptian, Greek, Roman beliefs, and in Babylonian rites, some of which were absorbed by the Jews into their religion while they were in exile after expulsion from their land by the Romans in 70 AD.

Today, the circle is no less prevalent as an important symbol, deep and widely used in almost all parts of the world. We can see its significance in the Kabbalah of Judaism, as the mandala, used to raise consciousness in Hindu and Buddhist meditations, the circle of the Freemasons, the Tao symbol of Yin-Yang, Tibetan prayer wheels, circles as part of tribal customs in the Americas and Australia, circles within the symbol for infinity and countless more. It does seem that the actual shape gives it a mystical aura, and that the shape itself has, somehow, inherently 'holy' properties. Not surprisingly, as we saw in the first chapter, it was the connection, in Medieval times, of zero to Eastern mysticism and 'anti-God' cults that threatened the Church's beliefs enough to ban its use in the counting system.

Whatever its origin and how it is perceived, neither the cycle of science with its rationality based on logical steps from previous ones, nor that of Buddhism with its mysticism, has tackled the problem of where it all began. Replacing the conundrum of *nothing* with that of the 'infinite cycles' presents a similar problem to that of 'eternity' and God, and cannot incorporate the beginning of time. As with Western religions, we are still left with the uncomfortable feeling that "Everything begins before it begins," as Jacques Derrida stated, albeit in a different context.[82]

Whichever way we look at it, with religions bending over backwards to deal with 'the beginning', one question stubbornly remains: what was the state of universe before *nothing* ostensibly became something? To add to the woes that come with that question, we have to bear in mind – how can we not? – that the universe was not in any sort of state then, and neither was there 'then' before there was time.

It's not all about cycles though. A claim by science that does take *nothing* into account to explain the existence of the universe is based on the idea that 'something is more natural than nothing', that it is more likely for the universe to exist than it is for the universe not to exist. At first sight, this seems hardly more satisfying than stating that it is more natural for God to exist than not to exist, along the lines of Descartes' point. Yet unlike Temple's equation that without God there is nothing, a world without God is eminently acceptable to non-believers.

By taking God out of the argument, it is no less trivial than it was when Descartes discussed it: that it is more natural for us to exist than not to exist; after all, we are only able to discuss it (or anything) at all because we 'are'. If we did not exist, not only wouldn't there be anything to discuss, but there would be *nothing*. Really, then, there is no choice between something and nothing.

It is no wonder that the very idea of *nothing* – non-existence – has been looked at with much skepticism and considered an unnatural proposition. The Greek philosopher Parmenides, some 2,500 years ago, was dead against the very idea of something not existing. As far as he was concerned, 'what is' is understandable, but 'what is not' is something that cannot be imagined.

Does Parmenides make sense? He does, but only partially. He

did not make the differentiation between two types of 'what is not': *nothing* and nothingness. He was referring to 'what is not' in the sense of *nothing*: the absence of everything. However, there is another type of 'what is not' – nothingness, the absence of something – and we know that it is possible to imagine an absence of what had once been present. What he was referring to, though, was the impossibility of imagining something that had never been present, even in our imagination.

It is no wonder that Parmenides dismissed the possibility of something coming from nothing. Something, he said, can only come from something, not from *nothing*. To put it another way, negation is only possible after presence: deletion can only be of something that is present. Positive comes before there is a negative, never the other way round.

Not only is something more natural than what is not, in other words, but that which is not is an impossibility if there is no thing to which it could refer.

That seems eminently sensible, until we think about it again and take a closer look at what science means about *something* being more natural than *nothing*. To do that we need to have a precise definition of *nothing*, which, luckily, physics can provide, since it deals with the physical properties of states (in this case, the non-physical properties of a [non] state). Physics can envisage a theoretical concept of *nothing* as a state that is the simplest of all conceivable states – no mass, no energy, no space, no time, no spin: nothing. Physics also demonstrates that simple systems tend to be unstable and often spontaneously transform into more complex ones, which theoretical models such as the inflationary model of the early universe bear out. Since *nothing* is as simple as it gets – so goes the argument – it would be completely unstable, and so naturally becomes something.[83]

As an argument, that may be palatable to non-believers, but is it really more successful than a religion-based one in explaining how something can be created from nothing and that something is more natural than nothing?

Nevertheless, it does bring up intriguing questions as to what *nothing* can or cannot do. Being *nothing*, we must assume that it does nothing. That's fair enough. But do we also assume that *nothing* necessarily **couldn't** do anything? After all, because it is *nothing* what is there to stop something happening? So while nothing comes from nothing, we cannot negate the **possibility** of something coming from nothing, since there isn't anything to stop it.

For believers, of course, that possibility means, well, nothing. As far as they are concerned, *nothing* is an impossibility, since *nothing* is not nothing if it contains God, for that would make it something. And neither could *nothing* have the potential of God spontaneously appearing, since God has supposedly always been around.

The problems with *nothing* and the notion of the universe coming therefrom don't end there. If *nothing* had no beginning, how did it end, which it must have done if it became something? Surely it could not have been *nothing* if it ended; only *something* can end. The very nature of *nothing* is that it has no beginning and no end; for it to begin, *nothing* would very reasonably come from *nothing*, since *nothing* cannot come from something; for it to end, it would most unreasonably mean that something can come from nothing.

The problem is not solved if we consider it possible that God was able to begin the universe from *nothing* (and somehow ignoring the galling fact that his presence would mean that there had been no *nothing*). Adding God to the equation still leaves us with *nothing* having a border – the point where *nothing* becomes something. *Nothing* could never have been *nothing* once a border – a beginning or an end – was placed on either side of it, similar to the situation of artists striving to represent *nothing* within a frame, as we saw in the previous chapter. *Nothing* is simply not nothing if it is limited in any way.

And so *nothing* cannot be measured in any way. This is obvious, considering that *nothing* was supposedly in existence before time and space began, and that it had been there for an eternity. Eternity, like infinity (and they are, presumably, similar) has no length as such. When we think of *nothing*, the eternity before time and space, we think of an inordinately long period. Yet it wasn't long and it wasn't short. With time not existing and no events happening to measure it against, *nothing* (eternity) did not last a long time or a short time; one cannot talk about it 'lasting' at all.

Nothing in the east

Now while all this is problematic within the monotheistic religions (but not for believers themselves, for whom faith doesn't have to be justified), for Eastern religions and faiths *nothing* is not a problem at all. On the contrary. For Eastern religions *nothing* is what they are all about, the centrality of their belief.

Nothing is real and actual within Eastern faiths; it is not a theoretical past background, but a state of perfection for which people are meant to strive in order to achieve self awareness; they do so through emptying the mind and taking out everything that is worldly and can interfere with what is really real. At that point of emptiness, when the mind is in a pure state, it is ready and able to accept what is true so that the person can become one with the true inner self, with nature and with reality.

One way, then, of looking at the difference between Western and Eastern religions is the way they deal with *nothing*. But in the light of what we discovered about *nothing*, it's not that simple.

There is, we recall, a difference that we teased out between *nothing* and *nothingness*. Is it *nothing* (the absence of everything) or *nothingness* (the absence of something) that Eastern faiths strive for? The theoretical state of enlightenment, when the mind is empty – is that a state of *nothing* or of *nothingness*? Surely it is *nothingness*, since however empty someone's mind is – a state of non-mind, rather than a state of mind – there still remains the person and, indeed, the universe; there would be *nothing* only when there is the absence of everything, including the person himself, since while he is present, there is still something.

So while commentators on Eastern faiths and mysticism refer to 'nothing' and often even to 'absolute nothingness', they can only really mean *nothingness* in the way we have defined it.

Despite some significant differences between Eastern faiths, that include Buddhism in its various forms (Theravada, Mahayana, Vajrayana, and sects, such as Taoism, Zen, Feng Shui, Shinto, the Kyoto School, and more), Hinduism, and a host of other faiths to which can be added New Age, *nothingness* is the centrality of spirituality that is their common denominator. For all of them, reality is not what we see in the world, but rather what is absent – an ultimate reality beyond the material universe – and that spirituality can only be reached through nothingness, emptiness, the void. We get to what there is, in other words, by first getting to what is not; unlike Western faiths that are concerned with what is, Eastern faiths, concern themselves with what isn't – in philosophical terms, it is *being* versus *non-being*.

Creating nothing

With such a huge difference between Western and Eastern religions in perception of the world and how it works, it goes without saying that the creation of the world is also considered very differently by them, with almost no emphasis on any beginning within Eastern religions.

Using the word 'Creation' is itself a giveaway. It is, in fact, heavily loaded, since it implies the presence of a creator who created the universe and everything in it, and that all of it came from *nothing*. For that reason, it would not be used by Eastern religions (nor, obviously, by scientists) to describe the beginning of the universe, before which could only have been *nothing*.

If for Western religions there was the beginning of everything, for Eastern religions there are no beginnings, but cycles without beginnings and endings.

For Creation, though, *nothing* is the essential, un-understandable background, since it is *nothing* that gives the creator his legitimacy and Creation its uniqueness. Creation is a miracle – the first miracle. Without putting too fine a point on it, for Western religions *nothing* is – has to be – the source of everything, including our finite selves. For Eastern faiths, on the other hand, nothingness does not play a similar role to that of *nothing* in Western religions. For Eastern faiths, nothingness is not outside, within a pre-past, but is the desired state in the here and now.

So unlike the Eastern religions, in which *nothingness* is something for people to aspire **to**, monotheistic religions accept the concept of *nothing* as being the inspiration that everything is **from**.

Nothing/nothingness, then, is an important dividing line. The position of believers is that, when we come from *nothing*, inherent within monotheistic religions, we gradually form ourselves by moving towards greater knowledge and progress as humans to an awareness of God and what he expects from us. Conversely, when we go towards *nothingness*, as within the Eastern faiths, knowledge is different: it is knowledge gained through losing worldly thoughts that would deflect from what is considered real knowledge and wisdom, or as an ancient Chinese proverb puts it: "To attain knowledge add something every day, to attain wisdom remove something every day."

The difference between *nothing* and nothingness could also be described, then, in terms of movement. While *nothing* represents the beginning of an accumulative movement towards something, nothingness is a reductive movement from something towards nothingness, and illustrates the way relationships between humans and nature are perceived.

When there is a creator, there is the created. The implication is that there is a separation between the creator and his creation. In fact, the doctrine of Creation within monotheistic religions teaches that all things are distinct from God, who is their efficient cause. In Genesis I, God looks at his work as he creates – all of nature and mankind – and says that "it is good."

But we do come across earnest expressions on the lines of 'God is everywhere' and that 'God is in every one of us'. As innocent and as valid as they sound, statements such as these make mainstream Western religions wary. Heavily influenced by New Age and Eastern religions, the sentiments obfuscate the separation between God and man.

As far as Western religions are concerned, God does not produce things from his own substance nor from any pre-existing reality, but by an act of his will brings them out of *nothing*. Unlike Eastern religions, which reject Western religions' positing of a gulf between God and man, but, rather, embrace the idea of God and man as one and that God is inside all of nature, for Western religions God is separate from nature and from people. For them, therefore, a faith that espouses union of God and man, and God and nature, is heresy. And no wonder, since it has its roots in paganism, alive nowadays mostly in the form of Animism, a belief that everything has a 'soul', an 'anima' (the Latin, for 'spirit'), including animals, plants, rocks, mountains, rivers, stars.

History is filled with people who were considered heretics because of such views and suffered in consequence. It doesn't seem like a big deal nowadays, especially as we so frequently come into contact with the popularity of Zen Buddhism and New Age views of 'god is in everything'; but in the past people were put to death for thinking along those lines, while others, in slightly more recent times, were expelled from their religion.

Most of the clashes were with the Church, but not all. Baruch Spinoza (1632-77) was excommunicated in 1656 by the Dutch Jewish community (after which he changed his first name to

Benedict – the Latin version of the Hebrew Baruch 'blessed' –
although the Christians didn't really accept him any more than
the Jews had) for his views, that were, in fact, pantheism: that
God and nature are one.

Pantheism

It is not surprising that pantheism is considered to be so bad. As
a repudiation of the fundamentals of Judaism (and, in fact,
Christianity and Islam), it can't get much worse. Because
pantheism claims that God created the world from himself and
that there is no separation between God, nature and humans, this
goes against the doctrine of God creating everything from
nothing. The implications go much further and deeper, though.
If everything that exists is part of the single substance of God,
who is identical with nature and is eternal, there are no goals for
man or the universe. Nature does not have a goal and neither can
it be evil, so it cannot be punished. The whole notion of sin and
punishment is invalid within the ideas that constitute pantheism.

Spinoza had no doubts about God. It was, rather, his doubt
about the importance of humans that got him into trouble. For
Spinoza, then, it was not that God is not special, but that humans
are not special. And for that, he was excommunicated.

As important as this scandalous affair was within the Dutch
Jewish community at the time, its repercussions swept through
the Jewish world and beyond, not least because Spinoza was a
respected philosopher, whose views counted, even if begrudg-
ingly. His pantheistic view of religion – with him believing
fervently in the orthodoxy of his views – obviously hit a chord
among the people, something that the rabbis felt threatened by.
And also by the Christian clergy, which explains their very
lukewarm embrace of Spinoza, not unjustifiably so; as Einstein
later famously said: "I believe in Spinoza's God who reveals
himself in the orderly harmony of what exists."

Potentially, though, the ideas inherent in pantheism were

much more dangerous even than thoughts about sin and punishment. The notion that God and nature are one could be taken further if one wanted. If the human soul is a part of the divine nature, then nature is divine in essence and therefore has no need of God. The fact that some Christian theologians did latch onto such thoughts made the established church very nervous indeed, especially as pantheism was vibrant in the East in the form of Hinduism and presented a real threat.

It's not surprising, then, that the Church didn't take to Spinoza's views any more than his co-religionists did. Mysticism – ideas from India and the East, of which pantheism was central – was in danger of becoming popular as a sort of thinking man's version of the established dogma. It was not that Spinoza adopted Eastern views – in fact, his emphasis on rigorous rational thought was the opposite of Eastern methods – but, because of pantheism, they were perceived to be as such by the Church.

In its holistic view of nature, pantheism, especially in its extreme form as the basis of Hinduism, is, no doubt, an attraction to those unwilling to adhere to a strict institutionalized religion. In Hinduism, the entire world and universe and everything within it is God (in his various forms). Unlike the personal God of the monotheistic religions, the Hindu God is an impersonal force that makes up everything in existence, and there is no difference between creature and creator as both are one. This is ultimate realty: everything is a part of a formless, inexpressible, unknowable force which is called Brahman. For Hindus the goal is to come to 'self-realization', which is the ultimate realization that they themselves are Brahman.

The powers-that-be lost the battle against mysticism, of course. Today, mysticism is not only a legitimate part of most religions, but has become almost a fashion item, what with pop stars and meditation, yoga, Kabbalah, Zen and the amorphous New Age that is all the rage. Spinoza, today well and truly rehabilitated, would be amazed to know that there are statues of him in Amsterdam and that streets in Israel bear his name.

Bringing nothing to the west

Madonna and Kabbalah, Paul McCartney promoting Transcendental Meditation (TM) among schoolchildren around the world and Oprah Winfrey's support and encouragement of mysticism are just three prominent examples of the widespread acceptance of Eastern mysticism in the West.

Whether those media stars care or are fully aware of the intricacies of Eastern faith behind their mystic persuasions is a moot point. Transcendental Meditation, for example, is more than just a way of relaxation or a cool system to calm schoolchildren; the purpose of TM, begun by the Maharishi Mahesh Yogi and spread so widely throughout the Western world, is to empty one's mind in order to 'reach enlightenment'.

The Maharishi was but the most famous of the spiritual gurus of the 1960s and attracted a glittering cluster of celebrity followers, including the Beatles, Mick Jagger and Clint Eastwood, instrumental in spreading 'Flower Power' and the message of universal peace and love.

Somehow lost in all of this was that the philosophy of the East, including that of Hinduism and Buddhism, is about diminishing one's self; there is a certain amount of irony in the fact that celebrity mega-stars with such larger-than-life egos would advocate a philosophy that believes in emptying individualism along a path towards nothingness. It doesn't help either that this path was advocated at the time by an Indian holy man who basked in the limelight or that nowadays a similar path is advocated by the celebrity French Buddhist monk and author, the Venerable Matthieu Ricard.

It was John Lennon, who, years after losing his enchantment with the Maharishi, nicely encapsulated the difference between Eastern and Western thought. "There is no guru, Lennon said.

"You have to believe in yourself. You've got to get down to your own God in your own temple. It's all down to you, mate."

To be or not to be

"It's all down to you" is as good a pithy summary of Western liberal ideas as it gets. Building oneself up – the notion of self as defined by operations of consciousness (exemplified by Freud's 'ego') including rationality, free will, and self-reflection – is the antithesis of the Eastern idea of emptying the self of everything material and mental. The difference is encapsulated in the now-clichéd 'to be or not to be', or, in the title *Being and Nothingness* of Jean-Paul Sartre's seminal book.

And so it is with Western, monotheistic, religions. The notion that the Creator of the universe, omniscient, omnipresent and omnipotent as he is, would care about each individual's welfare, is, let's face it, a good reason for people to feel important. How can it be otherwise when, according to the monotheistic religions, God created the world for humans and that everything he does is for them.[84] That this can lead to narcissism and arrogance is clear, even though the plea by religion for believers to be humble adds some sort of counterbalance.

And not just in religion. For while there is the urge in the West for humans to build themselves up and be more meaningful for themselves and society, there is at the same time a general counter-urge towards the opposite: towards self-effacement and nothingness in light of the wonder and vastness of nature and of space outside earth. So it is that we prove our greatness by building ever larger buildings and skyscrapers, with countries outdoing themselves to construct the tallest building (at the moment this is Burj Khalifa in Dubai at 828 m., double the size of the World Trade Center, NY, destroyed by terrorists in 2001) that at the same time literally belittle us, as anyone arriving in Manhattan for the first time can testify.

This conflict between *something* and *nothing* in the West is general enough to cross political boundaries and ideologies. Karl Marx, introducing the category of 'the proletariat' in 1843, illustrates it as 'I am nothing and I should be everything'. Whether later, in the Soviet Union or elsewhere, the proletariat succeeded in becoming 'everything' is a moot point.

On the right of the political scale, the same play is carried out. Fascism extols the supremacy and power of the individual, while at the same time claiming that citizens are nothing compared to the state, to which they need to subordinate and even sacrifice themselves. But we don't need to go so far to the right to discern the same something vs. nothingness in play. Capitalism, with its belief in the potential of the individual to achieve anything and everything, nevertheless has to rely on mass employment resulting in the blurred nothingness of individualism to make it work.

This is not surprising, since capitalism, at least in the USA, is based on a Protestant work ethic and connected to Calvinist and Puritan religious ideas, at the heart of which is the paradox of rugged individualism and self-effacement, the strong feeling of nothingness vis-à-vis God.

There is a double paradox here, within the Protestant work ethic. We are told that the more we know about God and the closer we are to him, the more we realize how little we know and the smaller, and closer to nothing, we become. On the other hand, coming from *nothing* – the supposed background to the existence of everything – should mean that we are continually growing as individuals and in the knowledge that we acquire, in this way moving closer towards God.

So do we understand more about God by understanding more about him, or is it that we understand more about how little we know about God?

As strange as it seems, what we have is a learning curve of ignorance: a coincidence of opposites, in which the more we are aware of our ignorance, the more we attain of true knowledge. So the more we know of our nothingness compared to the perfection of God, the more we learn about God. It is, then, in our interest to truly comprehend our nothingness.

On the other hand (and there always seems to be another hand when it comes to *nothing* and/or *nothingness*), there is the point of view that it is better to know as little as possible about God, for the more we know, the less great he would appear to be. Is that not what we can learn from the Bible story of Adam and Eve: that it is not for us to unravel God's mystery, because if we do, then we will understand him, which is not what God wants? Interestingly, the punishment that God dished out to Adam and Eve for daring to eat from the Tree of Knowledge was to make them aware of their humanness, including the realization of their own mortality.

It is no wonder, then, that believers think not only of themselves as nothing compared to God, but also that their understanding of God is nothing, or as Nicholas of Cusa, the fifteenth century German philosopher we came across in Chapter One put it: "The great Dionysius says that our understanding of God draws near to nothing rather than to something. But sacred ignorance teaches me that that which seems to the intellect to be nothing is the incomprehensible Maximum." In other words, there is no way that we can get beyond knowing nothing when it comes to understanding anything about God.

A severe limitation to all of this is the difficulty – the impossibility, even – of understanding that one understands nothing. One notable person who was purported to admit it was Socrates, who said: "All I know is that I know nothing," which is the basis of his most famous paradox, i.e. if it's true that Socrates knows nothing, then he knows something – he knows the fact that he knows nothing. Therefore, he didn't know *nothing*; he knew something.

In any case, how can one know nothing? When Socrates spoke about 'nothing', he presumably didn't go so far as to believe that he didn't even know that he was thinking and that he was alive. His 'nothing' was relative. And so, obviously, is the 'nothing' that people know about God. *Nothing* – the absence of everything – cannot, though, be relative; any 'nothing' that is relative is, according to our definition, *nothingness*.

What about the paradox of God being able to understand that he understands nothing? Now we are in a real tangle, since we need to ask if it is possible for God not to understand something. It gets worse: since everything is possible for God, would he be able to not understand something if he wanted? This is equivalent to asking whether God is capable of making a rock that he cannot move, or whether he would be able to create *nothing* in which he didn't exist.

Whatever the paradoxes and however much believers feel themselves close to God, when it comes to facing him they make themselves as small as possible, the end result being a condition as close as possible to the Divine. It is ultimate humility and total purification that involves annihilation of the self. One only has to look at the enormity of cathedrals (despite Christ's teachings to pray in one's own room and in solitude)[85] and the grandiosity of mosques (despite the Quran's injunction that God "is with you wherever you are")[86] to observe the urge of humans to minimize themselves as much as possible. And what is the bowing, kneeling and prostration when praying if not a symbol of subservience and self-denial to the point of invisibility when facing God?

It is natural to feel small compared to the hugeness of God. And in case people thought otherwise, there are many examples of having it spelt out, sometimes graphically. *Spiritual Combat* by Lorenzo Scupoli, published in Venice in 1589, is a tumultuous blood and thunder guide to worshipping God, that shows how humans are reduced to nothing as compared to God. To protect oneself from Satan, we are instructed to "choose for thy battlefield the safe and level ground of a true and deep conviction of thine own nothingness; that thou art nothing, that thou knowest nothing, that thou canst do nothing, and hast nothing but misery and sin and deservest nothing but eternal damnation." Pretty rough stuff.

Presumably one would need to be living a life of hell to carry out those thoughts and act upon them. One such person who dragged herself through it within a life of extreme subservience, the absence of corrupting materialism, and self-denial until her death at the age of twenty-four, was Thérèse of Lisieux, who, perhaps not surprisingly, was proclaimed a saint only two years after, in 1897. Dedicating herself to "nothingness, hiddenness, self-denied to the point of invisibility,"[87] she reveled in her life of loneliness, saying that "absence is God, God is human loneliness."

As a concept of where God is, Saint Thérèse's is interesting. God, she said, is where a person isn't. What she was doing, then, was to remove herself from the world, so that she could be closer to God! The implication, paradoxical in the extreme, is that God is absent where a person is present. Where there is nothingness, there is God, according to this concept.

Being nothing, knowing nothing

Monotheistic religions are big on making humans small. Self-denial is not merely the act of individuals who feel their inadequacy compared to God as the perfect being, but is also part of following clear messages in the Bible. Bringing oneself as close as possible to nothingness is a corollary of knowing nothing, reinforced by the scriptures.

After the unfortunate saga of Adam and Eve's punishment for daring to seek knowledge, there are many other instances where the search for knowledge is actively discouraged. Job, for example, was reduced to abject grovelings after he asked God too many questions. He couldn't do much more than to say, in effect, "I know nothing," after God reminded him that he wasn't there when the Earth was created (Job 38:4), within a long monologue (Job: 42: 2, 3, 6) about his unworthiness and "things too wonderful for me, which I knew not... Wherefore I abhor myself, and repent in dust and ashes."

For believers, the scriptures have a heavy hand in instilling the rhetorical question as to how much humans could possibly know compared to the all-powerful Creator, infinite in knowledge and wisdom ("In whom are hid all the treasures of wisdom and knowledge" – Colossians 2:3), while human knowledge is slammed as intellectual/academic pride in words, such as, "Knowledge puffeth up" (Corinthians 8:1).

It is no wonder, then, that religious believers would be comfortable in their efforts at self-denial, both within the mainstream of their religions, where it was sometimes frowned upon if it was perceived to go too far, and also in the smaller outshoots. And there are always methods to speed along the process towards nothingness. Opus Dei, the semi-secretive Roman Catholic sect, came under an unwelcome spotlight in Dan Brown's *The Da Vinci Code*, with its graphic description of the extreme self-flagellating monk. Fiction that may have been, but what to make of the surprising news that Pope John Paul II routinely beat himself with a belt and slept on a bare floor "to bring himself closer to Christ"?[88]

It doesn't have to be so painful, of course. Often it is enough to do, literally, nothing. This, from the Quakers, who wait for 'divine guidance' and are popularly known for their Pacifism, sums up the feeling: "Center down into abasement and nothingness... This is what I labored after: to be empty, to know nothing, to call for nothing, and to desire to do nothing."[89]

There is a price to be paid for the personal, religious downward spiral towards nothingness. How far can a person go with the idea that he/she is nothing in relation to God? After all, if we know nothing about God, then how can we even talk about him? This is the conclusion that proponents of what is known as

negative theology come to. Not that the idea is new; negative theology was a method of thought already in early Christianity (and earlier within Platonism and Neo-Platonism) as a way to comprehend the Divine by indicating everything it was not.

It is obvious, from this point of view, that anything that can be said about God would be inadequate because it does not, and can not, encompass what God is. So, to say, in the example given by James Faulconer, philosopher at Brigham Young University, that God is just, is a problem, since it uses 'just' in human terms but does not represent what it means when applied to God.

The point, Faulconer says, is that "God's justice surpasses ours, so much so that it is inadequate to use the same name for it." Now here comes the solution that is also the problem: In order to deal with the inadequacy of applying 'just' to God, one would need to say that God is not just! The problem, of course, is that it looks as though we are denying that God is just, whereas we are, in fact, saying that God is not just in the way that humans understand it.

It is, negative theology says, impossible to make affirmative statements about the nature of God. Whatever we say God is, he is not. Even to say that God exists is problematic, since God cannot exist in the sense that we normally mean existence.

The Kabbalah shows this through considering the Supreme Being as the *Eyn Sof* (Endless, Infinite), which contains within it the *Eyn* (Non-existent), and so having to think of what God is not, rather than what he is. The only way out of this conundrum is to speak of God only as far as he actualizes himself through what is known as the 10 mystical attributes of nothingness, called the *Sephiroth*.

Now while the negative theologian recognizes the necessity of speaking about God, he is, in fact, reduced to silence, for whatever he says would give the impression that he is comparing God to humans in some way. How, then, can one express the wonder of God?

However difficult it is to grasp, negative theology is not merely about showing what God is not (and certainly not that there is no God) or that God is not just. It is more than simply saying that we are too small to understand God's ways; the negative theologian reminds us of God's infinity by showing us the failure of our affirmative theology. We are, in other words, incapable of showing what God is, even though we are forced to continue to speak of God and to wonder at his justice.

"Whereof one cannot speak, thereof one must be silent," would sum it up perfectly. It was Ludwig Wittgenstein's pithy one-liner at the end of his first great philosophical work the *Tractatus*, in which he showed that really it is impossible to express anything through language; trying to discuss philosophical ideas, he said, would necessarily lead to failure.

On a similar tack, but in connection with literature, the French philosopher, Jacques Derrida, demonstrates through his theory of deconstruction that while language often 'fails' to say everything, it nevertheless says something, even about what it fails to say. The point is that, by being aware of what is not being said, we understand the meaning of what could not be said.

Whether he meant it or not, Derrida's thoughts covered also the negative theology of Eastern faiths, where the importance lies in what is not, rather than what is. Buddhism gives a solution to the need to escape from the world of the born with all its attendant troubles, and it does so by referring to the opposite, to the unworld. The Baha'u'llah, the Prophet-Founder of the Baha'i Faith, uses the word 'God' for what The Buddha called "the Unborn, Unoriginated, Uncreated, Unformed." Both agree, however, that these are only words used as a name for something that we humans can never fathom.

Now whereas negative theology within Western religions would leave it at that and accept human limitations as to understanding God, Eastern faiths are all about trying to understand the overtly un-understandable. Taking this to extremes is the

Hindu notion that everything is nothing – everything that we see, touch or feel in our physical world is actually just an illusion: it really doesn't exist. Only by withdrawing from the world of everything can one arrive at the real world of nothingness. A holy man sitting alone for years will eventually reach an advanced state of 'self-realization' and will be so withdrawn into himself that he no longer has a conscious awareness of anything in the physical world. When this state is reached the person is incapable of caring for himself and can no longer communicate with the physical world.

Robert Pirsig, in a newspaper interview about meditation, encapsulated the process descriptively: "If you stare at a wall from four in the morning till nine at night and you do that for a week, you are getting pretty close to nothingness."[90]

The enduring magnetism of nothing

From what we have seen, the powerful urge to reach towards nothingness is a common human trait, so that it is not surprising to have it manifested within religions and beliefs, almost without exception, as well as in the arts as we saw in the previous chapter.

The idea that there is – must be – something beyond what we can see or readily perceive or what we can talk about and beyond what is rational is encompassed within the notion of mysticism.

And what is mysticism if not the movement towards nothingness, the emptiness resulting from the eventual reduction of everything that can interfere in our journey to reach the core of understanding? From the Greek μυω (muo, 'to conceal'), mysticism is the pursuit of ultimate reality, the divine spiritual truth, through direct, personal experience (intuition or insight) rather than rational thought and analysis. It is the notion that there are objective realities beyond perceptual or intellectual understanding, and that they are directly accessible through intuition and personal experience. It is mysticism that is the centrality of Eastern religions, and it is the mysticism of direct personal experience with the divine to which Western and monotheistic religions are attracted.

Now while it is sometimes claimed that the mystical side of Western religions arose as a rebellion against the institutionalization of worship,[91] the opposite seems to have happened: that institutionalized rules were imposed in order to keep an already active mysticism in check and under control.

It is not a chicken and egg situation. Mystic elements were alive and well in the earliest history of the monotheistic religions, before institutions tried to bring them under control as part of accepted canon.

In Christianity, the first opportune moment came at the First Council of Nicaea in 325 AD, where the doctrine of the Christian Church was defined and where the Church leaders decided which of the Gospels would be part of the canon. Not included, because they were too openly mystical – and in the wrong way – were The Gospel of Mary Magdalene, The Gospel of Judas, The Secret Book of John, and others, collectively called Gnostic Gospels (with Gnosticism as a religious cult outlawed thirteen years later). Purported to be the secret writings of Jesus, the mysticism that they contained believed in direct communing with God, so taking away authority from the priests. This was a definite no-no, as important to the powers-that-be as was the problematic 'heretical' belief in Jesus more as spirit than a real historical man. As spiritual as were the early beliefs, the Church made it essential to think of Jesus as flesh and blood, of his human side.

Yesterday, no less than today, politics was everything, so that believing in the spirit and not in the flesh (rather than the spirit **and** the flesh in one, equally) placed a question mark also on the acceptance of priests as necessary earthly representatives. It is not surprising that the church opposed Gnosticism with a vengeance

Also Judaism had its own early problems with mysticism.

Thanks to the discovery by accident in a cave in Qumran in 1947 of the Dead Sea Scrolls, we have an insight into the ideas, through their own writings, of the Essenes, a branch of the Pharisees, one of the mystical sects that made up Judaism and that had been around for some two hundred years before the turn of the first millennium. Considering that Christianity arose from Judaism, it isn't surprising that there were similarities between early Christians and the Essenes, particularly in mystic beliefs, which influenced the way they lived. Both the Essenes and some early Christians espoused a pious, ascetic life, so deserting the city and the secular world for a life of solitary or communal prayer and self-denial. With the emphasis on individual communion with God and consequent non-reliance on priests, it goes without saying that this was not more eagerly accepted by the Jewish authorities than it was by the Christian authorities.

Of the three monotheistic religions, Islam was the wisest when it came to its approach to mysticism. Accepting it early on as part of human yearning towards understanding through an intuitive link with the Divine, Islam used mysticism – mainly Sufism, but other forms as well – and, by embracing them, helped to link the various strands of thought that spread the new religion far in a relatively short time.

Whether or not they wanted it, the established religions found their adherents gravitating towards questions that were more and more individually mystical in nature, sometimes alarmingly so. And whereas opposition was at various times heavy-handed and bloody, eventually ideas that were mystical in essence became not just accepted but often formed part of the institution-alized religion within its denominations and sects.

Ripples of mysticism

With all the diversity of the world's religions, it is surprising – or perhaps not – how similar their mystical elements are, even though the traditions are separated geographically, culturally, and by vast epochs of time. Understandable as it is that mysticism fits comfortably within Eastern religions and philosophy, it is somewhat more surprising to discern the natural absorption and acceptance of mysticism as part of Western religions, whose basis is so very different.

The West, as we have seen, sees its philosophy as based on what IS, whereas the philosophy of the East is based on what IS NOT. Western religions deal with God's existence (cataphatic theology – what God *is*), while mysticism is broadly but essentially based on Eastern faith and philosophy that believes in negative theology (apophatic theology – what God is *not*), the importance of *nothing* rather than *something*.

Within Christianity, mysticism is alive and well in Roman Catholic teachings, as well as in many sects of Protestantism, even while largely frowned upon by mainstream Protestantism. In other monotheistic religions, it is seen in the practices of, for example, the Kabbalistic Jews and Sufi Muslims.

But what is it about mysticism that makes it similar to Eastern philosophy and Eastern faiths?

For a start, it is the notion that *nothingness* is more important than *something*, that 'what isn't' is more important than 'what is' – so much more important, in fact, that only through 'what isn't' can a person reach ultimate reality and truth. In terms of monotheistic religions, this ultimate reality and truth is, of course, God. The point is, though, that it is not just a matter of reaching the ultimate truth and seeing it, but of uniting with the ultimate truth and becoming one with it. At its most extreme, this is a union between man and God.

It is fairly certain that followers of Kabbalah, considered an authentic Jewish outgrowth, wouldn't take kindly to the idea that it has basic similarities to Buddhism, Hinduism, Yoga, and even Native American spirituality. Yet what are we to make of the following statement from Kabbalah: "When the self becomes nothingness, the will of man becomes identical with the will of

God"? Or this, about *nothing*: "Nothing is infinitely more real than all other reality"?[92] And deemed to be of symbolic significance is that the letters in Hebrew of 'the self' (a-n-y) and 'nothingness' (a-y-n) are the same, although in a different order. It follows, then, that the Kabbalist, Isaac of Acre (b. 1291?) would write, in the same vein, of the soul being absorbed into God "as a jug of water into a running well," or that the Hasidic master, R. Shneur Zalman of Liady (1745-1812) referred to a person as a drop of water in the ocean of the Infinite with an illusory sense of individual "dropness."

Also Islam was infused with the same notion. The Sufi mystic al-Husayn al-Hallaj (858-922), for example, proclaimed, "I am God," and was hounded for it and, inevitably, executed for heresy. The Christian mystic, Meister Eckhart (c. 1260-1327) faired no better after similar identity-declarations, although he was lucky to have died naturally two years before being declared a heretic.

Meister Eckhart, negative theologian and mystic, is an interesting character from our point of view. His delving into nothingness demonstrates the similarity between Christian mysticism and Eastern faiths, notably Vedanta and Mahayana Buddhism. In fact, if in the fourteenth century he could be portrayed as heretical, by the twentieth century his insistence on the existence of the divine spark within the individual could be seen in a world context as the European parallel to Buddhist metaphysics. "The mystical search," he said, "is the search for the God who is nothing. It's the realization that God is a hidden god."

Meister Eckhart made nothingness his be-all and end-all, because for him that was the key to God. Even Creation wasn't *something* as such – a notion that went against the orthodox teachings. All of Creation, he said, was pure nothingness, and existed only because God recognized it, at which point it became divine. From this point of view, the answer to our earlier question, "Why is there something rather than nothing," is simple: because God recognized it. To the mystical claim that 'God is Nothing, He is Utterly Other; He is the Void', Eckhart proclaims, "Thou shalt love God as He is, a Non-God, a Non-Spirit, a Non-Person, a Non-Form." In a strange double negative, then, humans are nothingness and also God is nothingness.

But if God is nothingness, how could we possibly understand him? Only – as in Eastern philosophy – by emptying our selves in order to reach nothingness and our highest perfection (which, for theists, is God) so that we can unite with the nothingness of God.

And this, as we have seen in action, is one of the features of mysticism: aiming at a sort of self-annihilation and selflessness in order to unite with perfection, this perfection being the nothingness within, illustrated radically though the ideas of the Japanese philosopher Nishitani Keiji (1900-90) that within the self is an identical part that is non-self. Within Pantheistic Brahmanism of India, self-annihilation leads to a state of indifference in which the soul enjoys an imperturbable tranquility, and the means of bringing this about is the recognition of one's identity with Brahma, the all-god. For the Buddhist, it results in the quenching of desire and the consequent attainment of Nirvana, incompletely in the present life, but completely after death. For monotheistic believers in mysticism, it is unity with the perfection that is God (not too dissimilar to Shinto in Japan, where all men are believed to be capable of deep affinity with the Divine).

But let's not get carried away. Not all would agree that mysticism goes as far as unity with God, or indeed would want it to. Now while there are mystical strands of Western monotheistic religions' movement towards nothingness that stress 'the divine spark' within man, they by and large do not go as far as a mystical union between man and God, even though there is controversy and discussion as to whether 'union with God' actually means deification, man becoming God.

The mystical notion of union of man with God is an extremely radical way of thinking, since, as we have seen, monotheistic religions regard mysticism as a personalized movement towards closeness with God, but not man becoming God. That the idea of the unity with God is not only acceptable but also accepted as possible for anyone with enough devotion is quite amazing, since monotheistic religions have for a long time preached that only Prophets and extraordinary individuals could reach such a level of holiness, and even then it did not mean deification.

There are, though, monotheistic religions that hold to deification as the purpose to man's life. The Eastern Orthodox religions, including Greek Orthodox and Russian Orthodox churches have mysticism not as a strand of the religion (as say, Kabbalah is to Judaism), but as a tenet of their mainstream beliefs.

Now since the Eastern Orthodox religions follow an apophatic theology (negative theology), we feel the need to ask how they propose union with what is not. After all, union with God who is *something* is a concept that is just about understandable. But union with God who is not-something? As we saw, even saying that God **is** something is problematic in apophatic theology.

Just to recap on the mind-twister that is negative theology: To say that God is something – good or just or loving, or whatever – would compare him to humans; therefore negative theology can only say what God is not: he is not something. If he is not something, then how would it be possible to have union with not-something (nothingness)?

Eastern Orthodox religions get past this problem by differentiating between two parts of God, one of which, the something that is God, allows union, while the other, the nothingness of God, is unfathomable. While the ungraspable and unimaginable nothingness is so powerful that man cannot get to it and, in fact, is not allowed to, union with the energy of God is not only possible but is desirable.

It is not necessary to go into the theological niceties of Eastern Orthodox thought to get some idea of the problems that have theologians dancing on the tip of a pin when *nothing* and nothingness are brought up.

And neither are they any closer to solving the problem of the Creation and what was in existence before, which is as much a stumbling block for the Eastern Orthodox churches, who, despite the mystical nature of their canon, still need to hold on to the basis of Christian credo that God created the world from nothing and not out of pre-existing matter. And yet a glimmer of something else is apparent in the notion of the uncreated energies of God, with which, the Eastern Orthodox churches claim, he created the world.

The idea that God created the world from himself, is, of course, closer to the Eastern mystic ideas that lead to pantheism than to the monotheistic tenet of creation *ex nihilo*.

Judaism has it no easier. For the Kabbalah, a mystic arm of Judaism, there is no 'creation out of nothing' in the conventional Judeo-Christian sense. On the contrary, Kabbalah believes in emanation, that God created the world from the infinite revelation of himself and that everything that came afterwards did so as outflowings from the original, so that all of nature is part and parcel of God. Although not seen by Kabbalah as being pantheistic, this doctrine – for which, we recall, Spinoza was excommunicated – is the basis of many Eastern faiths and was also professed by Gnosticism as a number of emanations from a superior God (and another good reason for the exclusion of the Gnostic Gospels from Christian canon).

Unlike creation from nothing, where there is a Creator God standing apart from, even if intimately connected with, the universe, emanation is a gradual process of flowing, and downgrading, from the Absolute all the way to mundane reality, the physical world.

This Eastern concept of emanation was rejected no less by Islam than by Christianity and Judaism, and was introduced into Arabic philosophy by Avicenna (Ibn Sina, 980-1037 AD), the brilliant Persian philosopher, physician and scientist. In so doing, he rejected the classical Islamic theological doctrine of creation *ex nihilo*.

The difference between Eastern and Western religions is encapsulated in the way they respectively hold to emanation and Creation, so shining a light on the basic distinctness of their outlooks on *nothingness* and *something*. Similarly, emanation illustrates how basically different it is from evolution and secular Western thought.

As a way of describing the beginning of the universe, emanationism manages to get past the unimaginable *creatio ex nihilo* (creation from nothing). And it also avoids the problem that monotheistic religions have with Darwin's theory of evolution, which does not need God for species to evolve. Evolution is change; emanation is not: creatures *evolving* into other creatures necessarily result in the latter being different from the former. Emanation, on the other hand, is purely mystical: it is the becoming of something from something else that still retains its essence, even as it gets fainter; all further emanations are from the original, not from each other. Evolution involves improvement as the organism better adjusts itself to the environment, while, on the contrary, emanation is a diminishing from the original as each emanation moves further away from perfection.

It is clear, then, that emanation conflicts with *creatio ex nihilo*, and neatly demonstrates the difference between them – the Eastern approach: a diminishing from *something* towards eventual emptiness and *nothingness*, versus the Western approach: adding from *nothing* towards eventual fullness and *something*.

Is nothing good?

Unlike mysticism in monotheistic religions, mysticism in Eastern faiths does not necessarily mean union with a higher being (although it can do, in Hinduism and some forms of Buddhism), but rather, union with 'reality' that is 'the ultimate truth', when the mind is emptied of everything and is left with only the nothingness that is pure awareness, unsullied by thoughts or senses from the material world. What is left within this nothingness is the true self.

With the mysticism that is manifested as strands of monotheistic religions, the aim of contemplation and self-denial is to find one's way to God. When one finds one's true self, one finds God, who is within each person. This 'Divine spark', while not going as far as deification (the exception, to some extent, being the Eastern Orthodox churches among the monotheistic religions), is accepted by the Western religions as the soul.

Mysticism, then, sees the innate goodness of man. If God is in man – the 'Divine spark' – then man is necessarily good.

Not so, says Protestantism. Protestantism sees humans as inherently wicked through having been born in sin, carrying with them through the ages the original sin of Adam. For Protestantism, then, God, who is infinitely good, could not be within humans, and totally rejects that mystical concept.

Mysticism is, in fact, rigorously opposed in many Protestant circles. Unlike most other Christian denominations (and indeed the other two monotheistic religions, Judaism and Islam), mainstream Protestantism views the idea of mysticism with skepticism and a large measure of disdain. Protestantism – most extremely, the evangelical variety – is about faith found directly through the word of God, without recourse to outside influences and the necessity of explaining God's word through secular philosophy or science. It is not about feelings based on interpretations, about what there might be and what isn't, but about what there is: the word of God as written in the scriptures.

For mainstream Protestantism, then, mysticism is, at best, a highly suspect development, at worst, a highly dangerous one that is more attune with Eastern religions than with Christianity. For Thomas Merton, Roman Catholic monk, widely quoted by Christian mystics, to say that "At **the center of our being** is a point of nothingness which is **untouched by sin** and by illusion, a point of pure truth, a point or spark which belongs entirely to God..."[93] is for Protestants an aberration of Christianity and was cause enough for Merton to be accused of becoming a Buddhist. It didn't help his image among conservative Christians that he was a best-selling author dealing with self-help.

Typical, and in a similar vein, is the wrath directed against the Catholic author and speaker Brennan Manning, who advocates Eastern techniques of Meditation. As the Christian evangelist, John Caddock puts it:

> Contemplative spirituality is dangerous. Christian leaders should warn their people about it. Those who are interested in a comprehensive biblical understanding of true biblical spirituality and of the gospel of Jesus Christ should be warned that Manning is traveling on a wholly other path.[94]

It is not surprising that the way mysticism is perceived is a function of how humans are perceived. After all, mysticism is about possibilities and belief that humans are capable of reaching new heights of awareness. In the mysticism within religion, this means the potential to reach closeness with God, and as such is looked at quite differently from the points of view of the two largest Christian denominations, Catholicism and Protestantism.

As a way of illustrating differing viewpoints of potential, we could do no better than to look again at the Christian doctrine of **original sin**. As a doctrine it looks pretty grim, until one brings in the notion of potential to soften the blow.

In Catholicism humans have the potential (through God's grace brought about by penitence, devotion, good deeds, among other things) to overcome their original sin, while in Protestantism that potential is not available except for the elected (who won't know that they are the lucky ones till after death), so that every person is born into the world permanently tainted and cannot choose to accept salvation. For Catholicism, God is within, while for Protestantism God is without, so that in the former baptism can cleanse the taint of original sin (and for that reason infant baptism is a common practice), while in the latter baptism is recognized as an act of obedience to and identification with Jesus as the Christ, and that it has no sacramental (saving) power.

On the other hand, neither Judaism nor Islam, both of which contain important and influential strands of mysticism, subscribe to the notion that humans are born in sin. And unlike Christianity, Judaism and Islam teach that sin is something that is actually committed, not something that is a state of being.

Now while it is evident that there are close similarities in the mysticism accepted within monotheistic religions and that of Eastern faiths, there is one basic difference that alters the basic concept and so differentiates their viewpoints on sin: Western religions are contingent on the one omnipotent God, while Eastern faiths are not. The fact that Eastern faiths do not have the concept of sin exemplifies the basic difference. If sin can be roughly defined as a transgression against a moral code that was set out by God, it follows that Eastern faiths do not have that concept of sin, since there is no almighty God and there is no one to hand out rewards or punishments.

Transgressions against the codes within Eastern religions are seen in a different light, and punishment is internal; it is manifested in the harm that is caused to one's personal spiritual development. In effect, anything that disrupts one's movement towards nothingness and self-awareness is punishment, which can be avoided the closer one is to nothingness.

Putting that into less mystical terms, even if rather simply, we could say that if one does nothing, one will not sin, which happens to coincide with the Tao idea of not doing anything so as to flow with nature. This is how it is put in the Udana, a Buddhist scripture and one of the 'inspired utterances': "Where there is no movement, there is rest; where rest is, there is no desire; where there is no desire, there is neither coming nor going, no ceasing-to-be, no further coming to be..."[95]

That does not work for Western religions. The notion that sin is not present where there is nothingness is controversial and problematic.

The question is if there was anything that God did not create? If so, what was the non-created – the nothingness – that was left over after God created the universe? Surely, if everything that God created was good, the nothingness that he did not create would be not good.

On the other hand, how could it be that God did not create everything? And since everything that he created was good, he would not have created anything that was evil. That leaves us with yet another possibility: that evil is what remains when good is taken away.

For Protestantism, for example, the very idea of nothingness is an affront. The creation of the world from nothing is an accepted fact, but the existence of nothingness after the Creation seems to be alien, something that was beyond – the opposite of – what God created, and therefore analogous to evil.

It again comes down to the difference between *nothing* and nothingness. When all good is taken away, what remains is nothingness – the absence of good – which is necessarily evil but could, according to one's point of view, still be part of what God created. If, however, what remains is *nothing*, then evil cannot possibly exist, since *nothing* is the absence of everything (including the universe). To say, then, that evil is *nothing* would be to say that evil doesn't exist. Yet evil does exist and so, it would seem, it is not part of what God created.

For Judaism there is no problem. Since God created everything, including evil, he would have created nothingness as well.[96] For Judaism, then, nothingness is no more associated with evil than anything else that God created.

With nothingness being the absence of something, it is reasonable to expect it to be seen differently according to one's point of view. Nothingness can be good, as it is for Eastern religions; it is necessarily evil, according to Protestantism; or it might be evil but according to God's divine plan, according to Judaism.

It does not have to be one or the other, of course. Within religions that base themselves on balance, the two extremes live side by side so as to give an ultimate harmony to the world. An internal religious mutual deterrence, in fact.

Zoroastrianism, the ancient religion of Persia, founded possibly 2,500 years ago, is based on the struggle between eternal opposites, god and the anti-god (the creator of life and the creator of not-life), good and evil, light and darkness, truth and deceit. In true monotheistic mode, there is one God, Ahura Mazda, as source of goodness and purity, while faith accepts the two primal spirits, Good (*Vahyo*) and Bad (*Akem*), representing life and non-life that were in existence from the creation of the world and that cannot coexist. Because good and evil do not come from the same spirit, humans have to decide which path to follow.

Away from the harsh balance of good and evil in the linearity of Zoroastrianism is the balance within Taoism, the mellow belief that everything is basically good and that it is so because of the perfect harmony between nothingness and everything, as symbolized in the **Yin-Yang**, the easily recognized Taoist symbol of the interplay of forces in the universe.

In Chinese philosophy, yin and yang represent the two primal cosmic forces in the universe. Yin (moon) is the receptive, passive, cold female force. Yang (sun) is masculine force, movement, heat. Interestingly, but not surprisingly, in ancient Taoist texts it is the white – the nothingness – that represents enlightenment and it is the black – the everything – that represents ignorance, although they are each as important as the other, as are the Eyn and the Yesh (Nothingness and Being) of the Kabbalah and the white spaces between the black words in the Torah, representing the spiritual and the actual.

In Taoism, the less one thinks the better it is, so much so that even thinking about Taoism moves one away from what it really is. Death, then, is not something to be thought about, since it is completely wrapped up with life, so that death is no more of a big deal than is life. Death cannot exist without life, and life cannot exist without death. Nothingness cannot exist without everything, Tao says, and everything cannot exist without nothingness.

In the end

If religion supplies a human need – which it obviously does, seeing that the vast majority of the world's population believes in some religion, faith or cult – then it is reasonable to ask what that need is.

Although many thinkers, among them Karl Marx, Sigmund Freud and Emile Durkheim, have produced natural histories of religion, arguing that it arose to serve some social or psychological function, those conclusions were mainly arrived at through investigating the adherents of religions, rather than looking at a possible common denominator within all religions, faiths and beliefs themselves that would account for the rise and staying power of religion.

There is, though, no denying that religions vary widely in their fundamental beliefs and concepts. While it is fashionable to proclaim that all religions are equally true, or that all religions are actually different paths to the same truth, a thought that goes back to William Blake's declaration in 1795 that "all religions are one," this is simply not borne out. Yet, given the existence of beliefs since the dawn of human activity, with all human cultures having faith of some sort, it is likely that belief is connected to an evolutionary system of survival that all faiths supply for their adherents to hold on to.

Richard Dawkins, the evolutionary biologist and atheist *par excellence*, while not able to deny the power of religion, is skeptical that religion has any survival value, contending that its cost in blood and guilt outweighs any conceivable benefits.[97] In the meantime, though, religion is doing a good job at surviving, with the numbers worldwide not only increasing but believers actually becoming more devout and fanatical.

While Dawkins, like other scholars, is puzzled by the tenacity of religion within human behavior, he nevertheless approaches the puzzle through Darwinism, albeit in a backhanded manner, attributing religion to a 'misfiring' of something else that is adaptively useful: a child's evolved tendency to believe its parents and hence managing to survive (going against) a process of natural selection.

As attractive as that viewpoint is in its neo-Freudian approach, a look at the disparate beliefs spread over the planet seems to suggest a more fundamental and common instinct that supports an evolutionary tendency for survival: that religious beliefs and behavior confer adaptive advantages to individual believers.

While religions, faiths and beliefs differ in their explanations for the beginning of the universe and also possess differing rules of moral behavior, they all, without exception, have one thing in common: they do not accept that at the end of life there is nothing.

Every one, from the large established religions to the smallest cults, has something to say about death, yet none accepts that there is *nothing* at the end.

If we wish to discover what it is about religious belief that confers an adaptive advantage for survival, the answer lies in the avoidance of *nothing*. Not the avoidance of death, which involves specific rites and elaborate ceremonies to send the person off, but the avoidance of *nothing*.

The point is that death is not *nothing*. If *nothing* is the absence of everything, as we have defined it, it would include the absence of all states of existence or consciousness in any form and at any time.

There is no religion that accepts the finality of such a non-state when the physical body dies. Instead, religions accept death as nothingness in the sense that we distinguished it from *nothing*: nothingness as the absence of something, in this case the absence of life.

The fundamental difference, then, is between death (nothingness – how we, the living, think of death) and being dead (the unimaginable *nothing*).

As a way of relieving humans of the ultimate unthinkable – the thought of life simply ending – religion has the explanation of explanations: there is life after death. And hey presto, life is not futile. As an explanation for the rise of religion and why it was necessary, *nothing* is it. Heaven, hell, purgatory, reincarnation, the never-ending cycle of birth-death-birth, whatever it is called and however it is preached, the end result is the same for believers: there is no end.

In daily life there is, of course, more to belief than the dying part. There are the codes of behavior, the rules (and every belief has rules: even in those, like Tao, that believes in doing nothing), the acts of reverence, holy books and scriptures, the pomp and ceremony, sin and punishment and all the rest that are part of religion, whether it includes prayer to a divinity or an act of faith towards nature or oneself. As important as they all are, though, they perform a supporting role: that whatever one does in life affects what happens after life, or even, in some faiths, how to ostensibly avert physical death itself.

Is it a wonder, then, that priests are important as the ones who have the knowledge to instruct people how to best behave in order to live better in the next life? Priests, parsons, vicars, ministers, cardinals, bishops, monks, rabbis, imams, maharishis, lay functionaries and holy men (and, ever more women) – whatever they are called, their importance is knowing what others do not and so command our respect.

Very few and far between are religions that do not have clergy. One such faith is the Religious Society of Friends (Quakers), for whom life is a gateway to the next and where communal worship consists of silent waiting, with participants contributing as the spirit moves them.

Explanations for almost all faiths tread a line between the necessity to explain and the impossibility of doing so, between the priests' raison d'être and the necessity of making the higher Being or purpose a mystery that cannot be understood. It is at once a source of their power and their holding the ultimate mystery of what is being worshipped. The ultimate answer of all priests is that there are some things that we can't understand due to the limitations of the human mind and that even if we could, we don't have the words to describe what humans cannot fathom.

From the earliest worshipers of fire and the elements of nature, if people held the right ceremonies, honored their gods in the correct way according to the priests who knew best, people's voyage to the afterlife would be smooth and their existence on the other side would be good. It was a matter of doing the right thing: If they did, they would be rewarded in the next world; if they didn't, they would be punished in the next world.

Euphemisms help of course: 'passing away', 'passing on', 'passing over', 'being taken', 'ending one's days', 'kicking the bucket', 'no more', 'gone to meet his/her maker', 'resting in peace', 'shuffled off the mortal coil', 'joined the choir invisible', 'in a better place' are just some of the numerous verbal ways of allowing 'dead' to sound less final.

All beliefs are at it in normal daily speech and at funerals, which are often referred to as 'transitions'. Wicca, a pagan faith that is the modern version of witchcraft, refers to 'crossing the bridge', and in the Wiccan funeral ceremony the priest proclaims: "We are here, not to mourn the passing, but to celebrate the elevation of the spirit of [name of person] so that even in sorrow there may be happiness." Believing in the divine (usually god and goddess, but often just goddess) that is within each person and in nature, Wicca is essentially pantheistic. And while it claims that there is no such thing as sin and punishment, they do have the afterlife ('Summerland'), eventual reincarnation and the three-fold Law (commonly referred to as the Law of Return), which states that: "All good that a person does to another returns three-fold in this life; harm is also returned three fold."

Reward in the life after death is an essential part of religion. Now while there are differences as to how much is rewarded here and how much in the next world, the underlying principle, that of personal immortality, is the same. It is not ours to wonder why the seemingly unfair state of virtuous people who go unrewarded and even suffer, not to mention evil that goes unpunished. But because of the immortality of the soul and rewards in the afterlife, believers can be sure that justice will eventually prevail. Believing in immortality, then, is essential to their contentment and to helping them get through the travails of this earth.

Mostly it's straightforward: conscientiously following the rules means the possibility of salvation (the term used in Christianity) and a good time in the next life, while transgression means punishment and a rough ride in the afterlife. Because people never know whether they will actually get salvation, they have to work hard at it. Even when no amount of good deeds will help, as with the Protestants, born in indelible original sin, there is hope that in the next life they will know if they had been selected by God for salvation. Hope springs eternal, for all believers.

And there is **purgatory**, a concept subscribed to by many Christian denominations: a sort of halfway house for the soul – a state of temporary punishment and purification while it is decided whether the soul goes to heaven or hell. (Not, of course, for Protestants, who believe that one is either saved in one go or not). Mormons are generous when it comes to life after death and believe that one can repent after death and then go to paradise, while Judaism and Islam believe in a holding area for up to a year after death.

If all that fails or they end up where they shouldn't have, Christians, Jews and Muslims still have the ultimate event to look forward to: resurrection of the dead and Final Judgment Day.

Resurrection is certainly something to look forward to. Among Christians, the evangelists are most keen for the second coming of Jesus and the end of the world. Impatiently expecting the imminence of the second coming are Adventists (the Seventh-day Adventist Church), who are distinct as Christians not only in having the Sabbath on Saturday, but also in the afterlife scenario of 'unconscious state of the dead', where the immortal soul is in a state of sleep till the great day of resurrection occurs.

In contrast, Buddhism and Hinduism do not have the concept of eternal heaven and hell. It is just as likely for heaven and hell to exist in life, and it is up to the individual to regain freedom by rebirth into a better heaven. Dying is seen as a rebirth, so that eternal life is the cycle of death, life, death, life. No reason to fear death, in fact; in the "Life Span" chapter of the Lotus Sutra, the eternity of life is expressed by the passage: "There is no ebb and flow of life and death, and there is no existing in this world and later entering extinction" (LS16, 226).

If for Eastern faiths, life and death are *circular* without a beginning and without an end, for monotheistic religions life and death can be seen as a *linear* progression from life on earth to the afterlife. According to monotheistic religions, the earth is as real as heaven and hell, all of which are God's creation. So when people die, they go from one reality to another.

It's a nice way of putting it and certainly helps in making the inevitability of death not only palatable, but even something to look forward to. As put so calmingly by Sam Stoltzfus, an Amish woodworker, "A funeral to us is a much more important thing than the day of birth because we believe in the hereafter. The children are better off than their survivors." As a statement of belief, it does its job.

Christian Science has carried denial to a whole different level, where 'mind over matter' is taken so literally that death is accepted as occurring only as the result of not trying hard enough. With death as an aberration, Christian Scientists don't actually refer to an afterlife, as if dying is an admission of failure, of weakness. Where the mind – the spirit that is God – is every-thing, "Man is immortal, and the body cannot die, because matter has no life to surrender."[98]

Following its founder, Mary Baker Eddy (1821-1910), Christian Science claims that sickness, death, and even our physical bodies do not exist, but are only imagined. Its view of sickness as non-existent was summed up in *The Christian Science Sentinel* in 1906 in response to criticism of its uncompromising attitude: "We think our critic will agree that when disease disap-pears it vanishes into nothingness; that it is still not hovering about, but has actually gone to nothingness. We believe he will agree that something cannot be reduced to nothing; hence the disease must have been a nonentity to begin with."[99]

In any case, for them the thought of death is not only nothing to fear, but is actually welcome, since it is merely another false belief that stops one from concentrating on the spirit. "Death," it is written, "is not an enemy but a better friend than Life."[100]

But where is Christian Science when it comes to *something, nothing* and nothingness? For a start, it thinks of *nothing* as all other faiths do – it doesn't: the immortality of the soul does not allow for the possibility of non-existence. Its relationship to nothingness, though, is another matter. At first glance, Christian Science seems to go for nothingness in a big way as a negative theology with much in common with Eastern faiths, since it dismisses the body – indeed, all matter – and recognizes the mind only.

Yet far from emptying the mind in order to arrive at the nothingness that is the key to everything, Christian Science does the exact opposite: it strengthens the mind and it does so to such an extent that the mind is everything. The aim of Christian Science is not the non-being of nothingness, but the being of the spirit, which is definitely a big something.

Avoiding nothing

"Denial," Mark Twain said, "is not just a river in Egypt." Actually, it is also how all religions deal with *nothing* and, aptly, how the Ancient Egyptians demonstrated it most spectacularly though their burial habits. Like with many beliefs, they saw death as a journey, but one in which the body needed to be intact when it got to the next world so that the person's three souls 'ka', 'ba' and 'akh' could be reunited.

The point of embalming the body and wrapping it in bandages and amulets was to maintain it so that it could survive forever. Not just survive, but because the priest had performed the ritual of 'opening of the mouth', the deceased would have the power of speech, movement, and the ability to eat, when he was 'reborn' in the afterlife.

As with most religions – if we get past the hell-ish part of a few – the Ancient Egyptians believed that the next life could be an enhancement of this one, and since they didn't subscribe to the notion that 'you can't take it with you', their tombs were filled with food and drink, instructive texts, games, and jewelry.

They didn't get a ticket straight through, though. Before the dead reached the next world, Ancient Egyptian belief was they were led to a judgment hall by Anubis, the god of mummification, where their heart, containing evidence of their behavior in life, was then weighed against a feather. If their heart outweighed the feather it was heavy with the guilt of a life badly lived and was then eaten by Ammit, the creature combined of a crocodile, a lion, and hippopotamus. If the feather weighed more than the heart, the heart was pure and the owner made his way into the next life.

Now although the idea of taking one's body to the afterlife seems rather far-fetched, it is really only a variation of judgment and resurrection in the afterlife believed today by the monotheistic religions. While Christianity and Islam believe that people will have new bodies in heaven, Orthodox Judaism, although not believing that you can take earthly things with you, does insist on burying all parts of the body together and, based on the belief of resurrection of the body as it was, has severe prohibitions against moving it after burial.

The body is a problem. It is so for all religions, with believers in reincarnation having it no easier to reconcile the body within the mysticism on which their faiths are based. The Eastern faiths' cycle of life, consisting of continual rebirths, still can't ignore the fact that life takes place within a physical body.

But some can, and do. Hindus think of the body, and indeed all of life, as an illusion and unreal, since it is the result of what is perceived by the senses and so unreliable. For them, reincarnation – the cycle of the transmitted soul – is considered to be the wheel of life that turns from one illusion to another, with the spirit changing bodies in an endless cycle, even, according to Eastern Hinduism, the possibility of coming back as an insect, or a bird or even as a plant. The only escape from this terrible burden of reincarnation is to gain unity with Brahman. That is the ultimate aim, and when it is reached, the person at death no longer needs to reincarnate but can continue to exist in a formless spiritual state.

It's interesting that in the East reincarnation is considered a curse, while in the West it has become a fad within New Age as something desirable within one's immortality (and with the fervent hope that it will be a return to one's body, or a better one).

For Buddhists, it is the impermanence of life that is stressed. It's not so much a matter of moving away from illusion as such; it is of leaving behind the suffering of this life and reaching a higher plain with each rebirth that depends on the karmic forces which were built up each time.

While both Buddhism and Hinduism are concerned with attaining nothingness – emptying one's mind in order to reach a better state – the difference is that Hindus are in search of the perfect self, while the Buddhist's ideal is self-lessness. These are opposing ends, even if their approaches are similar. For each, the self means something different: Buddhism's self is existence as part of a whole, linked to humankind, while Hinduism's self is the perfect 'I', the perfect personal self.

Without going into the variations within Buddhist traditions or Hindu traditions, or between the more divine-driven Hinduism and the universalist aspects of Buddhism, it is the self-effacement through nothingness that is both the commonality and the difference between them. Both the fatalism that is inherent in, and accounts for, the caste system in Hinduism and the struggle in Buddhism for enhancement and release to be part of the whole that is humanity reflect on how both faiths deal with death as a continuation of the present, but that is, hopefully, better.

And that's the point. In one way or another, all religions and beliefs treat death as a continuation of life – a denial that death is the end of everything. It is a complete inability to accept the existence of *nothing*.

Nothingness and death

Since religions see death as the absence of life and not a conclusive end, it is made easier for believers to accept the notion that they will die. It is not death, the absence of life – nothingness – that is denied, but, rather, the absence of everything – *nothing* – that is inconceivable for all religions, faiths and beliefs.

Most religions have the notion of a soul, an eternal mystical spark within all humans, that religions accept as a reality in some way or other (a prominent exception being Buddhism, in which people are temporary vessels in this world and are born anew every time until they attain enlightenment). With a soul comes eternity.

Not always, though. Following the principle that the exception proves the rule, we have the Raelians, a UFO-based cult that claims to have 50,000 members in 85 countries, who believe that the soul dies with death, and overcome the problem of death by simply cloning themselves. Their key to eternal life is not, then, the soul but the re-creation of individuals from their DNA.

The sect, which believes humans were created by extra-terrestrial beings who had mastered genetic engineering, was founded in France in 1973 by a former journalist who worked for a racing car magazine. The religious connection – and the cult wants to be known as a religion – is that the founder, Claude Vorilhon, insists that in the spaceship that he entered in 1973 he saw Jesus, Buddha and Joseph Smith, the founder of the Mormons. Deeply impressed, Vorilhon was told by the extra-terrestrial beings who were hosting the prophets that humans were created 25,000 years ago in laboratories by people from another planet.

All members of faiths, however quirky, believe themselves to be immortal. Even young beliefs, such as the Rastafarians, a young Caribbean-centered religion with roots in Ethiopia, revolving around reggae and the ritualistic use of marijuana, talk about 'everliving' rather than 'everlasting'.

Whatever gets you through the night. Hallucinatory substances often help faith along its spiritual path. Shamans, powerful figures, popularly known as witchdoctors, are intermediaries between the human and spirit worlds. They can treat illness and are capable of entering supernatural realms to obtain answers to the problems of their community. It goes without saying that Shamanism is concerned that after death the human soul makes its dangerous journey to the underworld in safety, and it is the shaman who guides the souls across. He enters into a trance by taking hallucinatory substances so that he can be alert to dangerous spirits along the way. The Beyond, it is believed, consists of complete nothingness, a space totally devoid of all things abstract and material. The only true reality is found in death, at which point the true potential of the person is revealed.

It is not a coincidence that many faiths describe death as 'reality', so that life is, actually, an illusion. Death is then quite a casual thing – something good, in fact. In the shaman's world, the living can visit the Land of the Dead, and the dead the world of the living.

And neither is it a coincidence that so many religions link themselves with nature in a profound mystical sense. Pantheism is alive and well far and wide, not only in the intuitive sense of Western and Eastern mysticism, but also in the deep spiritual feelings and beliefs of native peoples.

Aboriginals are connected to the land and to all things in nature in a sense much more deeply than Westerners can comprehend. Aboriginal spirituality is the belief that all objects are living and share the same soul or spirit that Aboriginals share, so that for Aboriginals, as Eddie Murooro, Aboriginal writer and artist says, "Spirituality is a oneness and an interconnectedness with all that lives and breathes, even with all that does not live or breathe." Not just animals, in other words, but also rocks.

An Aboriginal's soul or spirit is believed to continue on after the physical form has passed through death. After the death of an Aboriginal person their spirit returns to the Dreamtime – a state that is a timeless combination of the present, the past and the future – from where it will return through birth as a human, an animal, a plant or a rock. The returned shape is not important because each form shares the same soul or spirit. The difference between this and reincarnation in Hinduism is that in the latter the reborn shape is the result of previous actions and hence very important.

It is no wonder that the notion of fusion with nature is as popular today as it ever was. More so, in fact. Not only because of the world's preoccupation with climate change and preservation of forests and animals, but because of the deep-seated belief in the continuity of nature and the perceived immortality that is achieved through being part of it. It melds in well with the upsurge of interest in pre-history and with native peoples that supposedly continue the pure life they led before contact with Western civilization.

One doesn't need to be religious, then, to believe in continuity after death; for non-believers, death as personal finality can always be mitigated by the thought of energy never dying and so becoming one with the cosmos. Non-believers, like religious believers, can accept nothingness but not *nothing*.

Nothing now

It is perhaps no wonder that New Age came along when it did. During a period when instant gratification is shown as the aim of life, the idea that eternity can be achieved effortlessly is much more attractive than the lifelong dedication that has to be invested within religions, their codes and strictures.

New Age concentrates on living. Death is so not in the picture as to be almost eradicated within the realm of what will be. It's as if the absence of bad thoughts averts the unthinkable.

Purity is the name of the game. Purity of life, of body, of soul, of the spirit. Achievable with the minimum of effort, it is the undefined theme of New Age wisdom on the road to happiness, contentment, well-being and satisfaction that lead to eternity.

New Age, a mishmash of Eastern faiths and philosophies made easy, is tailored to fit whatever is easiest to fulfill. If its main theme is the movement towards inner purity and fusion with nature, its method is the search for nothingness that rids the mind of extraneous worldly matters.

Its attraction, though, is that it can be achieved effortlessly and quickly, as encapsulated in the title of the book *The Power of Now* by Eckhart Tolle, an enormously successful author and advocate, largely thanks to Oprah Winfrey's enthusiastic endorsement of New Age and its wonders. Oprah herself has a banner headline on her website: "Awaken joy and get more happiness", while the title of Robert Holden's book, *Happiness Now! Timeless Wisdom for Feeling Good Fast*, sums it up nicely. Holden is also director of the Happiness Project in the United Kingdom, while in the USA James Baraz, a meditation instructor and founding teacher of Spirit Rock Meditation Center in Woodacre, California, teaches a class called "Awakening Joy", a series of exercises, lectures, and meditations, which is designed to bring more happiness to people's lives.

The idea that one can achieve contentment with as little effort as possible is New Age's big selling point and fits into the 'Age of Aquarius', with its television reality shows, the obsessive interest in celebrities' lives and the instant gratification that is part of it all.

When Eckhart Tolle describes his message as both simple to learn and potentially world changing, it is its wide acceptance and acclaim that shows how far the world has come in its thirst for simplistic solutions to the meaning of life. Tolle's belief that followers should turn off the mind's chatter, embrace the present and drop the ego, which he describes as a manipulative and divisive force, is actually the credo of Buddhism and its call to nothingness. But with its attendant lack of effort and promises of instant gratification, it is a pop version that ignores the suffering that Buddhism believes is part of life. Holding out the promise of achieving nothingness effortlessly, it offers, in fact, the instant satisfaction of getting everything from nothing.

New Age strikes a chord. Sometimes it uses pop versions of Eastern faiths, as does the American spiritual teacher Baba Ram Dass (born Richard Alpert), who has been bringing Buddhism to the masses, helped by his 1971 bestseller *Remember, Be Here Now*.

Very often, though, New Age wisdom is religious syncretism, the reconciliation or fusion of differing systems of belief that is a combination of strands from a variety of Eastern faiths, including Zen Buddhism, Taoism, meditation, yoga, as well as Kabbalah and mysticism from elsewhere. Recent self-help stars like Deepak Chopra are teaching very Tollean messages – like embracing silence and living in the moment – on television and on tour, while his gimmicky *Ask the Kabala Oracle Cards*[101] clearly embraces different popular fads as its marketing ploy.

The attraction of New Age is that it enables people to take whatever they want from a union of different and often opposing principles. We would be hard put to find anything less compatible than the mixture of negative philosophy of Eastern religions, the notion of 'positive thinking', advocated by Tolle, plus New Thought ideas such as 'The Secret', which claims that the mind is so powerful that it can cause us to achieve anything.

Because its purpose is to make people feel good, New Age is not restricted by the sometimes gloomy rules of religions. So when Vietnamese monk Thich Nhat Hanh, one of the best known Buddhist teachers in the West, offers a practice of 'mindfulness', a method of becoming aware of the inner workings of the body, this suits Western sensibilities, as does his coined term **Engaged Buddhism**, that seeks to apply the insights from meditation practice and dharma teachings to alleviating social, political, and economic injustice. As a politically activist movement, it certainly appeals to Western thought more than would the more passive Buddhism in its original form.

Obviously, in all the mix-and-match of New Age wisdom, it is not only Eastern religions that are being mangled on the path towards eternal happiness. Through 'Buddhist-Christian studies', it is just as easy to be a Christian New Ager, making Christianity easier to swallow with a theology of so-called 'radical openness' in, for example, Beverly J. Lanzetta's book *The Other Side of Nothingness: Toward a Theology of Radical Openness*, which espouses a religious pluralism that is willing to accept mystical strands from all faiths.

New Age is obviously not monolithic, and we would be hard-pressed to call it a new religion. On the other hand, there are very few religions that do not have within them strands radically different from one another. Mysticism, which was originally faith-based, has come a long way from its original search for nothingness through the emptying of one's mind as a way towards union with what is true and real. Whether New Age is part of mysticism or whether it is a synthetic search for what is easy and instant, like all faiths it provides a way of accepting nothingness.

New Age, by celebrating life NOW, keeps at bay thoughts about THEN.

Ever forward

When Brian Epstein, the Beatles' mentor, their guide and best friend, committed suicide in 1967, they were devastated. Help came in the shape of the Maharishi, who, according to John Lennon's then-wife Cynthia, called them into his quarters, where he sat yoga-style in the center and, asking them to sit down on the floor, talked to them about "life's journey, reincarnation, release from pain and this life being a stepping stone to the next." In Cynthia's words: "The Maharishi's words helped us all to feel a little less bleak."[102]

The Maharishi had touched the core of what it is that can make people feel content: the notion of certain immortality. Just as calming was his assured connection between this life and the next life. The crown in the jewel was his promise that not only is it okay to die, but that it can be even better when that happens.

As a summing up of what is common to all faiths, it was spot on.

There is no faith in the world that does not have a solution to the unthinkable *nothing*, that it all ends when the body dies. In that sense, New Age is no different from any other belief. In fact, the only difference between faiths is how one can make sure that the afterlife – in whichever form the belief subscribes to – is better than the present one.

Faith stands on one thing, without which there would be no religious belief: it is how humans go about accepting the reality of death while at the same time denying the possibility of *nothing*. Because nothingness is merely the absence of life, believers continue living as if there will always be a tomorrow.

Neatly summing this up are the New Thought teachings of Esther Hicks, who states categorically that, "You cannot die; you are everlasting life." And what strength of conviction it is for Cynthia Bourgeault, leader of the Christian New Age "Contemplative Society" to title one of her books: *Love is Stronger than Death*!

With death perceived as merely the absence of life, it is perhaps not surprising that believers imagine anything to be stronger than death. God certainly is, as far as the monotheistic religions are concerned. Dying for God. In fact, he often wants us to, with the motivation of suicide bombers and the promise of paradise for martyrs proving the point.

If death is not to feared, but rather is something to be embraced, it may go some way in explaining the atrocities that have been carried out in the name of religion. The obvious question has always been: How, if the teachings of most beliefs have the injunction to lead a life of goodness and follow the rules that contain a code of morality in order to benefit from rewards in the afterlife, can we reconcile that with atrocities carried out in this life? Put another way, as Andrew Brown does, "Does a belief in heaven make people more or less likely to behave atrociously?"[103] Referring to the wanton slaughter and almost unbelievable cruelty carried out by the Crusaders in the name of religion and where the fear of damnation was universal, Brown comes to the conclusion that the perpetrators did not really believe in life after death; if they had, he maintains, they would have acted differently.

Yet every religion, then and now, believes in an afterlife. Fighting for God was just as good a way of getting to paradise as any other, especially as the Crusades were religious in nature. God was obviously on their side (just as those being slaughtered believed he was on *their* side). Being part of the Crusades was being part of God's will, so that whatever had to be done for victory was following the rules that would get the followers to paradise.

There remains an awkward question: Had the Crusaders not thought that paradise awaited them, would they have continued with such zeal? Not having any way to answer that, we can but speculate that if they had thought that there was no afterlife in which awaited their reward, they would have been less keen to throw themselves to the task.

The Nothing gene

The survival instinct, the evolutionary thrust to perpetuate the human species, is inherent in the urge to live. Not just to live, though. It is to live a life of purpose, since without purpose humans would not find it necessary to propagate. With the majority of the world having a faith of one kind or another, it would seem that purpose is strongly bound up with belief.

If belief is important to evolution, it seems tempting to

subscribe to the presence of a God gene, proposed by molecular biologist Dean H. Hammer. In his book, *The God Gene: How Faith is Hardwired into Our Genes*, Hammer suggested that spirituality – the feeling of transcendence – is part of our nature and is due to our genes, and that a universal penchant for spiritual fulfillment explains the growing popularity of non-traditional religions and the presence of thousands of religions throughout the world.

The idea of a God gene was, and is, attacked by scientists and also by theologians, who object to the idea of religion being hardwired in the brain. For scientists, it is inconceivable that there could be empirical proof of religious experience, and also they criticize the attempt to link genes with particular personality traits. Theologians, no happier about the notion of a God gene, are totally against the cutting down of faith to the lowest common denominator of genetic survival. Atheists, of course, don't see why a faith gene should be proposed, since they simply don't have it.

Yet as a survival strategy, the God gene seems like a good idea. As the sole species – as far as we know – capable of contemplating its own death, humans would have needed something larger than ourselves to make that knowledge tolerable.

The 'God gene' is, of course, a misnomer. Not every religion believes in a god or in any sort of divinity. And neither would a 'faith gene' cover it, since it is too general to cover all religions, faiths and beliefs.

Tempting as it is to look for a 'denial gene' as representing the limits to acceptance of death present in all faiths, that would not cover it either. After all, what is it that all faiths are denying? Certainly not that the body is likely to die, since all beliefs deal with this in one way or another.

It is not, then, our capacity to understand that we will die that is in question, but, rather, as we have seen, our **inability** to comprehend that there can be *nothing*.

It is, though, more than that. 'Inability' seems to indicate the possibility of 'ability' at some point and in certain circumstances. But in the case of *nothing*, inability means the absolute impossibility of the mind to grasp the very concept of *nothing*, the absence of everything, including oneself. It is not the inability to understand death that is inherent within us, but the inability to understand *nothing*.

It is not a God gene or a faith gene or a denial gene that we need to look for in our genetic make-up, but a more fundamental adaptation that acts in a survival role.

It is the **Nothing gene** that is likely hardwired into our system with a specific function: it blocks out the capacity to comprehend *nothing*, and so gives humans the ability to contemplate the inevitability of their own demise.

If, according to the behavioral neuroscientist Michael Persinger, the God gene is a brilliant adaptation as a built-in pacifier for facing one's own death, the Nothing gene is much more than that: the mind is in no need of a pacifier for something that, as far as it is concerned, does not exist, so that the non-understandability of *nothing* is a crucial trait that would be stamped deep into our genome.

The Nothing gene is not present in order to instill fear of the unknown. There is no faith that advocates that. On the contrary, in fact. When there is fear – of eternal damnation or of reincarnation to a lesser state, for example – the fear is not of the unknown. It is not even fear of the unknowable. The Nothing gene is a block to fear. The closest we can get to understanding what it is that we can't understand is to claim that the Nothing gene gives the delusion that there is no unknown.

Nothing at the end is not a problem only for believers. Even many non-believers claim that since energy cannot be destroyed, bodies die but consciousness is converted to energy and so continues in some way. That, of course, does not really give them much to look forward to, but would cause them to make the most of what is here, expressed rather plaintively by French artist

Christian Boltanski: "I love life so much, also because I know I am going to die." It is not surprising that thanatophobia, the obsessive fear of death, is a condition that is more common to agnostics and atheists than to believers. Even more plaintive was the cry from Woody Allen, who said, "I do not want to achieve immortality through my work. I want to achieve it through not dying."

But how can one be afraid of *nothing*? So asks Julian Barnes in his aptly titled book *Nothing to be Frightened of*, echoing Socrates' memorable: "To fear death is to think that we know what we do not know." For Freud, the fact that humans are aware of their own mortality is part of the internal clash between the life instinct and the death instinct: "If we are to take it that everything dies for internal reasons – becomes inorganic once again – then we shall be compelled to say that 'the aim of all life is death'..." strangely, and surely unintentionally, similar to the religious notion that life is preparation for death.

In a similar vein, Jacques Derrida mentions that ever since Plato, the old philosophical injunction has been that "to philosophize is to learn to die," to which he adds, "I believe in this truth without yielding to it. I have not learned to accept death."[104]

And although Mark Twain dealt with death in his usual healthy way – "I do not fear death, in view of the fact that I had been dead for billions and billions of years before I was born, and had not suffered the slightest inconvenience from it" – it was Diogenes of Sinope some 2,200 years earlier who hit the nail on the head when, being asked whether death was an evil thing, replied, "How can it be evil, when in its presence we are not aware of it?"

Long before philosophers and theologians drove themselves and everybody else crazy by asking why we are here, Diogenes understood that the ultimate mystery is not why we are here but what it means to not be here.

Four

Thinking about Nothing

The struggle to understand the concept of absolute emptiness, the absence of everything, has been going on for some two thousand years, for at least as long as there have been written records of what people thought is important. Those who have made it their business to think have been puzzling at 'nothing', wondering what it was, whether it was anything at all, whether it existed, in fact, and if it did, how it affected things around it.

There is patently a fundamental human need to pursue the mystery that is the negation of everything, not just within the obvious framework of philosophy, but, as we have seen, within the arts, science, religion; everything, in fact, that humans do. As the opposite of everything, *nothing*, it is somehow felt, is the key to one of the most basic questions: what does it mean to exist?

And here lies a problem: treating 'nothing' as if it were another examinable entity: treating 'nothing' as something, in other words.

From the time of Parmenides, whom we met in Chapter Three, and Melissus of Samos (also born, later, in the 5th century BCE), there have been objections to the possibility of emptiness, a void, existing at all, in the way that an object exists. Full of conviction, Melissus said: "Nor is there any void, for void is nothing, and nothing cannot be."[105] And there was Aristotle, whose arguments against the very possibility of emptiness were so persuasive that they were accepted for 1500 years.

In the 20th century, the problem of treating 'nothing' as something had still not been dealt with, even though it was more the effects of 'nothing' that were looked at, rather than defining what it might be, with philosophers such as Jean-Paul-Sartre and

Martin Heidegger making it the backbone of their speculations.

They were all barking up the wrong tree, or, rather, different trees. As difficult as it is to tackle a concept that implies non-existence, the task is made even more so if one frequently and erroneously uses terms that seem to be similes but confuse the issue. Included are Aristotle's refutation of the **void**, with the Stoics and Hero of Alexandria arguing **vacuums**, while Galileo, Kepler and Descartes referred to the notion of **empty space**, as did Newton, whose law of gravitation assumed the whole universe to be filled with a subtle substance. Then along came Einstein who referred to **space** as an abstraction, in that it exists only because there are objects and that the objects affect space itself. And as mentioned, both Sartre and Heidegger referred to **nothing** and **nothingness**, with seemingly no differentiation between the terms.

Really it should come as no surprise that ferocious arguments have continued over the millennia, when discussions supposedly about absolute emptiness were actually about something that had attributes. People were beating their heads against a wall because mostly they weren't discussing the notion of *nothing*, the absence of everything. They thought they were, but they weren't. Mostly they were investigating the absence of something, not the absence of everything.

Aristotle, who had a lot to say about everything important, looked at the sky and couldn't accept that absolute emptiness was out there. If something moved, Aristotle said, it would have to move something else; there was no such thing as emptiness, in other words. And in any case, he pointed out, how could things that were not touching actually move unless something moved them? Galileo and Descartes, each in his own period and with his own reasoning, didn't accept the concept of emptiness either or that actions could be affected across distances. How could tides on earth be influenced by the moon, for example? Also Newton was unable to conceive of emptiness, which is why he was careful to attribute space as being filled with an ether-like substance when he described gravitation.

The confusion, now, is clear: *nothing* (space, a void, emptiness, nothing, nothingness – whatever it was called) does not have any attributes or properties, and neither can it do anything or affect anything. That is what *nothing* is: it isn't! Finding attributing characteristics in *nothing* and then being puzzled as to why is bound to end in more puzzlement.

While sometimes scientists and philosophers make attempts to tackle *nothing*, as, for example, in the famous question 'Why is there something rather than nothing', as we saw in the previous chapter, more often they aren't thinking of *nothing* at all, even when they think they are. What can we make of the *nothing* described by the French philosopher, Maurice Merleau-Ponty?: "Being is nothing; it is nothing but explosion, radiance, and opening – never fully is."[106] That opening, he says, is one in which the invisible world becomes visible for "every visual something... gives itself as a result of a dehiscence of Being," of a "deflagration of Being."[107] Surely, giving such attributes to *nothing* immediately stops it being *nothing*.

Shakespeare, brilliant as he was about everything else, was as lost as the rest when it came to *nothing*. So when Macbeth says, "Nothing is but what is not," we now realize that it is not that simple.

But that is the point. *Nothing* is an enigma. Since *nothing* is the absence of everything, anything at all would stop *nothing* from being nothing. Or to put it another way: anything makes *nothing* something. And let's go for another mind cruncher: *Nothing* is where everything is not.

We have already seen how spectacularly unsuccessful dictionaries are with defining *nothing*. Not surprising, of course. One of the problems, as we will see again, is in the very attempt; to define means 'to set boundaries' – which, as soon as you do, no longer leaves you with *nothing*. *Nothing* does not have a frame in any way: no beginning, no end and no thing within.

None of these problems, though, appear with *nothingness*. In fact, all the arguments about *nothing* over the thousands of years would have been avoided had it been realized that they were not about *nothing* at all, but about a different 'nothing', that has attributes, that which we have preferred to call *nothingness*.

The difference between *nothing* and nothingness is not a technicality. It is essential if we want to get any way towards finding about what it means to exist and where we as humans fit into it all.

Vacuums

Ever since Parmenides, vacuums have been equated with absolute and utter emptiness. This is reasonable because a vacuum was considered an area empty of matter, and so it is understandable why vacuums were the center of controversy for such a long time. Either they were empty or they weren't. When confronted with a barometer, Descartes, sure that there was no such thing as an empty vacuum and that the mercury was held up by something, vehemently disputed those, like Evangelista Torricelli and Blaise Pascal, who said that the mercury rose and fell according to atmospheric pressure.

Since a vacuum was considered to be absolutely empty, the innocent observation that 'there is a vacuum in this flask' was seen as a contradiction, since, as Melissus said, "A void is nothing, and nothing cannot be," so how could there be something that doesn't exist in the flask?

We are, though, in a position to look at it differently. Because we teased out the difference between *nothing* (the absence of everything) and nothingness (the absence of something), the seemingly strange phenomenon of 'nothing' in the flask now makes sense. What the flask contains is the absence of something (matter), and that a vacuum is not *nothing*.

By stating that 'there is a vacuum in the flask' we are affirming the existence of something in the flask: what we have in the flask is the absence of matter. We can, as we know, see, feel or sense an absence: an absence is something. It is because of that something we are aware of that there is no *nothing*.

The fact that we can actually produce a vacuum also puts it on another level from *nothing*, if only because we are able to produce *something*.

So let's ask the question: Can we produce *nothing*? Production must, surely, be of something. If we produce *nothing*, then we aren't producing at all. And if we are already thinking along these lines, we can't help wondering whether it is at all possible for *nothing* to come from something. The problems encountered when positing the formation of something from *nothing* – Creation and the Big Bang – are, so it seems, not any simpler when contemplating the opposite, the formation of *nothing* from something, since *nothing* that has a beginning is not *nothing*. In any case, how would *nothing* begin? We will look at that a little later when we ask 'where is *nothing*?'.

Adding to all the woes connected to the notion of producing *nothing* is the thought that anything that produces *nothing* would itself have to disappear, since the producer's existence would itself render *nothing* something. After all, *nothing*, the absence of everything, would not be able to have anything around, since then it would become *something*.

Vacuums, though, are reproduced naturally all the time. Large meteorites pass through the atmosphere in about one second leaving a hole – a vacuum. The fact that the air cannot rush in quickly enough to fill the gap explains why rock vapor from the impact shoots back up into the atmosphere and later rains down widely on the surface. During a meteorite shower, multiple vacuums are produced in the atmosphere.

Are these multiple nothings? Obviously not. For a start, a vacuum produced in space is no more *nothing* than a vacuum produced in the laboratory. They are the absence of matter, but not the absence of everything. In any case, with *nothing* as the absence of everything, it is nonsensical for there to be more than one, just as it is for there to be more than one everything.

The good news in all this is that we may be wasting our time ruminating on the philosophical issues of vacuums, since the latest from the world of physics is that vacuums aren't empty at all. Particle physics demonstrates that space is teeming with matter and anti-matter, with the Large Hadron Collider run by CERN, the European scientific project, 100 m under Geneva, smashing particles into each other in order to discover many more particles that form the basis of matter.

So what we so fervently believed to be true, that 'nature abhors a vacuum', turns out to be true after all. There is no such thing as empty space.

Nothing does not exist physically, then. As justification for the problems we have with understanding *nothing* as a concept, this is exciting. When it comes to the foundation of existence, both science, dealing with the building blocks of matter, and philosophy, looking at the basis of consciousness, seem to come to a similar conclusion: *nothing* isn't anywhere.

It seems every time we think we've found *nothing*, something turns up!

The opposite of everything

It might be possible to make sense of *nothing* by looking at its opposite: *everything*.

In order to satisfy ourselves that the opposite of *nothing* is *everything*, rather than *something*, we can do a small test.

Let's try 'There is nothing in the box'; the opposite would be 'There is something in the box'.

As we reasoned in Chapter One, when we say the box is empty, we mean that the box is empty of something or perhaps of many things; it is not, though, empty of everything – it does, after all, have air and dust and bacteria, whatever.

The reason that the opposite of 'There is nothing in the box' is not 'There is everything in the box' is because the box did not, and could not, contain the absence of everything (*nothing*).

Can we, though, imagine the box (or any box) containing everything? Of course not. It cannot contain everything in the same way that it cannot contain *nothing*, both of which are all-embracing.

The limitless possibilities of *everything* is the opposite of the non-possibilities of *nothing*.

All said and done, though, there is a huge difference in the way we think of *everything* as compared to *nothing*. There seems to be no problem for us to understand *everything*, in fact. But is the concept of *everything*, in fact, as clear as it seems?

We need to ask, first of all, whether there really is such a thing as everything. In theory there is: everything in the world. So – again in theory – it should be possible to have everything in the world in a box. This box would have to be a HUGE box, so big, in fact, that it would have to include everything in and on which it rested – and itself.

And here comes the problem. Although we understand what 'everything' is, which we know would include material objects, life forms, gases, viruses, bacteria, ideas, and so on, it is not easy to conceive of the actuality, even though we seem to be able to grasp the concept itself.

And we are talking about everything of everything, not just two-by-two (and they were only of all the animals!) that went into Noah's ark. And we haven't even gone into whether 'everything' would include things that we can't think of or haven't yet been discovered!

And if we are really talking about everything, we would have to include non-material things. *Everything* would have to include mental images, thoughts, memories, dreams, etc. Not only all of those, but since everything has to include everything, it would have to include *nothing* as well! *Nothing*, after all, is part of everything.

But that statement – 'everything contains nothing' – is problematic: because of the enigmatic nature of *nothing*, it is a statement that is riddled with contradictions and so cannot be proven true or false:

If the statement 'everything contains nothing' is true, then everything does not exist (everything has to contain something, whereas nothing is the absence of everything. Everything cannot contain the absence of itself, even though it would have to include the idea of its own absence).

If it is untrue – that everything does not, in fact, contain nothing – then we can go no further, because we cannot begin a statement claiming that everything doesn't contain something (even if that something is nothing), since that is a contradiction in terms.

Interestingly, our statement would not be a contradiction if it referred to nothingness, because nothingness (the absence of something) is something.

All in all, it seems that *everything* is as difficult to define as *nothing*, which makes sense considering that they are opposites. One is too all-encompassing to conceive, while the other is too non-encompassing to conceive.

Our paradox 'everything contains nothing', has, though, thrown up another point about *nothing* and everything: that the problem with *nothing* is not so much one of definition, but of something more fundamental – whether we can actually perceive of *nothing* and *everything*. However difficult it would be to think about what *everything* could include, it is not an impossible thought. In other words, 'everything' is *conceivable*; just because we don't know what everything could actually consist of doesn't mean that we can't conceive of the idea of *everything*. Can we, though, conceive of *nothing*?

That is a much more doubtful proposition. Because there is always something, even of ourselves thinking, there is never *nothing*. With *nothing* being the absence of everything, including ourselves, *nothing* cannot share the same space as we do, since when we are present we cause *nothing* to be something.

How, then, can we conceive of an absence of everything that includes ourselves as well? Or, putting it differently: How would it be possible for us to not conceive of anything at all?

The unfortunate conclusion is that looking at the opposite of *nothing* does not get us any closer to understanding it. It does not help at all to know that *nothing* is the negative of *everything*. All we know is that *everything* is everything that *nothing* is not.

Uniqueness and infinity

Is *nothing*, then, unique, different from anything else that we can't conceive of?

Very much so, it seems. We can imagine unicorns, for example, even if they don't exist as actual live creatures in nature; imagining a horse with a horn will give us a picture of a unicorn in our minds. We can even understand the notion of the bending of space and time, even though we can't grasp the concept itself; we know what it means when something is bent and accept physicists' explanation of the phenomenon occurring within our universe,

We can, though, not imagine what is ungraspable. However innovative sci-fi movies are, they have never come up with aliens different from what we can imagine; little green men or slimy blobs with three heads, or whatever, are just combinations of what we know.

What about infinity? We can't imagine infinity, but, like emptiness, we can understand what it means for there can be something that has no limitations. We cannot, though, grasp the concept of infinity precisely because it is unrestricted.

Long connected, *nothing* and infinity are seen somehow as two sides of the same coin, since with *nothing* having no beginning and no end, it does seem infinite.

When applied to numbers, infinity is not merely an enormously large number. Infinity is beyond that. You could keep counting (or measuring) for ever, and never reach infinity; it is not a description of something that is, but is a description of a theoretical possibility. As hard as that is to grasp, infinity is something that one can understand, even if it isn't attainable.

The problem of infinity was famously captured by the German mathematician, David Hilbert (1862-1943). He proposed the Infinite Hotel, now known as Hilbert's Hotel, as an illustration of how to deal with treating infinity as a number.

This hotel has an infinite number of rooms and despite being always full it can cater for any number of extra guests that arrive.

If a guest arrives at the hotel even though it is full, the guest will be given a room. How? No problem: everyone shifts to the next room. The person in room 1 moves to room 2, the person in room 2 moves to room 3, and so on. Since the hotel is infinite, there will always be a next-door to move into. This leaves room 1 free for the newly-arrived person to move into.

The same happens when any number of guests arrive, requesting rooms. If thirty turn up, the receptionist gets everybody to shift to the room thirty numbers down – the person in room 1 moves to room 31; the person in room 2 moves into room 32, and so on. The newly-arrived group will take rooms 1 to 30.

But wait, wasn't the hotel full already? Yes, but this shows how infinity can't be regarded as a number in the normal sense, because infinity plus a finite number is still infinity.

The possible scenario gets still more bizarre.

Imagine that an infinite number of guests arrive. Would the hotel be able to accommodate them? No problem in the Infinite Hotel. The receptionist gets everybody to move to the room which is double the room number they have already, so that the person in room 1 moves to room 2, the person in room 3 moves to room 6, and so on for ever. This leaves all the odd-numbered rooms free, and since there are an infinite number of them, there will be no problem in accommodating an infinite number of guests.

As much as it would be useful in Florence in August, Hilbert's hotel will never be available other than as a way of showing that two times infinity (or, in fact, any finite number times infinity) is still infinity.

Hypothetical and weird it may be, but the concept is graspable. Aristotle put it succinctly, as was his wont: "The infinite has a potential existence... There will not be an actual infinite."[108] While he didn't believe that infinity is reachable, he could not rule out indefinite time sequences, because to do so would have allowed time a beginning and an end. It was his way of getting out of the quandary of reconciling his opposition to the notion of emptiness and his acceptance of the concept of infinity.

If the concept of infinity is understandable, the same cannot be said for *nothing*, even though they seem, at first glance, to have the characteristic of endlessness in common.

We could demonstrate this by deducting numbers until we reach... ? As a demonstration of infinity, it would work, since there would be no end number. As a model for *nothing*, though, it breaks down at some point. There is no common endlessness between infinity and *nothing*. Whereas with numbers towards infinity there will always be another number that could be deducted, on the movement towards *nothing* eventually we will get to something that cannot be deducted: us. At that point, when all that will be left is us, we would need to stop deducting, because there will never be *nothing* when we are around making it something.

Deducting ourselves would create an imponderable. With infinity, we can understand the concept, even if we can never reach it, whereas with *nothing* we cannot even grasp the concept of a situation in which we don't exist and that even imagining such a situation would make it something.

Nothing is not, then, infinite. And neither is it for another reason. While infinity is obviously unreachable, it is so because whatever is being applied (numbers, time, whatever) is ever-moving beyond us. *Nothing*, on the other hand, as a theoretical state of non-existence, does not move beyond our reach, or indeed move anywhere. In that sense also, *nothing* is not infinite.

So while we can grasp the concept of infinity, even if we could never actually attain it, *nothing* as a concept is impossible to grasp, to imagine or to understand, since it would require us to think of a situation that includes our non-existence. That is not to say that we can't image a world without ourselves in it; of course we can. But if we do think of such a world, it necessarily is through 'our mind's eye', present but invisible.

Nothing has the uniqueness of being finitely infinite.

Can *nothing* exist?

The **word** 'nothing' exists, that's sure. We have been using it in order to discuss the concept *nothing*. But apart from the word itself, how can *nothing* exist in any way? Asking that, though, might lay us open to an answer on the lines of US President Clinton's memorable words: "It depends on what is, is."

The British philosopher Thomas Baldwin envisaged a situation where each object in the world vanishes in sequence.[109] Eventually you get to three objects, two objects, one object and then *poof!* There's nothing.

But are we left with nothing? Let's illustrate that practicably by drawing a smiley. If we then erase the feature that gives the smiley its human characteristic – the mouth – we are left with a blank circle, a zero shape. Now erase the ring. "Nothing is a zero [0] without the [bold] ring," said an otherwise-forgettable Francis Schaeffer. After taking away the drawn circle, are we, though, left with nothing? Actually we aren't. What we have is the page or surface, and we have ourselves looking at it: we, the perceivers.

In order for something – anything – to exist, there must be at least that one thing. Without at least one thing, there is *nothing*. As Paul Dirac, the British theoretical physicist and Nobel laureate put it: "A place is nothing; not even space, unless at its heart – a figure stands."[110]

It's not any figure, though. The one figure that has to be left is us, the observer. The one thing that makes *nothing* something is us.

Even if one object is left – and it would have to be us, otherwise there would be more than one object – there is not *nothing*.

It is not only 'things' – concrete or non-concrete objects. The world is full of abstract ideas, such as the equator, the weight of the moon, the speed of light, the future. All of these ideas can, in theory, be subtracted, but only if one remains after all have been subtracted: us.

If you were the only thing in the universe, what would you see? You would not see *nothing*; you would see a different 'nothing' – nothingness. Nothingness exists because you exist, and, in a double-sided derivation, you exist because nothingness exists to distinguish you from the absence of you.

In the scenario where you are the only thing in the universe, *nothing* would not exist because your presence would make it something. If you, the last thing in the universe, disappeared, nothingness would disappear with you; there is no nothingness where there is nothing: *nothing* is the absence of everything, including nothingness. Nothingness, the absence of something, would naturally not exist where there was *nothing*.

Nothing, though, is in a category of its own. We can neither say it exists nor that it doesn't exist. To think of *nothing* existing in any way would imply that nothing does something; even 'not existing' is an exaggeration when it comes to *nothing*. On the other hand, to claim that *nothing* doesn't exist is as nonsensical as to claim it does exist when there is no observer of its 'existence' or 'non-existence'. Unlike unicorns, which we can 'see' in our minds even if they don't exist as real animals, *nothing* doesn't exist even in our imagination. No matter how hard we try, we won't be able to imagine *nothing*.

The French philosopher Henri Bergson thought of *nothing* differently. He reckoned that *nothing* can be conceptualized, but only by suppressing the awareness of being. The problem here is that the argument is circular: one needs to suppress awareness in order to conceptualize *nothing*, but to conceptualize *nothing* one has to have no awareness. Not being aware of anything would, admittedly, be similar to being aware of *nothing*; but as the person would not, and could not, be aware of *nothing*, he/she wouldn't be aware of anything else either.

Is, then, *nothing* and 'not-being' the same? After all, we have been saying that *nothing* means the absence of everything, including ourselves. The answer is that they are not the same, since any description of non-existence would necessarily be from the outside, by the observer discussing a theoretical problem. That would not be looking at *nothing*, but rather at nothingness, since it would be the non-existence not of oneself, but of someone else. It would be, in other words, the absence of something, not of everything (including oneself)

But is it true that we can't conceive of *nothing*? This is an important question that needs to be asked again. Surely we can conceive of our not being present? Yet as hard as we try, we can't. What we actually imagine is the absence of ourselves in the world. This is not *nothing*, since we are looking at the world as if we were invisible in that world. We cannot envisage our non-being within a world that we are not looking at. *Nothing* could exist only if we were around to observe it – but if we were, then *nothing* would not exist.

In a way, this is a version of the 'anthropic principle' applied to the universe: that if the universe weren't the way it is, we wouldn't be around to observe it. But that is precisely what is involved in any discussion of *nothing*: any theory of *nothing* would have to propose a situation in which humans didn't exist, since any alternative situation would not be *nothing*. To propose instead that there may **not** be *nothing* when all humans disappear and that there would be *nothing* when everything else disappeared at some later point, is, as shown earlier, conjecturing about a possible scenario imagined by humans.

And since *nothing* isn't something, we can't even begin to define it, or, we hasten to add, even refer to *nothing* as 'it'. With all its non-characteristics, we can't combine *nothing* with a verb, even a stative verb, so that even saying that 'nothing is…' is wrong (which is why looking up its definition in a dictionary is doomed).

Where is nothing?

At first glance, *nothing* seems less of a mystery when it is thought of as what there was before we were born. As the philosopher Arthur Schopenhauer put it: "After your death you will be what you were before your birth."

But equating what was before birth with what will be after death is problematic. Of course from the point of view of the person who is dead, he/she is the same state of 'nothing' (except that one doesn't have a point of view then). But, in fact, that isn't saying very much. Schopenhauer meant it to be considered by those still alive, and it is here that the comparison breaks down.

Once we know what there is, i.e. what happened after birth, the 'nothing' that was there beforehand was not *nothing*, and, in fact, was never *nothing*. The state of not-yet-being not only had the potential of being something, it did actually become something. *Nothing*, though, has no characteristics: *Nothing* does nothing and does not have the potential to be something.

The situation before birth – the state of not-yet-being – is not the same as not-being (or, indeed, of not-having-been). We were not born from *nothing*, but as a result of the fertilization of an egg with sperm. If the sperm had not fertilized the egg, you would not have been born; if that had not happened, try imagining the state you would be now! Impossible to imagine, of course, since that would be *nothing*.

Invariably, that brings us back to the larger question asked in the previous paragraph in relation to religion, as to whether there was *nothing* before there was humankind, i.e. before human consciousness.

An interesting question, asked by nuclear physicist Frank Close is, "Could there even be nothing if there were no one to know that there was nothing?"[111] In a way, this is a trick question, since the question itself assumes not only that there is such a thing as *nothing*, but also that it could be possible for someone to be aware that there was *nothing*. The point about *nothing*, though, is that it is unknowable, since knowing about it would make *nothing* something. Trick question or not, it is spot on, bringing us to the heart of what could possibly be said about *nothing* within the realm of human consciousness.

Because the concept of *nothing* is in itself so difficult, we are going to look at trees for a while. At least we know that trees exist. Let's consider that proverbial tree in the forest, in a problem raised by George Berkeley. The original, well-known question is:

> **If *a* tree fell in the forest and no one heard it, did the tree make a sound?**

To non-philosophers, it's an annoying question to which the answer is intuitively that, of course, it made a noise if it fell. However, in the light of our foray into *nothing*, that reaction might not now be as quick in coming. With the risk of making it even more annoying, but in order to make it more relevant to our subject, we will change the question slightly to:

> **If a tree fell in the forest and no one knew about, did the tree fall?**

This is basically the same question that Frank Close asked ("Could there even be nothing if there were no one to know that there was nothing?"), except that a tree has replaced *nothing*, so that his question has now been paraphrased to: ***Could there even be a tree if there were no one to know that there was a tree?***

The question is, actually, about perception and human consciousness: whether something can be said to exist if people don't know about it. And it is the same trick question that asks whether something – anything – happens if no human ever knows about it.

It is a question that infuriates because of its seemingly anthropocentric bias. Humans are not the center of the universe, we are told; animals would know about the tree falling; the world existed before humans and will continue after humans.

All of those objections may or may not be valid. And that's the point: we have no way of knowing. And not having any way of knowing could just as easily mean that nothing happens that we don't know about.

It needs to be clear that 'we' does not refer to us as individuals. Obviously if you don't know about something, it doesn't mean that it hasn't happened or that it doesn't exist. 'We' refers to all humans, who share a common consciousness. If even one person was aware of the tree falling, or knew about it afterwards, then the tree fell.

For whom do things 'happen'? Perhaps that tree fell and scattered a group of bears. Yes, perhaps it did. On the other hand, perhaps it didn't. Perhaps, in fact, no tree fell. That means that a tree falling and a tree not falling comes to the same thing. If we don't know whether something happens or doesn't happen, then what makes us even consider things about which that we have no inkling?

And here is why it's a trick question – one that has a mine buried within the question itself: as soon as we use the word 'know', even in its negative 'don't know', we are assuming that there is a particular something somewhere that we might (or might not) know. When we query if a tree fell, we are assuming that a tree might have fallen. The mine, then, explodes before we get to the end of the question. The question, in fact, cannot be asked at all, since it already contains the *possibility* of the tree having fallen.

Whether we are the center of the universe is immaterial. The point is that as far as we are concerned, the universe is what it is possible for us to conceive and only what it is possible for us to conceive.

Anything that we refer to has to be something we know about, and everything that we can think about has to be part of our conception. There is nothing else, since even what we are able to speculate as being out of what we can conceive, is, actually, within our conception in the first place.

As infuriating as the above argument may be, it is the only one in town that is relevant to us as humans. Any other argument would allow all and everything to happen that we as humans don't know about, which would mean that anything *could be* happening and that anything *could* happen. It would mean, for example, that there might be a spaghetti monster at the bottom of your garden, and that perhaps he or she is running the world. Or perhaps we really are part of a matrix, run by aliens. Or perhaps stones are alive and go for walks when we aren't looking.

It doesn't matter how wild the 'possibility' is; by allowing that anything *may* be happening, we accept the things that we do not know to be as valid as the ones that we do know. Scientific theories would, then, be useless; in a world where anything can happen, we would have to form scientific rules so wide that they would have to account for all eventualities. The rules would have to include events for which we have no evidence and that would possibly go against the scientific rules that cover data for which we do have evidence. We are pretty sure that the sun will rise tomorrow morning, and we are pretty sure that the reason our feet stay on the ground is because of gravitation and not because there might be an invisible elephant holding us down that we don't know about. Scientific rules do not cover the possibility of that invisible elephant, which they would have to do if we consider it possible that anything, including that elephant holding us down, may or may not happen.

If anything **can** happen, in other words, then we don't know what actually **is** happening. If it is possible that anything might be happening because there is a chance that we may not know about it, then we are paralysed: we can't deal with anything, since we don't know what isn't happening anywhere. Basically, knowing everything would be knowing nothing.

Our long foray into the forest was necessary. Essential, even, to illustrate the connection between *nothing* and us. In the sense that we refer to human consciousness, *nothing* is like that proverbial tree. The contention that if humans don't know about something then, for humans, it isn't relevant, applies to possible falling trees and to *nothing*.

With *nothing*, though, the whole question of awareness takes on an added dimension. Trees exist – we know what they look like and we can imagine a tree falling. Not so with *nothing*. While we can prove that a tree fell by knowing about the incident, we aren't that fortunate when it comes to *nothing*, which we can't know about in any circumstances. We cannot solve anything about *nothing*, because it can exist only when we aren't around: when we don't exist, in fact.

Our tree leads us to conclude that the question 'does *nothing* exist?' is itself nonsensical. *Nothing* is much more incontrovertible than the past existence of dinosaurs, where one can argue about bone fragments. *Nothing* is out of our conception because we simply can't conceive of our own non-existence.

The meaninglessness of even attempting a discussion on the existence of *nothing* is different to arguments over the years about the problem of proving the existence of what is not, which troubled Parmenides and all the rest. When John Carey, in his book *What Good are the Arts?*, tried to define art first by attempting to show what it is not, he found the task impossible. If that is so with art, what can we expect when we try to find out what *nothing* is by showing what it is not?

As troubling as negatives are, they refer to absences. Unlike *nothing*, nothingness can begin and it can end, as we have seen. In fact, total illusionary absence is already on the way. Scientists at the Nanoscale Science and Engineering Center at the University of California are creating new types of materials that can bend light the wrong way in order to fashion an 'invisibility cloak' over buildings so that they will not be seen from the air, thus creating artificial nothingness. Science is catching up with the magic of Harry Potter, it seems.

Nothing, of course, is different; we showed that it cannot end, since it would then not have been *nothing*. Can *nothing* begin, though? If humankind dies out, could we say that *nothing* begins at that point? The only answer would have to be with the question: For whom would *nothing* begin if there were nobody around?

If we want, then, to know where *nothing* is, we have an answer: *Nothing* is where everything is not.

The attraction of nothing
On the face of it, there is something perverse about looking for *nothing*, when everything else is out there for us to find out about. What is education about after all if it isn't about learning as much as we can? The direction, generally speaking, is towards knowing more, rather than less, obviously.

Just a cursory look at any online bookseller will bring up a plethora of books whose marketing ploy is 'everything'. They include, in no particular order: *A History of Almost Everything* by Bill Bryson, *A Brief History of Everything* by Ken Wilber, *The Interruption of Everything* by Terry McMillan, *A Reason for*

Everything : Natural Selection and the British Imagination by Marek Kohn, *Everything Bad Is Good for You: How Today's Popular Culture Is Actually Making Us Smarter* by Steven Johnson. And there are the more specialized books that are concerned with everything about a particular subject, for example, *How to Cook Everything: Simple Recipes for Great Food* by Mark Bittman, *Everything Scrabble* by Joe Edley, John D. Williams Jr., *Everything Belongs: The Gift of Contemplative Prayer* by Richard Rohr.

Of course, none of those books actually get anywhere remotely near *everything* even about their particular topics. Not surprising, of course, since, from what we have seen, *everything* is a nigh impossible situation.

As interesting as a macro view of topics is, the fundamentals of life are in the micro. The building blocks of existence are minute. It is quantum mechanics that is looking to what matter consists of, and it is the search for the basis of consciousness that might go some way to answering what makes us tick. The idea is for nature in all its complexity to be explained by the parts that makes it work, with the feeling that the smallest point we can reach will give us answers.

The puzzle as to what was around before the universe existed, or why there is a universe and not nothing, or what human consciousness is, these are questions that touch upon the mysteries of our very existence. It is not by chance that people have been wondering about *nothing* for so long, why it is looked upon with such aversion and reverence, why artists grapple with trying to represent it, and why all religions have something to say about it.

It is the uniqueness of humans that they attempt to understand *nothing*. There seems to be no other animal that is concerned with what isn't, and certainly not with trying to understand its own existence. The fascination with 'nothing' (in both senses of *nothing* and nothingness) is a reflection of the integral part that *what isn't* plays within the urge to find out *what is*.

And it is because of *what isn't* that we can see *what is*. Unlike *nothing*, that we can't get to, nothingness is everywhere that we are.

Exemplified by the stars that we see only because they have space as a background, everything is set off against the space that surrounds it. Without that space, there would not be anything to distinguish objects, or, indeed, mental images, ideas and concepts. Words on a page or on a computer screen show this nicely. The only reason that you can discern the words that you are now reading is because of the space that separates the letters from each other, the space between words and the space between sentences. This space is not *nothing* – it is nothingness,

So things – concrete and non-concrete – exist because of the space around them. Nothingness is the backing that we need if we are to see anything, or as Merleau-Ponty put it: "Our perceptual field is made up of 'things' and 'spaces between things'."[112] This space, the absence of the thing itself, is the nothingness that defines everything.

It goes the other way as well: all things define nothingness. The holes in cheese are, after all, the absence of cheese; these holes are defined by the cheese that surrounds them. Shadows – the absence of light – are similarly defined by what is around them.

This is not how Newton had characterized space; for him, space was an eternal and infinite entity that had been empty of objects for an infinite period before Creation, at which point things were placed into space. Space, for him, would exist with and without anything else.

Since then, pioneered by the work of Einstein, we have come to know that space is an abstraction from relations between objects. Without things, there would be no space. Space, the absence of something, which we have been calling nothingness, is the framework that depends on what it frames. Consequently, space can be described as having characteristics; space can grow bigger, or it can be curved or warped or have holes. Since space depends on objects (concrete or non-concrete) just as objects depend on space, nothingness is every bit as important as the objects it defines. This is what Hegel posited, already some two hundred and fifty years ago, that Being and nothingness are merely equal and opposite.

Nowhere is this shown more clearly than with shadows, which, while considered as the absence of light, can be objects in their own right. Take, for example, shadow puppets, or the well-known allegory of 'Plato's Cave', in which prisoners are forced to sit all their lives and stare at a wall on which they see only shadows projected by people passing in front of a fire behind them. For the prisoners, the shadows are reality.

Although nothingness is relative – the absence of food, of noise, of light, of anything, is always seen as relative to what it replaced or to what is still present somewhere else – that does not mean that we treat 'stuff' and nothingness the same way. In our normal lives, objects are what we relate to, not the surrounding nothingness. We are, after all, more interested in what 'is', rather than what 'is not'.

That does not mean, though, that 'what is' is more fundamental than 'what isn't'. The opposite may be the case. As the background to what everything is, nothingness could be considered as more fundamental. Just as photos represent what we want to look at, it is nevertheless the negatives from which the photos are made.

Yet this goes against the intuitive notion that space (nothingness) is dependent on what it surrounds, rather than then other way round, or as Jean-Paul Sartre, in his book *Being and Nothingness* puts it: "Nothingness, *which is not*, can have only a borrowed existence…"; by this he means that nothingness has a place only because of Being, and that if Being disappeared so would nothingness.

So having earlier asked the non-question as to whether

nothing exists as such, we can now ask the question 'Does nothingness exist?'. The answer is an unequivocal yes. It has to exist. Nothingness separates things from each other. Without nothingness there would be no things.

Nothingness, by separating things from other things, and thus differentiating between them, shows where one object begins and ends, and, by extension, where nothingness begins and ends. To put it another way, an explanation of how something exists is an explanation of how that something began. Trees are there because they grew from seeds, and clouds are formed from condensed water that forms visible cloud droplets. Without pointing to its beginning, it is hard to see how there could be an explanation of its existence, which is why the perplexing question of whether the chicken or the egg came first drives everyone crazy. Everything begins from something – which would bring us back to the previous chapter. The universe began from something: as a result of the Big Bang, or of God, or whatever.

In fact, though, all somethings begin from nothingness, just as nothingness begins from something. Where one begins, the other ends.

Human progress has to do with filling in gaps. We are beguiled more by what we do NOT have than about what we do have. Exploration and search for knowledge is, after all, a search for what we do not yet know, the continuing challenge of humankind.

Nothingness is part of what we are. We are not 'complete' in that we are always striving for something that is absent. It is that nothingness that we constantly try to fill. We never will, of course. Sometimes we do so temporarily, but it is an ongoing battle. When we are hungry, for example, we experience the absence of food and strive to fill the absence. We work in order to fill the absence of money or power or personal fulfilment.

In the sense that an object is absent, it is negative. Yet that doesn't make it any less significant than objects that are there, and a number of thinkers have referred to the place of 'negation' within their investigations into the meaning of reality. Kant referred to "negative magnitude"[113] as the object that we are constantly looking for and that is real even though, but because, we aren't in possession of it, while Freud opined that through asserting what is not, people actually affirm what is.[114] Nothingness is not only an absence that needs to be filled, but also an absence that may never be filled. The urge to move into the void (called 'the death wish' by Freud) is what makes us continue living.

Often the nothingness that needs to be filled is an ideal: God, beauty, strength, whatever. But being an ideal, it can never be attained; its place is just beyond the horizon. Seen in that light, the saying 'Absence makes the heart grow fonder' is not an endearing or encouraging truism, but, rather, a sobering commentary on relationships that require distance to keep the idea alive.

The only absence that is not relative is *nothing*: the complete absence of everything. *Nothing* has no potential, in contrast to nothingness that is the potential to become what is from what isn't. The importance of nothingness, then, is not what it 'is', but what its possibility is of becoming.

It is not surprising that we can attempt to understand nothingness but we can't even attempt to understand *nothing*. If nothingness is the result of our pursuit of Being, *nothing* does not tell us anything about ourselves, because it can't. If it could tell us something, it would be about our non-existence.

Nothingness has to do with our potential as humans, while *nothing* brings us face to face with what is beyond us.

Nothing at the end

Jean-Paul Sartre's seminal book *L'etre et le Néant* is known in English as "Being and Nothingness". The translation is misleading. Although Sartre's 'néant' is commonly translated into English as 'nothingness', the French word means 'absolute nothing' (equivalent to our *nothing*); he chose to use 'néant', rather than 'rien', which has a much looser meaning, somewhat akin to our 'nothingness'.

There are similar problems with the translations of Heidegger's works. Heidegger's original German term was 'das Nichts', an amorphous term that, with the definite article ('the nothing'), was clearly intended to mean *nothing*.

Is that important? Why would it matter? The reason, as is by now clear, is that if we want to look into the basis of existence, it is essential to differentiate between *nothing* and nothingness, each of which plays its separate part in how we can possibly conceive of our own existence.

It is not a matter only of translation. Both Sartre and Heidegger – as seen from the original languages – mean to deal with *nothing*, but in fact are referring to something else.

With Sartre, the problem is illuminated as soon as he defines his central term. When he states that 'néant' (*nothing*, in its clearer translation) is the absence of Being, and later qualifies *nothing* as the state after death, he, in fact, gives it characteristics that make *nothing* into something. This is compounded when he claims that *nothing* is a state that one can imagine.

When Sartre wrote that "nothing [néant] lies coiled in the heart of being," he defined *nothing* as the absence of being. His intention was to demonstrate that the notion of non-existence – death – was essential within that of existence: not only that death has a role to play within life, but that existence has no meaning when its opposite is not taken into account.

Earlier, Freud, in his theories of psychology, had also referred to opposites, but he saw them balanced in terms of human drives – life and death instincts.

For Sartre, though, existence was not a drive as such, but a human deep-seated awareness that 'nothing' was part of life. For Martin Heidegger, who also saw 'nothing' [das Nichts] as the basis for existence, 'nothing' is what makes it possible for us to be aware that there is something, and also because it draws our attention to the fact that there could be 'nothing' instead. Anxiety is experienced when 'nothing' slips away and we are left with our 'being-towards-death'. We are born to die, in other words.

Both Sartre and Heidegger based their claims on 'nothing' as an absence, that which we define as the characteristic of *nothingness*.

For Sartre, Heidegger and the Danish philosopher Søren Kierkegaard before them, the dread of death, of a future not-being, was so terrible as to be the controlling thread of one's life. The fear of death is imbued so thoroughly that living is itself a horror, since it will one day be sure to end. Or as a recent book title has it: *The Thing About Life is that One Day You'll be Dead.*[115]

Interestingly, the dread of death as described by philosophers is different to the way religions deal with death, where, rather than dread, it is a continuation of life, albeit in a different way.

The point is, though, that while we can imagine dying, we cannot imagine the state of our being dead.

Death is, after all, not an experience at all. At the most it is second-hand knowledge – but knowledge of nothingness, not of *nothing*. It is knowledge of someone else's death, which, as the French philosopher Emmanuel Levinas puts it: "The experience of death that is not mine is an 'experience' of a death of *someone*, someone who from the outset is beyond biological processes, who is associated with me as someone."[116]

Is there a whiff of hope within all the gloom? Most certainly there is, since death is always of someone else. Levinas, while claiming that the overwhelming fear of one's annihilation is an essential part of what it means to be aware of one's existence, nevertheless talks about the doubt associated with *nothing*. Levinas implies that we can't know everything, certainly not about what happens after death. The result is a big question mark on *nothing*.

Nothingness is different, though. Nothingness is an absence that we can feel, so that when it is the absence of life it is always the absence of others' lives. And it is certainly reasonable to have fear of it, considering the inevitability of death. Yet it has never happened to us as individuals! We ALWAYS reach an event for which we had been waiting, no matter how far ahead it was originally. Only those who have died don't reach that event – never us.

As far as we are concerned, we are immortal. Whatever fear we may have of dying, of nothingness, we – 'I' – never get to it. Wittgenstein put it like this: "Death is not an event in life: we do not live to experience death. If we take eternity to mean not infinite temporal duration but timelessness, then eternal life belongs to those who live in the present. Our life has no end in just the way in which our visual field has no limits."[117]

Our feeling of immortality is not based on logic, reason or intuition. Of course we know we will die; it just never happens to *us*. It is a feeling based on *nothing* – literally. Or, to put it accurately, the non-acceptance of *nothing*.

It is the Nothing gene that protects us from the concept of *nothing*, so that even an awareness of others' deaths does not allow us to grasp the notion of the world without us, our non-being. In this way the Nothing gene is a survival gene, in that it gives hope within the illusion of our personal mortality.

Unlike nothingness and existence, that depend on each other, *nothing* is not dependent on anything and so is not part of a duality. *Nothing* is the absence of everything but is not dependent on it. *Nothing* does not come into existence with the disappearance of everything. When everything disappears, so do we.

It stands to reason, then, that *nothing* is not part of competing inner drives, on the lines of Freud's life instinct and death instinct. The Nothing gene does not subscribe to Freud's notion that 'the aim of all life is death', which would, in any case, apply only to others, not to 'me'. As a survival gene, the Nothing gene is the opposite of what is proposed by Freud's 'death drive' (which Freud speculated as countering the pleasure principle). In any case the aversion to *nothing* is not psychological, since otherwise it would not be a universal human characteristic. The key is a Nothing gene. The Nothing gene does not 'do' anything, but is, rather, as demonstrated with religions, a blocking gene that disallows our understanding of a personal state of non-being.

It is the impossibility of understanding *nothing* that allows people to accept the dichotomy of life and death with equanimity. It is not ambivalence, that philosopher Havi Carel claims, "links love and hate, beauty and transience, life and death, a link that stands at the basis of the unified view."[118] If there is acceptance, it is of dying (nothingness), not to the state of being dead (*nothing*). It is the **not** being able to understand *nothing* that facilitates the acceptance of our future demise.

Limits, language and understanding

Within discussions of fundamental problems, the question is often raised as to whether there really are such things as philosophical problems or whether, as Ludwig Wittgenstein claimed in his *Tractatus Logico-Philosophicus*, that philosophy boils down to nothing more than a series of linguistic puzzles. That is what caused his depressing conclusion that since we can't stand outside language and the world and describe the relationship between them, we can't say anything at all about philosophical problems.

Later, Wittgenstein changed his opinion about this conclusion, admitting in his *Philosophical Investigations* that perhaps the *Tractatus* had been over-simplified as opposed to "...the multiplicity of the tools in language and the ways they are used." Problems within philosophy are, in fact, a problem of language, he claimed, which need to be solved through looking at how language is actually used.

Is our inability to define *nothing* due to the nature of language and not to the impossibility of our conceiving *nothing*? In a nutshell: Is the problem not *nothing*, but one of language? Or perhaps limitation of language is the other side of the coin to limitation of imagination. When it comes to the concept of *nothing*, then, the question is whether problems transcend language, or whether the whole notion of *nothing* is simply not within the realm of ordinary language.

Or perhaps it is something else: of the human mind being limited, so that the most profound problems are just too much for it. This has been a not-too popular suspicion discussed through the ages. Plato, Kant, Wittgenstein, Chomsky, and latterly with much gusto, Colin McGinn, take the position that there are questions that are beyond our capacity to answer.[119]

The fact that there are questions that we can't answer should not come as a surprise. There are questions that we will never be able to answer if only because we are human! We will never, for example, understand what it means to be a whale, or to be inside the head of a bird. Constituted the way we are makes us incapable of becoming a whale or a bird.

It's even worse: we can't even 'be' another person; however close we are to someone and however much we 'feel' that person's pain, we do not feel that actual pain. All we can do is to imagine the pain – and only because we feel pain in our way. Language has nothing to do with this incapacity to 'be' another person, and neither does our intellectual capacity.

Mysterianism, a new-old theory that claims we aren't capable of understanding fundamental problems such as consciousness, was propounded by, among others, Gottfried Leibniz in the seventeenth century, Dr Johnson in the eighteenth, and Thomas Huxley in the nineteenth. The most active modern exponent is the philosopher Colin McGinn, whose basic point is that there are some problems – 'mysteries' – that lie outside the capacities we have as humans. "We have," he says, "gaps in our cognitive skills as we have gaps in our motor skills,"[120] and he gives the example of humans being unable to fly unassisted due to lack of the right 'organs', which he applies to unanswerable thought questions. The same limitation applies to all creatures who have structures that can deal with certain functions and not with others.

A strong argument against this is that a solution may present itself at some point in the future. Just like past insoluble mysteries were solved, so may current ones. We don't, after all, know that what seems to be beyond our mental capacity at any point is so only because we haven't yet been able to take advantage of new knowledge.

Could that apply to the concept of *nothing*? Is it simply that our human limitations, or that of language, stop us from understanding *nothing*? Perhaps for intelligent aliens, the concept of *nothing* is no problem at all!

There may be another possibility. Perhaps *nothing* is an example not of knowledge that we can't grasp, but, rather, of a concept that we simply can't convey to someone else. This would be a problem of *articulable* language, which is held out as the reason for the difficulty in getting across the notion of God and beliefs. What is felt as intuitive knowledge can often not be communicated further. It may be impossible to communicate the nature of God, as we have seen, but that doesn't mean that believers don't accept God's existence and know his attributes. For them, they and God are in the world. Understanding an issue while at the same time not being able to explain it does not mean that it doesn't exist, only that the information cannot be passed on. (Knowing that the tree fell means that it did, even if we don't communicate that to anyone.)

Now if all or any of those possibilities apply to difficulties understanding fundamental problems, such as, for example, human consciousness, free will, thoughts and their link to a physical brain, they do not hold water when it comes to *nothing*. *Nothing* is unique, so much so that it is erroneous even to say that it is in a class of its own; putting it in any class, even if it were alone, would make *nothing* something.

Admittedly, there is a problem when it comes to the declared position that we are simply not capable of understanding something. For a start, though, *nothing* is not something. Other notions that seem to reach the limits of our understanding are available as concepts for us to puzzle out. *Nothing*, on the other hand, is not.

The claim that some problems are incapable of being solved contains its own destructive weakness, for it means that humans have been built in some way that we will **never** be able to understand some fundamental problems. The paradox here, as pointed out by Nicholas Fearn, is that we would not know if we are capable of knowing enough about an issue until we know something about it. How far along we would need to go in order to come to a conclusion is what makes the paradox deliciously crazy.

That may be so, but there is no paradox when it comes to one issue: *nothing*. We will never know anything about *nothing*, for anything we know will put us in the same world as *nothing*. And that, as is clear by now, would make *nothing* something.

Nothing is not, in fact, a problem. *Nothing* isn't anything. *Nothing* just isn't.

As complex as are the issues commonly grouped together as The Meaning of Life, both *nothing* that isn't and *nothingness* that is get us closer to the most fundamental issue of all: our own existence.

While nothingness shows us what is, *nothing* allows us to understand our own limitations. Both show us what it is to be human.

Above all, one thing is clear: *Nothing* is impossible. Very much so.

Notes

1. The earliest indication of rudimentary counting in the Stone Age was the discovery in 1937 in Moravia, then-Czechoslovakia of a wolf bone some 30,000 years old that had on it notches within varying series.
2. Kelvin, 1889.
3. Roman numerals do have a limited positional system, particularly with the placement of the number I to the left or right of certain other numbers. To the left it reduces the number, while to the right it adds to the number. V = 5, IV = 4, VI = 6; X = 10, IX = 9, XI = 11. This does not take away from the fact that the numerals themselves always have the same value: I is always 1, V is always 5, X is always 10.
4. Based on a sentence composed by Noam Chomsky – "Colorless green ideas sleep furiously." – as an example of a sentence which is grammatically correct but is nonsensical.
5. In his work, the Brahmasphutasiddhanta in 628, Brahmagupta set out rules for arithmetic on negative numbers and zero which are quite close to the modern understanding. Brahmagupta failed when he attempted to define division by zero, which cannot be done with real numbers and is left undefined in modern mathematics. His definition is, literally, empty; for instance, he states that $0/0 = 0$.
6. Three hundred years later the division by zero in Einstein's equations lead to the acceptance of an Expanding Universe.
7. Sura 19:67.
8. Shlomo Sela, 1977.
9. Quoted in *Numbers Through the Ages* by G. Flegg.
10. A recent book to tell us that is *Zero: The Biography of a Dangerous Idea* by Charles Seife.

11. Called as such by Tobias Dantzig, 2005.

12. Published in "Proceedings of the National Academy of Sciences," February 2006.

13. It is interesting to note that some animals also have number sense (although none have the ability to count), and although none has been discerned in higher mammals, some birds and certain wasps do have number sense. See Barry Mazur, Tobias Dantzig, Joseph Mazur.

14. Sartre, 1969 (p. 41).

15. Words & music by Roy Turk and Lou Handman, 1926. Recorded by Elvis Presley April 4, 1960.

16. The many examples of what the Church accepted with much reluctance included:
    - the Mendicant orders of St. Francis and St. Dominican
    - originally-pagan customs in its calendar of festivities: May Day, Whitsun, All-Fools Day, Halloween, days of the months and weeks with pagan/Emperor names
    - property and wealth in opposition to Apostolic poverty
    - the idea of a Just War in opposition to the teachings of pacifism
    - the idea of icons that it had opposed in the Byzantine Church
    - principles of classical humanism in the arts
    - secular investiture, nepotism, and simony.

17. Monty Python and the Flying Circus: Vocational Guidance Counsellor, 1969.

18. From the translation by J.B. Geijsbeek, Ancient Double Entry Bookkeeping: Lucas Pacioli's Treatise, 1914.

19. Some examples are: *Leonardo da Vinci* by Kenneth Clark, *Leonardo da Vinci and a Memory of His Childhood* (1910) by Sigmund Freud, *Cosmic Trigger III* by Robert Anton Wilson, *The Heretic's Feast* by Colin Spencer, *Mary Magdalene: Christianity's Hidden Goddess* by Lynn Picknett – in which the author discusses the possibility that the *Mona Lisa* is

really a self-portrait of Leonardo in drag, as well as the suggestion that Leonardo used himself as the model for St. Anne in *The Virgin and Child with St. Anne* (c. 1510), *The Templar Revelation* by Lynn Picknett and Clive Prince.

20. Number 1216 from *The Notebooks of Leonardo da Vinci* edited by Jean Paul Richter, 1880.

21. Jesus was born in the reign of King Herod, who died in 4 BC, according to Matthew and the historian Josephus. If he did die then, Jesus would have had to be born before that date.

22. Different calendar calculations have given Christmas for the Armenians on January 6th, and for the Coptic, Jerusalem, Russian, Serbian and Georgian Orthodox churches on January 7th).

23. BC (Before Christ) is the English translation of Bede's *Ante Christum Natum*.

24. Part of the calculations of Easter and other Christian dates – see Cheney, 2000.

25. Naomi Klein, "Baghdad Year Zero" *Harper's Magazine*, 2004.

26. Bosley Crowther's critique in the New York Times of the movie *Goodbye, Charlie*, November 19, 1964.

27. Interestingly, the symbol he used was a circle, although it was not more than a punctuation mark, certainly not a mathematical symbol or even a place holder.

28. Interview with Tim Adams, *Sunday Times*, November 19, 2006.

29. http://filmsound.org/QA/creating-silence.htm

30. *The Day of Battle: The War in Sicily and Italy*, 1943-1944, 2007.

31. "The Aesthetics of Silence", (1983).

32. Grove Press, 1967.

33. The term "minimalism" was adopted from a 1965 essay entitled "Minimal Art" by British philosopher Richard Wollheim. Wollheim was referring, though, not to the art

itself, but the minimal conditions that might satisfy the definition 'work of art'. The term 'minimalism' was borrowed from his speculations and applied to the work of artists such as John McCracken, Donald Judd, and Robert Morris, to the great distaste of most of the artists to whom the term applied.

34. *The Absence of the 20th Century*, translated by Jorge Jauregui: http://www.lacan.com/frameXVIII5.htm

35. Warhol's actual statement, in 1968 was that: "In the future, everyone will be world-famous for 15 minutes." In 1979 he referred to it again: "...my prediction from the sixties finally came true: In the future everyone will be famous for fifteen minutes."

36. Details about this blue stamp have been described by John Held Jr. in "The Formidable Blue Stamp of Yves Klein" – http://www.mailartist.com/johnheldjr/YvesKlein.html

37. Silence, Lectures & Writings, 1961 (pp. 7, 8).

38. Absolute silence has been associated with death. John Cage stated that: "Until we die there will be sounds." He came to the same conclusion regarding silence as Jacques Derrida did regarding death – that the *I* can never experience it.

39. Jenny Diski, *On Trying to Keep Still*, 2006.

40. Jean Baudrillard, *America*, 1988 (p. 7).

41. *Stealing the Mona Lisa*, 2002.

42. The Guardian, April 2004. http://www.johnpawson.com/essays/minimalism.

43. May 10, 2007, in an interview on the occasion of the opening of first major Spencer Finch exhibition at Massachusetts Museum of Contemporary Art.

44. K.C. Cole: *The Hole in the Universe: How Scientists Peered over the Edge of Emptiness and Found Everything*, 2001.

45. *From Art as Art, The selected writings of Ad Reinhardt* (undated).

46. *A Nocturnal upon St. Lucy's Day*, stanza 2.

47. Kasimir Malevich, trans. Howard Dearstyne, 1959.

48. Malevich was not the only Russian artist painting monochrome squares as part of a Russian movement that wanted to analyze the primary elements of all experience: to go back to a modular two-by-four art, to strip away everything until only the fundamental, elemental basics of art remained. An example of this is Rodchenko's 1921 three squares of *Pure Red, Pure Yellow, and Pure Blue*. But by representing art itself and not anything outside it (like feelings), he was closer to Ad Reinhardt than to Malevich. Rodchenko survived longer in the brave new world of the Soviet Union than did Malevich, mainly by his later art and architecture "in the service of the Soviet Union."

49. The first time the color white was the actual subject of a picture was in mid-18th-century France, when Jean-Baptiste Oudry used only tones of white to demonstrate the relativity of whiteness in a series of still-life paintings. A more recent – and more well-known – image using white is the Beatles "White Album" cover designed by Richard Hamilton in 1968.

50. The association of *nothing* with virginity and purity, mentioned earlier, takes on added color (pun intended) when it is linked to white with a similar allusion so inherent in Christian symbolism. **White** symbolizes the purity of the soul, innocence, and holiness from whence derives the tradition of the white wedding dress and the white robes and collars worn by Christian clergy. The Virgin Mary holding the white lily and often portrayed wearing white symbolizes the Immaculate Conception. Artists from the Renaissance to the 20th century have used lilies, doves, lambs, horses and white clothing to signal innocence, purity, or heroism.

51. http://theartofmemory.blogspot.com/2007_04_01_archive .html

52. *With a Little Help from My Friends*, Lennon/McCartney, 1977.
53. *William Hazlitt, Complete Works*, 1930.
54. There is a surprisingly long list in Nicolas Slonimsky's *Lexicon of Musical Invective* of now popular pieces that were lambasted when they were first heard.
55. "Art and Elitism: A Form of Pattern Recognition" *Britannia Blog*, November 14, 2007.
56. http://www.artrenewal.org/articles/2003/Claudio_Lombardo/lombardo1.php.
57. Camille Gizzarelli's Art Appreciation Site: http://www.bellaonline.com/articles/art46268.asp.
58. *The Madonna of the Future*, 2000.
59. Ecclesiastes 1:9-14 NIV: "What has been will be again, what has been done will be done again; there is nothing new under the sun."
60. Most memorably performed by Pete Seeger in 1962, it was recorded by a number of artists, including Nina and Frederick, Elvis Costello and Malvina Reynolds herself.
61. *The Emotion Machine*, 2007.
62. *Pictures of Nothing*, 2003.
63. This statement would be challenged by many Eastern faiths, as we will see in the next chapter.
64. BBC News, 23 September 2002.
65. Katie Siegel, Artforum International Magazine, Inc. 2001.
66. "Collected Poems, 1956-1998".
67. First published in *Die Neue Rundschau*, 1922.
68. *The Independent*, March 4, 2007.
69. July/August edition.
70. "The Art World", 1964
71. *What Good are the Arts?*, 2005.
72. "Mark Rothko at Tate Modern" by Rachel Campbell-Johnston in *The Times*, September 24, 2008.
73. A later interpretation is given in the Second Book of Maccabees, which is accepted as part of the Bible by many

Christians (including Roman Catholics, but not Protestants) but is missing from the Hebrew biblical canon. "Beholding the heavens and the earth, and seeing all that is there, you will understand that God has created it all from nothing" (2 Macc. 7:28). Within Christian canon, creation from nothing is mentioned later, as, for example: "All things were made by him; and without him was not any thing made that was made." (John 1:3). In the Quran, reference is made to creation of man from nothing: "But does man not bear in mind that We have created him aforetime out of nothing?" (19:67).

74. From 'Carolingian debates over Nihil and Tenebrae: A Study in Theological Method', *Speculum*, 59, (1984), (pp. 757-795).

75. XXVII.

76. While not mentioned specifically in the liturgy that sums up the creed of most Christian Churches, creation from *nothing* is certainly alluded to. The first line, with slight variations, of the Nicene Creed, the profession of faith, says "I believe in one God, the Father Almighty, Creator of heaven and earth, of all things visible and invisible."

77. Birch.

78. Bede Rundle, *Why there is Something rather than Nothing*, 2006.

79. Prigogine, *The End of Certainty*, 1996.

80. Marcus Chown: *The Never-Ending Days of Being Dead*, 2007.

81. *The Human Touch*, 2006

82. He applies this mystical description to the existence of commodities, in his description of Marxism – 1994.

83. Victor Stenger, in his book *God: The Failed Hypothesis,* states that something is more natural than nothing, and that the universe appeared as a natural, uncaused phase transition of nothing to something analogous to water changing to ice. We have all emerged, he states, from an original state

of frozen nothing. The analogy is flawed, though, since it is only *something* that can be frozen. Anything frozen is something, not nothing. It is interesting that water is used as an analogy in an anti-God book, considering the same scenario is described, albeit as physically true, in many theistic accounts of the creation of the world.

84. In Protestantism, the centrality of humans is even more emphasized. It was Luther who stated that everything depends on the conviction that God became man 'for us'. To believe in Christ, he argued, is to believe that God has presented mankind with a visible exact image of himself.

85. See Mt 6:5-6 and Lk 6:12.

86. See 57:4.

87. Kathryn Harrison in *Saint Thérèse of Lisieux*.

88. *Why He is a Saint: The True Story of John Paul II* by Slawomir Oder and Saverio Gaeta.

89. Elias Hicks (1748-1830], the American Quaker, echoing the train and style of Robert Barclay, one of the most important Quaker writers.

90. Interview with Tim Adams, *Sunday Times*, November 19, 2006.

91. As suggested, among others, by Nicholas Wade in *The Faith Instinct*, 2009.

92. David ben Abraham Ha-Laban, 1300.

93. *Conjectures of a Guilty Bystander*, 1968.

94. "What is Contemplative Spirituality and Why is It Dangerous?" 1997.

95. Udana 8:3; Khudda Nikaya, in *Minor Anthologies*, (p. 98).

96. "I form light, and I create darkness: I produce well being, and I create evil, I Yahweh do all these things" (Is. 45:7); "... I am shaping evil against you and devising a plan against you" (Jer.18:11); "does evil befall a city, unless the Lord has done it?" (Amos 3:6).

97. *The God Delusion*, 2006.

98. *Science and Health* 426:23.
99. *The Christian Science Sentinel*, May 5 1906.
100. *S&H* 486:14.
101. Deepak Chopra & Michael "Zappy" Zapolin with Alys R. Yablon, 2006.
102. "The Beatles, the Maharishi and Me." *The Sunday Times*, February 10, 2008.
103. Andrew Brown's blog: http://www.guardian.co.uk/commentisfree/andrewbrown /2010/jan/05/religion-islam
104. Interview in *Le Monde*, August 18, 2004.
105. Guthrie, 1965.
106. *Primacy*, 190.
107. *Primacy*, 187, 180.
108. Aristotle, Physics, Book 3, Chapter 6.
109. "There Might be Nothing", 1996.
110. *Principles of Quantum Mechanics*, 1982.
111. *Nothing: A Very Short Introduction*, 2009.
112. *Phenomenology of Perception*, 1962.
113. *Theoretical Philosophy* 1755-1770.
114. "Negation" in *The Standard Edition*, 1925.
115. David Shields, 2009.
116. *God, Death and Time*, 1975.
117. *Tractatus Logico-Philosophicus*, 6.4311.
118. Havi Carel, 2006.
119. Nicholas Fearn, 2005.
120. McGinn, 1993.

Bibliography

Atkinson, Rick. 2007. *The Day of Battle: The War in Sicily and Italy,* 1943-1944. (Volume Two of the Liberation Trilogy.) Henry Holt & Company

Baldwin, Thomas. 1996. "There Might be Nothing", *Analysis* 56.4 (pp. 231-238)

Barnes, Julian. 2008. *Nothing to Be Frightened Of.* Knopf

Barrow, John. 1992. *Pi in the Sky.* Oxford University Press

Bataille, Georges. (1994 [1976]). *The Absence of Myth. Writings on Surrealism* (trans Michael Richardson). NY/London: Verso

Baudrillard, Jean. 1988. *America.* London: Verso

Beckett, Samuel. 1967. *Stories and Texts for Nothing.* Grove Press, NY. Originally published as Noevelles et Textes pour rien, 1958, by Les Éditions de Minuit, Paris

Ben Abraham Ha-Laban, David. 1300. Mesoret Habrit. In *Mekitzi Nirdamim,* 1306

Birch, Cyril, Fowler, Rosamund. 2000. *Tales from China (Oxford Myths and Legends).* Oxford University Press USA

Born, Max. 1969. "Symbol and reality", in *Physics in my Generation*

Brown, Dan. 2003. *The Da Vinci Code.* Bantam Press

Bryson, Bill. 2003. *A Short History of Nearly Everything.* Doubleday

Caddock, John. 1997. "What is *Contemplative* Spirituality and Why is It Dangerous? A Review of Brennan Manning's *The Signature of Jesus.* Journal of the Grace Evangelical Society, Autumn 1997 – Volume 10:19

Cage, John. 1961. *Silence: Lectures and Writings,* Wesleyan University Press, Hanover

Carel, Havi. 2006. *Life and Death in Freud and Heidegger.* Rodopi, New York

Carey, John. 2005. *What Good are the Arts?* Faber and Faber

Carroll, Lewis. 2007. *Alice's Adventures in Wonderland.* Vintage Classics

Cheney, C.R. 2000. *A Handbook of Dates*. Cambridge University Press

Chimnoy, Sri. 1974. "Between Nothingness and Eternity". *Poet Seers* – www.poetseers.org

Chopra, Deepak, Zapolin, Michael "Zappy", and Yablon, Alys R. 2006. *Ask the Kabala Oracle Cards Guidebook*. Hay House

Chown, Marcus. 2007. *The Never-Ending Days of Being Dead*. Faber and Faber, London

Clark Kenneth, Kemp Martin, 1993. *Leonardo da Vinci*. Penguin Books

Close, Frank. 2009. *Nothing: A Very Short Introduction*. OUP Oxford

Cole, K.C. 2001. *The Hole in the Universe: How Scientists Peered over the Edge of Emptiness and Found Everything*. Harcourt

Crean, Thomas. 2007. *God is No Delusion: A Refutation of Richard Dawkins*. Ignatius Press, San Francisco

Critchley, Simon. 2008. *The Book of Dead Philosophers*. Granta Books

Crosby, A.W., 1997. *The Measure of Reality: Quantification and Western Society*. New York: Cambridge University Press

Danto, Arthur C. 1964. "The Art World", *The Journal of Philosophy*, lxi 19

– 2000. *The Madonna of the Future – Essays in a Pluralistic Art World*. New York: Farrar, Straus & Giroux

Danzig, Tobias, Joseph Mazur, Barry Mazur. 2005. *Number: The Language of Science*, The Masterpiece Science Edition. Pi Press

Dass, Ram. 1971. *Remember, Be Here Now*. Lama Foundation, San Cristobal, New Mexico

Dawkins, Richard. 2006. *The God Delusion*. 2006. Bantam Press, UK

– 1986. The Blind Watchmaker. W.W. Norton, NY

Derrida, Jacques. 1994. *Specters of Marx, the state of the debt, the Work of Mourning, & the New International*, translated by Peggy Kamuf, Routledge

Dirac, P.A.M. 1958. *The Principles of Quantum Mechanics*, Oxford University Press

Diski, Jenny. 2006. *On Trying to Keep Still*. Little, Brown

Ebert, Theodor. 2009. *Der rätselhafte Tod des René Descartes*. Alibri; Auflage: 1. Germany

Eco, Umberto. 1994. *The Island of the Day Before*. Trans. 1995 by William Weaver. Harcourt Brace & Company

Eddy, Mary Baker (1875/1906). *Science and Health with Key to the Scriptures*. The Christian Science Publishing Society. Boston MA

Farthing, Stephen. 2007. *1001 Paintings You Must See Before You die*. Universe

Fearn, Nicholas. 2005. *Philosophy: The Latest Answers to the Oldest Questions*. Atlantic Books, UK

Flegg, G. 1989. *Numbers Through the Ages*. Macmillan, London

Flew, Antony, Varghese, Roy Abraham. 2007. *There Is a God: How the World's Most Notorious Atheist Changed His Mind*. HarperCollins

Frayn, Michael. 2006. *The Human Touch*. Faber

Freud, Sigmund. 1910. *Leonardo da Vinci and a Memory of His Childhood*. Norton, NY

– 1925. *The Standard Edition of the Complete Psychological Works of Sigmund Freud*, Volume XIX (1923-1925)

Golding, William. *1956. Pincher Martin*, London: Faber and Faber

Guthrie, W.K.C. 1965. *A History of Greek Philosophy*, vol. 2, Cambridge University Press

Hamer, Dean H. 2005. *The God Gene: How Faith is Hardwired into our Genes*. Anchor Books

Harrison, Kathryn. 2003. *Saint Thérèse of Lisieux*. Weidenfeld & Nicolson

Haught, John, F. 2007. *God and the New Atheism: A Critical Response to Dawkins, Harris, and Hitchens*. Westminster John Knox Press, Louisville, Kentucky

Heidegger, Martin. 1996. "What Is Metaphysics?" in *Basic

Writings, ed. D. Farre'l Krell. London: Routledge

– 1996. *Being and Time*, trans. J. Macquarrie and E. Robinson. London: Blackwell

Herbert, Zbigniew. 2007. *Collected Poems, 1956-1998*. Ecco/HarperCollins

Hopkins, Jasper. 1985. *Nicholas of Cusa on Learned Ignorance: A Translation and an Appreaisal of De Docta Ignorantia*. Minneapolis: The Arthur J. Banning Press

Howe, P.P. ed. 1930. *William Hazlitt, Complete Works. Centenary Edition*. J. M. Dent and Sons, Ltd., London

Hugo, Victor. 1862. *Les Misérables*. Norman Denny, trans. Penguin Classics

Idel, Moshe. 1988. *Studies in Ecstatic Kabbalah*. State Univ of New York Press

Johnson, D.D.P. (2005) God's punishment and public goods: A test of the supernatural punishment hypothesis in 186 world cultures. *Human Nature* 16, 410-446

Johnson, D.D.P. & Bering, J.M. 2006. Hand of God, mind of man: Punishment and cognition in the evolution of cooperation. *Evolutionary Psychology* 4: 219–233

Kafka, Franz. 1992. *The Metamorphosis and Other Stories*, trans. Malcolm Pasley. Penguin Books

Kant,Immanuel. 1755-1770. *Theoretical Philosophy*. Translated and edited by David Walford in collaboration with Ralf Meerbote. Cambridge: CUP, 1992

Kaplan, Robert. 2000. *The Nothing that Is: A Natural History of Zero*. New York: Oxford University Press

Kelvin, W.T. 1989. "Electrical Units of Measurement" in W.T. Kelvin, *Popular Lectures and Addresses*, Macmillan

Kiesler, Frederick. 1964, 1966. *Inside the Endless House: Art, People, and Architecture: A Journal*. New York: Simon & Schuster

Klein, Naomi. 2004. *Baghdad Year Zero*. Harper's Magazine

Kline, Morris. 1972. *Mathematical Thought from Ancient to Modern Times*, Oxford Univ Press, New York

Klosterman, Chuck. 2007. *Chuck Klosterman IV*. Faber

Koyré, A. 1973. *The Astronomical Revolution: Copernicus-Kepler-Borelli*. New York: Dover

Lanzetta, Beverly J. 2001. *The Other Side of Nothingness: Toward a Theology of Radical* Openness. Albany: State University of New York

Leader, Darian. 2002. *Stealing the Mona Lisa*. Counterpoint, NY

Leanhardt, A. *et al.* 2003. *Science* 301 1513

Leeming, Joseph. 1953. *Riddles, Riddles, Riddles*, New York: Franklin Watts, Inc

Lem, Stanislaw. 1974. *The Cyberiad: Fables for the Cybernetic Age*. Seabury Press

Le Poidevin, Robin. 2003. *Travels in Four Dimensions*. Oxford Univ Press, New York

Levinas, Emmanuel. 2001. *God, Death and Time (Meridian: Crossing Aesthetics)*, foreword Jacques Rolland, trans. Bettina Bergo. Stanford University Press

Logan, Robert K. 1986. *The Alphabet Effect: The Impact of the Phonetic Alphabet on the Development of Western Civilization*, St. Martin's Press, New York

Lydiat, Anne. 1999. *Lost For Words*. Lydiat

Lyotard, Jean-Francois. 1991. "The Sublime and the Avant-Garde", in *The Inhuman: Reflection on Time*, trans. Geoff Bennington and R. Bowlby. Stanford: Stanford University Press

Malevich, Kasimir. 1959. *The Non-objective World*, trans. Howard Dearstyne, Paul Theobald

Mather, G.A., Nichols, Larry A. (eds). 1993. *The Zondervan Dictionary of Cults, Sects, Religions and the Occult*. Zondervan

McGinn, B., 2001, *The Mystical Thought of Meister Eckhart: The Man from Whom God Hid Nothing*, New York

McGinn, C. 1993. Problems in Philosophy. Oxford: Blackwell

McGrath, Alister E., McGrath, Joanna Collicutt. 2007. *The Dawkins Delusion?: Atheist Fundamentalism and the Denial of the Divine*.

IVP Books, UK

Merleau-Ponty, Maurice. 1962. *Phenomenology of Perception* trans. by Colin Smith, New York: Humanities Press

– 1964. *The Primacy of Perception*. Evanston, Ill: Northwestern University Press

Merton, Thomas. 1968. *Conjectures of a Guilty Bystander*. Image

Minsky, Marvin. 2006. *The Emotion Machine: Commonsense Thinking, Artificial Intelligence and the Future of the Human Mind*. Simon & Schuster

North, John D. Some Norman horoscopes, in *Adelard of Bath. An English Scientist and Arabist of the Early Twelfth Century*, ed. Charles Burnett, London, The Warburg Institute, University of London

Paulos, John Allen. 2007. *Irreligion: A Mathematician Explains Why the Arguments for God Just Don't Add Up*. Hill and Wang, NY

Picknett, Lynn, Prince, Clive. 1998. *The Templar Revelation*. Touchstone

Picknett, Lynn. 2003. *Mary Magdalene: Christianity's Hidden Goddess*. Carroll and Graf

Prigogine, Ilya. 1997. Trans. from French 1996. *The End of Certainty*. The Free Press. NY

Richter, Jean Paul (ed). 1880. *The Notebooks of Leonardo da Vinci*. Dover Press

Rotman, Brian. 1993. *Signifying Nothing: The Semiotics of Zero*. Stanford University Press

Rundle, Bede. 2006. *Why there is Something rather than Nothing*. Clarendon Press

Russell, B. 1993. *History of Western Philosophy and Its Connection with Political and Social Circumstances from the Earliest Times until the Present Day*, London: Routledge

Sartre, Jean Paul. 1969. *Being and Nothingness*, trans. H.E. Barnes, New York: Washington Square Press

– Elkaim-Sartre, Arlette, Webber, Jonathan (Translator). 2004. *The Imaginary: A Phenomenological Psychology of the*

Imagination. Routledge

Schimmel, Annemarie. 1975. *Mystical Dimensions of Islam*. Univ of North Carolina Press

Scupoli, Lorenzo. 2002. *Spiritual Combat: How to Win your Spiritual Battles and Attain Inner Peace*. Sophia Institute Press

Seife, Charles. 2000. *Zero: The Biography of a Dangerous Idea*. Viking Press

Sela, Sholom. 1977. Micelánea de Estudios Árabes y Hebraicos, *Revista del Dpto. de Estudios Semíticos, Universidad de Granada*

Shields, David. 2008. *The Thing about Life is that One Day You'll be Dead*. Knopf

Slonimsky, Nicolas. 1965. *Lexicon of Musical Invective*. Washington University, 1965

Sokal, Alan, Bricmont, Jean. 1988. *Fashionable Nonsense: Postmodern Intellectuals' Abuse of Science*. Picador

Sontag, Susan. 1983. "The Aesthetics of Silence" in *A Susan Sontag Reader* ed. E. Hardwick, Harmondsworth: Penguin

Spencer, Colin. 1995. *The Heretic's Feast: A History of Vegetarianism*. University Press of New England

Stenger, Victor. 2007. *God: The Failed Hypothesis*, Prometheus Books

Stewart, Matthew. 2006. *The Courtier and the Heretic*, Yale University Press

Struik, Dirk J. 1967. *A Concise History of Mathematics*, 3rd ed. Dover Publications, NY

Suzuki, Daisetz T. 1972. Essays and a reprint of "The Essence of Buddhism", an invited lecture to HM The Emperor of Japan in April, 1946 in *What is Zen?* Harper & Row

Varnedoe, Kirk. 2003. *Pictures of Nothing: Abstract Art since Pollok*. Princeton University Press

Vila-Matas, Enrique. 2000, trans 2004 Jonathan Dunne. *Bartleby & Co*. New Directions Books, NY

Wade, Nicholas. 2009. *The Faith Instinct: How Religion Evolved and Why It Endures*. The Penguin Press

Weinberg, Harry. 1959. *Levels of Knowing and Existence: Studies in General Semantics.* Harper & Bros, NY

Westgeest, Helen. 1996. *Zen in the Fifties: Interaction in Art between East and West.* Wanders Uitgevers, Zwolle

Index